Restraining
Great Powers

Restraining
Great
Powers

Soft Balancing from
Empires to the Global Era

T. V. PAUL

Yale UNIVERSITY PRESS/NEW HAVEN & LONDON

Published with assistance from the foundation established
in memory of Amasa Stone Mather of the Class of 1907,
Yale College.

Yale University Press books may be purchased in quantity for
educational, business, or promotional use. For information,
please e-mail sales.press@yale.edu (U.S. office) or
sales@yaleup.co.uk (U.K. office).

Set in Minion type by IDS Infotech Ltd.
Printed in the United States of America.

Library of Congress Control Number: 2018934742
ISBN 978-0-300-22848-9 (hardcover : alk. paper)

A catalogue record for this book is available from the British
Library.

This paper meets the requirements of ANSI/NISO Z39.48-1992
(Permanence of Paper).

10 9 8 7 6 5 4 3 2 1

Contents

Preface

Balance of power is one of the most enduring themes in international politics. Its antecedents go back to antiquity, to the classical era of warring Greek city-states, and it has been considered the bedrock of great-power stability since the seventeenth century. Yet it is also arguably the most contested concept and strategy in world politics. The pivotal question of whether it promotes peace or war has yet to be fully answered.

In this book, I argue that balance of power is not an immutable strategy, as some scholars and policy makers believe, but a concept shaped by the international politics of the day. Countries have used different techniques in different epochs to balance and restrain powerful or threatening states. It is often assumed that during much of the European imperial age, great powers balanced one another with formal alliances and arms buildups. But they also used international institutions and economic sanctions as means of soft balancing to restrain the power and threatening behavior of other states. The Concert System among European powers in the nineteenth century is a prominent example.

Soft balancing continued into the twentieth century. The League of Nations and its successor, the United Nations, became arenas of great-power contestation and balancing. During the Cold War, lesser powers under the rubric of the Non-Aligned Movement also engaged in a weak form of soft balancing against superpower dominance. Economic sanctions, often with the approval of an international institution, were used as a soft-balancing instrument to restrain or punish a threatening power. With the end of the Cold War, the traditional instruments of balancing, such as arms buildups and formal alliances, became less salient. For about two decades—approximately from 1991 until 2010—the United States as the preponderant power faced a surprising absence of balancing efforts against it. The U.S. outshone others not only in its aggregate power but also in using that power to initiate wars against secondary states in restive regions such as the Middle East. Similarly, China became the world's second most powerful economy with rapidly growing military might and began a program of territorial expansion in the Pacific, especially in the South China Sea. But it has faced only limited balancing by the affected states. Vladimir Putin's Russia has received limited hard-balancing responses, especially from the U.S. and its NATO allies, to its aggressive actions toward Ukraine and Baltic states.

All of these cases remain anomalies for balance-of-power theory. Why is this so? Is it because traditional instruments of power have become less effective than they used to be? My contention in this book is that states have increasingly relied on international institutions, limited ententes, and economic instruments to balance power and restrain threatening behavior. Military capabilities remain important, but they are not the only feasible instruments of balancing in the contemporary world. The availability of less threatening instruments allows states to resort to nonmilitary means more often than before because these instruments change the cost-benefit calculations about balancing.

This trend toward using less coercive instruments of balancing can continue only if globalization advances and states become more interconnected through economic links and improving technologies. A massive failure of globalization to bring sustained growth and prosperity, or the resurgence of expansionist or nativist nationalism in key countries, could alter this pattern and make military power once again the balancing instrument of choice. Globalization has brought greater prosperity to almost all nations, making zero-sum competition for resources less bitter than in previous eras, when European great powers fought massive wars in an effort to add to their material wealth and power. If globalization and resulting economic interdependence fail to foster sustained cooperation, competitive international politics could reemerge with a vengeance. The inauguration of Donald Trump as U.S. president in 2017 and the possibility of other right-wing leaders coming to power in Europe have brought a return of hard balancing as a topic of discussion. However, restraining the forces seeking the comeback of geopolitical competition and isolation may require greater use of soft balancing.

After the Cold War, the twin forces of globalization and global norms against aggressive territorial expansion restrained but did not prevent the U.S. from intervening in Iraq and Afghanistan. To some extent, these same forces simultaneously encouraged rising powers such as China and Russia to mellow their behavior. Since 2009 or so, however, China has actively expanded into contested waters such as the South China Sea and, increasingly, the Indian Ocean, and in most cases the responses of affected states have been less assertive than expected. India, a third rising power, is globalizing in every key dimension, especially economically, and is being quickly integrated into the global order. It has formed limited strategic ententes with the U.S., Japan, and some Southeast Asian countries such as Vietnam.

We should not assume that the United States or rising powers will never use military power or asymmetric strategies to achieve their goals. Since 2010, Russia and China have both employed military means to assert dominance in their immediate neighborhoods. The affected states have responded with limited hard balancing in addition to soft-balancing efforts. A massive economic decline or the imposition of protectionist trade barriers in key countries could reignite the competition for resources and wealth.

Prudent statecraft grows ever more important in preventing the world from sliding into intense rivalries and potential military conflicts. Balance-of-power strategies relying on traditional military means alone cannot guarantee long-term peace and stability in an interconnected world. A hybrid approach that includes both hard and soft balancing, relying on adequate defensive military capabilities to provide a deterrent, is necessary to preserve peace in the coming decades. The success of these approaches will depend heavily on how great powers, both established and rising, view the legitimacy of the international order and of our era's dominant institutions. If these institutions remain robust, with strong normative bases, peaceful power transitions can take place. Established powers can accommodate rising powers without violence through a mixture of soft- and limited hard-balancing techniques along with deep economic and diplomatic engagement.

This book was inspired by the attention soft-balancing literature has received in scholarly debates on state behavior during the first decade of the twenty-first century. An original proponent of the soft-balancing approach, I was also impressed by the comments of its critics. As I began to read historical records, it became clear that the strategy of soft balancing among great powers is nothing new, meaning that the United States in the post–Cold War era was not the sole case of a soft-balancing target. The records show that soft balancing became prevalent in the early nineteenth century when international institutions began to develop. Now, it seems, it is being used increasingly by China and Russia as well as by others affected by those countries' aggressive policies. None of this implies that soft balancing always works. But then, hard balancing has not always worked either. The historical record tells us that both hard and soft balancing sometimes failed to restrain aggressors and may even have encouraged them to become more belligerent. Yet countries employ both methods in the face of a threatening state because they are better than doing nothing.

The book explores the use of soft balancing by great powers and their allies in the contemporary world starting with nineteenth-century Europe. My goal is to bring out key episodes from the rich diplomatic history of the past two hundred years and explore whether great powers pursued soft balancing even in times when hard balancing remained the most dominant approach. If so, under what conditions has soft balancing been employed? What lessons do these cases hold for diplomacy and the peaceful conduct of great-power politics in a more globalized and interdependent world? Under what conditions can we expect intense traditional hard balancing to reemerge?

In answering these questions, this book concludes that in the complex international system of the twenty-first-century world, when economic globalization and resultant interdependence have increased among rising and established powers, soft balancing remains a key strategic approach to restrain the threatening behaviors of both categories of states. This does not mean soft balancing always succeeds or will inevitably lead to peace, but it is a better strategy under many circumstances than relying purely on costly arms buildups, alignments, and escalation to wars. Even if the targets ignore these "balancing lite" strategies, affected states may not have much else to rely on and they may have to use soft balancing as a hedge while awaiting opportune moments to apply different strategies, including hard balancing.

Acknowledgments

T he research for this book has been greatly facilitated by several research assistants and graduate students working with me over the past six years: Fritz Lionel Adimi, Jean-François Bélanger, Noor Bhandal, Matthew Castle, Alice Chessé, Colin Chia, Yilang Feng, Erik Underwood, and Han Zhen. Bélanger, Castle, and Underwood provided able editorial service and valuable suggestions for improvements to the text. Funding came through research grants from the Social Sciences and Humanities Council Canada (SSHRC), Fonds de recherche du Québec—Société et culture (FRQSC), and the James McGill chair. I have conducted field research in several countries, including Australia, Austria, China, India, Japan, Russia, and Singapore. Seminar presentations at various institutions in these countries and in the U.S. helped to sharpen the arguments. These include: the University of Adelaide; the Aoyoma Gakuin University, Tokyo; University of Arizona, Tucson; Australian National University, Canberra; Beijing Foreign Affairs University; Bilkent University, Ankara; Brunei Diplomatic Academy; Chinese Academy of Social Sciences, China Institute of International Studies, Beijing; Diplomatic Academy, Vienna; FLASCO Ecuador; Fudan University, Shanghai; Griffith University, Brisbane; Higher School of Economics, Moscow; Institut Barcelona d'estudis internacionals (IBEI); Japan Foundation, Tokyo; Jawaharlal Nehru University, New Delhi; Jinan

University, Guangzhou; Kerala International Center; Kerala University, Trivandrum; Koç University, Istanbul; Kyoto University; Mahatma Gandhi University, Kottayam; Universiti Malaysia, Sabah; Malaysian Ministry of Foreign Affairs; Murdoch University, Perth; Nagoya University; Nanjing University; Nanyang Technological University, Singapore; National University of Malaysia; Naval War College, Goa; University of New South Wales, Sydney; Observer Research Foundation, New Delhi; University of Chicago; Ritsumeikan University, Kyoto; University of Salzburg; Sasakawa Foundation/International House of Japan; Shanghai Institute of International Studies; Society for Policy Studies/India International Center, New Delhi; State University, St. Petersburg; Sun Yat-sen University, Guangzhou; Sydney University; Tongi University, Shanghai; Tsinghua University, Beijing; UN University, Tokyo; University of Western Australia, Perth; and Yokohama University.

A book workshop organized by McGill's Center for International Peace and Security Studies (CIPSS) in November 2015 provided critical analysis from my colleagues and graduate students. Comments by Megan Bradley, Mark Brawley, John A. Hall, Michael Lipson, Vincent Pouliot, Norrin Ripsman, and Anatassio Tasso were very useful. I thank John Ciorciari, Kai He, Steven Lobell, Mahesh Shankar, and Jeffrey Taliaferro for offering excellent suggestions on various chapters of the manuscript. A workshop at the University of Chicago yielded many critical comments by Alexandra Chinchilla, Charles Lipson, and others. At the S. Rajaratnam School of International Studies, Singapore, where I spent time as a distinguished visiting scholar in 2014 and 2016, I benefited from seminars and a book workshop organized by Rajesh Basrur, Barry Desker, Anit Mukherjee, Evan Resnick, and Pascal Venesson. In Japan, Kenki Adachi, Kumiko Haba, and Hiro Katsumata enabled my interaction with Japanese scholars. Others who offered valuable comments are Husaini Alauddin, Richard Harknett, Markus Kornprobst, Vendulka Kubalkova, Cheng-Chwee Kuik, Lawrence Prabhakar, Rajesh Rajagoplan, K. M. Seethi, David Shambaugh, Raju Thadikkaran, Anders Wivel, and Lai YewMeng. I was also helped in one way or another by Amitav Acharya, Navnita Behera, C. Uday Bhaskar, Nick Bisely, Roberto Dominguez, Rajat Ganguly, Ian Hall, Andrej Krickovich, Antonia Maioni, Hudson Meadwell, CMA Nayar, Venu Rajamony, Maria Rublee,

T. P. Sreenivasan, Ashok Swain, and Joseph Liow Chin Yong. The keynote addresses I gave at regional meetings as president of the International Studies Association (2016–17), especially the Mexican International Studies Association convention in Huatulco in October 2017, also sparked many useful conversations on the arguments presented here. Sections of chapter 2 are drawn from my article "Soft Balancing in the Age of U.S. Primacy," *International Security* 30, no. 1 (Summer 2005); 46–71 (with permission from MIT Press).

I am grateful to Yale University Press for showing interest in this book and to my editors, William Frucht and Robin DuBlanc, who did much to improve the text. Don Fehr at Trident Media Group worked sincerely on my behalf for this to materialize. I am also much appreciative of my family: my wife Rachel, my daughters Kavya and Leah, my son-in-law Daniel, and my brothers Varkey and Mathew for their constant support.

Balance of Power Today

For more than three centuries, balance of power has been the primary instrument of stability among great powers. Yet since 1991 the world has witnessed a great imbalance in power. After the end of the Cold War, the United States emerged as the unquestioned hegemon and has not been directly challenged by a major balancing coalition. China has risen to global power status within just three decades, approaching the U.S. in gross national wealth and engaging in threatening behavior toward some of its neighbors. Yet Beijing also has not been the subject of serious balancing activity during these decades. Only since 2010 have the U.S. and affected regional powers resorted to limited military balancing toward China.

The dominant theories of international relations cannot explain this lack of intense balancing behavior against contemporary great powers. The anomaly is especially pronounced for realists, many of whom seem to give balancing almost the force of law. Hard balancing—involving formal military alliances and matching military buildups—appears to have been sidelined by most states as a foreign-policy tool, at least for now. At most, contemporary balancing has largely consisted of limited arms buildups and informal alignments. Until 2016, despite its provocative behavior against Georgia, Ukraine, and the Baltic countries, even Vladimir Putin's Russia had attracted only limited hard balancing. What accounts for this lack of intense balancing?

Will this state of affairs continue? The Trump administration's maverick foreign-policy positions have raised questions about many of the assumptions underlying international relations theories. In the system now emerging, will we see more reliance on arms buildups and formal alliances as states revise their perceptions about who their friends and enemies are?

This book argues that in the first two decades of the post–Cold War era, countries engaged more often in soft balancing, relying on informal alignments, international institutions, and economic sanctions to restrain threatening powers. The capabilities of established and rising powers appeared to be perceived by other states as giving less cause for concern than in the past because they could no longer easily be used to conquer territory. Hard balancing did not disappear, but in many circumstances, it became a less attractive option.

This progression from hard to soft balancing needs an explanation. I propose that from the seventeenth to twentieth centuries, when European great powers dominated the international system, the continental states had cause to worry about one another's increasing power capabilities, since such power was being actively used for conquest. Balancing was an essential strategy by which a state avoided conquest and retained its sovereign independence. An exception was the Concert era (1815–53), when the European great powers relied on an institutional mechanism to prevent one another's aggressive behavior. Hard balancing reemerged during the late nineteenth century, when almost all European powers viewed territorial conquest and mercantilist policies as necessary for their economic prosperity and security. Economic interdependence among some of the great powers could not prevent them from sliding into competitive outbidding and hard balancing, and ultimately into two major wars. In the interwar period, the victors of World War I attempted soft balancing through the League of Nations, but they generated resentment and nationalism in Germany, Italy, and Japan.

Hard balancing reached its apogee in the Cold War, with the two superpower-led blocs competing with each other through formal alliances and arms buildups augmented by nuclear weapons. The post–Cold War era, however, brought deepened globalization and a perception that outright military conquest has few payoffs. Economic interdependence, generated through globalization, has required states to adopt less threatening economic strategies, since economic prosperity demands access to the markets, technology, and the goodwill of others, especially the dominant economic powers. Active military balancing against these states might lead them to shut off market access, with significant security and welfare implications for the balancing state. More important, for reasons I will discuss, powerful states are unlikely to conquer others directly. Excessive efforts at balancing can lead to economic decline and loss of power. For the same reasons that second-ranking states are hesitant to balance against major powers, countries are also reluctant to form alliances with a threatening power. The alternative, therefore, has been to focus on soft balancing or limited hard balancing as and when threats emerge. Such behavior is sometimes born more out of "making virtue of necessity" than by choice alone. The case studies in this book suggest that other options may not be seen as viable when the target state is too powerful or the balancing state is too reliant on the other's markets and protection.

Today, increases in the power capabilities of states do not automatically entail threats to other states' sovereignty or territory, the twin fears that led to intense hard balancing in the past. While increasing economic interdependence has been the most important reason for this transformation, other normative and material changes have also made hard-balancing behavior more costly. These changes include a territorial integrity norm that forbids altering national boundaries by force; increased sovereignty and nationalistic aspirations; the asymmetric capabilities of weaker states; the availability of weapons that allow deterrence and defense rather than offense; and the absence of a territorially expansionist ideology among the contemporary great powers. It is possible that a reversal of these factors could bring a return of intense hard balancing. President Trump's statements, if followed through, could generate conditions favorable for hard balancing, especially by China. My point here is that balancing is a human-created activity and the instruments states choose determine their outcomes more often than structural theories suggest.

The Need for Balancing

In the twentieth century, wars were the number one cause of death after natural causes such as diseases and old age. Great powers participated either directly or indirectly in most of these wars. Since the European great-power system emerged around AD 1600, there have been nine major wars in which almost all great powers of the time participated.[1] World War I reportedly resulted in some 37 million casualties, and World War II caused 72 million.[2] Thus the two wars together generated 109 million casualties. During the Cold War era, the proxy wars fought by the two superpowers also killed millions: according to one estimate, U.S. interventions caused 20 to 30 million deaths in the developing world.[3] The post–Cold War conflict in Iraq has generated over a quarter of a million casualties so far.[4] Great-power interventions and proxy wars have other consequences for regional order and peace. The ongoing conflicts in Afghanistan, Iraq, and Libya, for instance, result to a great extent from failed great-power interventions that produced extraordinarily violent consequences for those three countries. Largely because of these failures, groups with extreme religious ideologies such as ISIS, the Taliban, al-Qaeda, al-Shabaab, and Boko Haram have taken control of many poorly governed spaces in the most violent fashion imaginable.

In the past, great powers regularly fought major wars, but with the exception of the Korean War, there have been none since 1945. But the great powers have been more prone to engaging in intense rivalries and generating instability by starting proxy wars in volatile regions. Surprisingly, however, our understanding of how these wars are generated and how they might be restrained is rather limited. The international community takes it for granted that great powers have an inherent responsibility and capacity to maintain order, even though they are the main causes of the violence. Advanced countries invest a great deal in medical research programs to cure and prevent diseases. But there is no analogous effort to prevent wars that can kill millions of people. And, to reiterate, great-power politics and reckless policies account for many of these wars in the first place.

Great powers have managed to legitimize their aggressive behavior through propaganda and sheer dominance accrued over half a millennium of European-, Russian- and American-led world systems. It is astonishing that even in the most democratic nations, decisions for war among great powers are made by small groups of powerful individuals. These elites' decisions have not often been met with widespread social opposition except when casualties began to mount. The U.S. wars in Vietnam during the 1960s and 1970s and in Iraq beginning in 2003 testify to the illogical—and highly politicized—nature of war decisions in democratic great powers. The Soviet Union, which of course was not a democracy, invaded Afghanistan in 1979 and also found itself trapped in a disastrous, unwinnable war. Even worse were the choices made by leaders of great powers in 1914, which historian Barbara Tuchman called an example of "the march of folly."[5] Many leaders in great-power states showed terrible judgment, but they had the power to command their citizens to make the supreme sacrifice on behalf of the nation-state.[6] As Jack Snyder powerfully argues, great powers have often engaged in counterproductive aggressive policies that generated insecurity for themselves and other states. Snyder attributes these self-inflicted disasters to the logrolling coalitions that form among domestic interest groups and bureaucratic elites that "justify their self-serving policies in terms of broader public interests in national survival."[7] The social contract that binds the citizen to the state has worked to the advantage of decision-making elites. Although many economic and technological factors contribute to the rise and decline of great powers, the elite-crafted grand strategy of the state has always been a major cause for aggression and warfare.[8]

Great powers can also be the makers and reformers of international and regional orders, of course.[9] The question is whether they accomplish these goals through peaceful means, such as the creation of institutions and norms. Great powers have certainly shaped or built international and regional orders through economic openness, market access, and protection of smaller actors. They have often helped to create international law and legal norms, even though they sometimes violate the same laws and norms. They try to obtain regional peace and order while creating conditions for regional rivalries to persist. They have attempted to prevent the spread of nuclear weapons but have looked the other way when a few smaller allies acquired them. This is one of the paradoxes of great-power behavior.

The rise of China and the resurgence of Russia in the second decade of the twenty-first century have generated many worries about
these two powers' growing material capabilities and behavioral patterns.
Will China's rise be followed by intense wars like those fought between
European great powers during the past five centuries, or can the key con-
tenders be restrained through military and nonmilitary instruments?
Will the declining powers peacefully accommodate the rising powers?[10]
These general questions could be rephrased in more specific terms:
will Russia attempt to reconquer its former empire, including Ukraine
and the Baltic states? Will China's foray into the American-dominated
Indian and Pacific Oceans—now considered global commons—
generate military responses? Will the U.S. retreat or face its challengers
violently?

In international relations scholarship, power-transition and power-
cycle theories generally predict that as leading states approach parity,
they will most likely go to war.[11] But many now believe that great-power
wars are obsolete.[12] Some think that international norms, reinforced by
economic interdependence, are strong enough to prevent great-power
wars. To others, the mutual assured destruction (MAD) generated by
nuclear weapons makes it impossible for one great power to wage war
against another. But this restraint is limited to big wars. Great powers can
still fight smaller wars, especially in peripheral regions, and these smaller
conflicts could escalate into larger ones. As we advance toward the third
decade of the twenty-first century, deterrence may be weakening in great-
power relationships, especially in the territories adjacent to China and
Russia.

Intensified globalization and increased economic interdependence
since the 1990s should give us some hope for sustained peace among
great and aspiring powers. Rising powers such as China and India have
both benefited from greater international trade and investment. Historically, great powers fought over territory, ideology, wealth, status, and
prestige. While many observers see the post–Cold War period as characterized by a lack of military balancing, I argue that this is because states
have been using different tools—soft balancing—to accomplish the same
objective of restraining threatening powers. I further argue that after two
decades of soft balancing, great powers today have also increasingly en-

gaged in limited hard balancing, relying on asymmetrical arms buildups and quasi-balancing coalitions. Whether intense balance-of-power competition returns or states continue to use soft balancing or mixed strategies will depend on the threat environment, the dominance of offensive over defensive and deterrent weapons, the presence or absence of intense nationalist and expansionist ideologies, the existence or absence of norms against territorial expansion, and whether territorial expansion once again becomes necessary for maintaining or acquiring great-power status. More important, perhaps, is how much value great powers accord to the norms and principles of international institutions and the legitimacy of nonmilitary mechanisms for maintaining their power positions.

What Is Balance of Power?

For the past four centuries, balance of power has been the bedrock of international politics and of realist international relations theory. The traditional instruments for restraining great powers are the acquisition of military capabilities (internal balancing) and the building of formal military alliances (external balancing) to prevent a great power from threatening other powers. Other realist approaches to peace include deterrence and containment of a rival or threatening power to prevent aggression. Deterrence is achieved through the threat of retaliation or denial of victory, while containment is intended to limit a threatening state's power by isolating it. The security policies of major powers have relied more heavily on balance of power than on deterrence or containment.

Observers trace balance of power's antecedents to antiquity. Before it had a name or theoretical explication, balancing was employed by the Greek, Chinese, and Indian civilizations as well as by various empires and kingdoms.[13] The Greeks practiced it in forming a league against Athens before the Peloponnesian War (431–404 BC). The Delian League of Greek city-states formed in 478 BC to fight Persians was another example of a balancing coalition. Balance of power in the Roman era was scant: as Raymond Aron writes, "Rome was able to conquer her adversaries one after another, for they were unable to conclude in time the alliances which would have saved them."[14]

References to balance of power appear in the diplomatic history of Christendom against the Ottoman Turks. The medieval writers Dubois (1306), Marsilus of Padua (1326), and the king of Bohemia (1458) all proposed to go beyond "a single preponderant papal power against the Turks," instead forming "a confederation, or something similar, of several powers united by alliances."[15] The Italian city-states practiced balance of power during the fourteenth and fifteenth centuries along with their fine arts of diplomacy. The Treaty of Westphalia (1648) gave birth to the modern nation-state and the beginnings of the contemporary international order by developing the principle of sovereignty, by which states had the independent right to existence within an agreed-upon international order characterized by rules that limited the use of power.[16] The Treaty of Utrecht of 1713–14, which ended the War of the Spanish Succession (1701–14), mentioned balance of power explicitly, noting that it would "secure and stabilize the peace and tranquility of the Christian world by a just equilibrium of power (which is the best and most solid basis of mutual friendship and durable harmony)."[17] In many respects, the Treaty of Utrecht "was the diplomatic watershed between the mediation for a mythical unity by divine law and preponderance of power, and the mediation of estranged states by international law and balance of power."[18]

The concept of balance of power was also underscored in correspondence between the French and British monarchs. In a letter of patent sent to Queen Anne of England along with the Utrecht treaty, King Louis XIV stated that Spain's renunciation of rights over the French throne was driven by a hope of "obtaining a general Peace and securing the Tranquility of *Europe* by a Ballance of Power."[19] According to the French monarch, the Spanish crown had acknowledged "the Maxim of securing forever the universal Good and Quiet of Europe, by an equal Weight of Power, so that many being united in one, the Ballance of the Equality desired, might not turn to the Advantage of one, and the Danger and Hazard of the rest."[20]

Jean-Jacques Rousseau was among the first to appreciate what had changed. Previously, he wrote shortly after Utrecht, balance of power in Europe had been "more the work of nature than of art. It maintains itself without effort, in such a manner that if it sinks on one side, it reestablishes itself very soon on the other."[21] This perspective had led European observers to conclude that "the greatness of one Prince is . . . the ruin or the diminution of the greatness of his neighbor."[22] Now balancing became "art": something to be deliberately created and maintained by great powers.

The trajectory of balance of power has changed with the contours of European politics. From the 1648 Treaty of Westphalia to the 1792 French Revolution, the concept of a balance of power found expression in monarchs' foreign policies, but the stakes for competition among them were relatively limited as the monarchs did not envision conquest on a Napoleonic scale.[23] Following the Napoleonic Wars, conceptions about alliances, and thus the application of balance of power, came to reflect conservative states' fear of resurgent French imperialism and the onset of revolutions. Later, the Concert of Europe and the League of Nations strengthened the notion of the nation-state. The League of Nations gave currency to the idea of national self-determination, which would be embraced all over the world following the world wars.[24] As the dynastic era—based on close links between individual monarchs—gave way to the nationalist phase, the "policies of a collectivity such as the nation" came to the fore.[25]

Balance-of-power politics underwent three critical phases in the nineteenth century, beginning with the Concert System created by the Congress of Vienna in 1815. During the first phase, pursuant to the Concert rules, territorial changes could be made only with the consent of great powers. This phase also generates questions about strict definitions of balance of power that rely on techniques such as alliances and arms buildups. In 1870, the Prussian statesman Otto von Bismarck began the second phase by attempting a different balance-of-power strategy relying on crafty alliance relationships. Bismarck had maintained a close alliance with Russia but kept open the possibility of a conflict between Russia and Austria-Hungary in the Balkans. When Russia expressed unhappiness over his acting as an honest broker, Bismarck formed a secret alliance with Austria-Hungary in 1879. For the next decade, this treaty would lead both Russia and Italy to seek a closer alliance with Germany, preventing both a Franco-Russian alliance and the emergence of hard balancing.[26] A third phase followed in the 1890s, after

Bismarck's dismissal from office. Germany abandoned its alliance with Russia, forcing St. Petersburg to ally with France. German policies would further alienate Britain, which would join the Franco-Russian alliance, leaving Germany in a tight alliance with Austria-Hungary. Thus a bipolar alliance system emerged. What was missing was the flexibility and intra-alliance interactions that Bismarck had cultivated.[27] Of these three phases, Gordon Craig and Alexander George note in their book *Force and Statecraft,* "In terms of effectiveness, the first came closest to fulfilling the purposes for which it was formed. The second embodied all the ingenuity of its creator but was too complicated to have much inherent stability; and the third was little more than an exercise in desperation."[28] Germany's rise as a continental and maritime power toward the end of the nineteenth century had the most transformative effect on the politics of Europe. Balance-of-power alliances among European powers drew the fault lines that led to the First World War: the Entente Cordiale between Britain and France in 1904, the Anglo-Russian agreement establishing the Triple Entente among France, Russia, and the United Kingdom in 1907, and the Triple Alliance among Germany, Austria-Hungary, and Italy, in existence since 1882 but now invigorated.

From 1919 until the end of World War II, when nationalism became global, Europe was the focal point of intense balance-of-power politics.[29] The critical point was the failure to prevent a second cataclysmic war, as revisionist Germany, Japan, and Italy, despite their aggregate material weaknesses, attempted to break the balance of power in their favor. They succeeded at first, and it took the intervention of the United States and a determined Soviet Union under Stalin to eventually reverse the revisionist states' victories. With the onset of the Cold War in 1949, balance of power took on global and regional dimensions. At the global level, the heyday of balance of power was during the Cold War era, when nuclear deterrence and containment became the dominant strategies of the two superpowers. The nuclear revolution added a new dimension to balance of power as the unprecedented buildup of destructive weapons helped maintain the system's stability.[30] The superpowers kept building new weapon systems in an arms race that was very much devoted to maintaining the balance of power. Deterrence was obviously the objective, but balancing was required for deterrence, and the two concepts became intimately linked. For the Soviets, survival depended on catching up with the United States, first by acquiring a robust nuclear force and then by building a second-strike capability involving ICBMs and hydrogen bombs. Thus, an unending race to acquire balancing capabilities was a key characteristic of the Cold War.[31] The newly emerging states in the Non-Aligned Movement (NAM) engaged in soft balancing against both superpowers, although with limited impact.

The end of the Cold War in 1989–91 heralded a period of dramatic change in world affairs generally as well as in balance-of-power politics. The twin features of the post–Cold War era have been the rise of American power and the intensity of economic globalization. Both these features have helped to shape and refine balance-of-power approaches. In a near-unipolar world, restraining the most powerful states needed subtler instruments than arms buildups and formal alliances. Since 2010, however, balance-of-power politics has once again entered a transition, with a mixture of hard and soft instruments emerging as crucial for restraining the aggressive behavior and increasing capabilities of rising and resurgent powers. Russia and China have also used asymmetric strategies, including cyber warfare, to achieve their balance-of-power objectives. Nevertheless, a full-fledged balance-of-power competition comparable to previous eras has yet to emerge.

Balance of power, then, has not remained static, but the realist treatment of it has not changed much. According to realists, states maintain security and stability at the international level largely through military balancing. Great powers invariably engage in balancing against other great powers, because if they didn't, one such power could gain the ability to dominate the others and thereby jeopardize their security. From this perspective, the key strategy for achieving great powers' security goals has hardly changed.[32] Realist scholars such as Kenneth Waltz and John Mearsheimer have described the persistence of balance of power as perhaps the most important recurring phenomenon in world politics.[33]

As understood by realists, balance of power has at least two key dimensions that should be distinguished from one another: balance as an outcome and balancing as a strategy. Balance-of-power diplomacy and balance-of-power politics are strategies aimed at achieving outcomes based on an equilibrium of power. Both the strategy and the outcome rest on the following premises. First, the international system is anarchic, with no central governing authority to protect individual states. Second, a state's paramount goal is to survive as an independent entity, since without survival it cannot pursue any other goal. Third, no state can truly know another state's intentions—and even if it thinks it knows those intentions today, they could change at any time. Fourth, these three inescapable facts mean that power competition is a perpetual condition of international politics. To ensure their survival, states must have sufficient power to at least deter others whose intentions they cannot know. Differential growth rates and technological innovations endow states with ever-changing military and economic advantages. States seek to increase their capabilities in order to widen their interests and thereby seek more power as a way to protect their increasing assets and thus their survival itself. Fifth, when a powerful state attempts to become dominant, affected states will form defensive coalitions and/or acquire appropriate military wherewithal through internal or external sources so as to oppose the power of the rising or hegemonic state. If the rising power is not restrained, it will inevitably engage in aggressive behavior and cost others their independence and sovereign existence.[34] When confronted with the prospect of domination or elimination by a hegemonic power, weaker actors band together to form balancing coalitions.[35] As former British prime minister Viscount Palmerston said: "Balance of Power means only this—that a number of weaker states may unite to prevent a stronger one from acquiring a power which should be dangerous to them, and which should overthrow their independence, their liberty and their freedom of action. It is the doctrine of self-preservation."[36] Under a balance-of-power system, no state is allowed to obtain preponderant status over others; equal distribution of power is necessary for an equilibrium that preserves peace. With proper balancing, this equilibrium will restrain a rising power or a hegemonic state from challenging the status quo, as it is unlikely to win a war or succeed in its coercive policy. This traditional balancing, whose key mechanisms are formal alliances and matching or superior weapons systems, can be termed *hard balancing*.

In general, two conditions must be present for states to actively pursue traditional hard balancing. First, they must perceive the existence of a rising or hegemonic power that, if not opposed, will threaten their sovereign existence and territorial integrity; and second, they must find allies with which to match the power of the rising or hegemonic state if they cannot accomplish this by their own internal efforts. A great power with rapidly growing power capabilities could eventually make other great powers relatively weak, jeopardizing both their physical existence and their status as independent centers of power. For international stability, according to the proponents of balance-of-power theory, the rise of a hegemonic power has therefore to be prevented through coalition building, arms buildup, or preventive war.

The fundamental reasons a state pursues balance-of-power politics are to maintain its survival and sovereign independence as well as to preserve the state system and ensure that no single state predominates.[37] For a great power, the strategy may also serve other goals, such as maintaining the independence of other great powers or smaller allies, but these are always secondary. As Jack Levy puts it, "Maintaining the independence of one's own state is an irreducible national value, whereas maintaining the independence of other great powers is a means to that end, not an end in itself."[38] Even during the heyday of balance of power, great powers were occasionally willing to sacrifice the independence of smaller states (like Poland) to advance their own interests. The ultimate aim of balance of power for a great power remains protecting its own and its closest allies' sovereignty and physical security. When strategically vital smaller powers are occupied by a threatening great power, other great powers can perceive that the threatening power's eventual goal is domination over all states. This is why the European great powers feared expansionist France (under Napoleon) and Germany (under Wilhelm II and Hitler) so much that they formed defensive coalitions.

Scholars disagree about whether balance of power is deliberately managed as a conscious strategy, or whether it happens automatically through a law of political behavior.[39] Jean-Jacques Rousseau was one of the pioneers who believed that balance of war was "more the work of nature than of art."[40] On the other side are scholars such as Nicholas Spykman, who contended that "a political equilibrium is neither a gift of the gods nor an inherently stable condition. It results from the active intervention of man, from the operation of political forces. States cannot afford to wait passively for the happy time when a miraculously achieved balance of power will bring peace and security."[41] Spykman pointed out that the balance of power has a subjective dimension: countries tend to prefer a military balance in their favor over an equilibrium of power. Moreover, the test of relative strength is war, whose outbreak means that the balance of power has failed.[42] In the years before 1848, three monarchical continental powers of Europe—Prussia, Russia, and Austria—thought a preponderance of power on their side was needed to prevent France from reemerging as a threat. During the 1880s and 1890s, many continental statesmen viewed the preponderant power of a German empire as necessary for peace. They thought the British affinity for balance of power was designed to uphold its naval dominance.[43]

Scholars also debate whether balancing occurs against a rising power or a threatening power, which assumes that not all rising powers are threatening.[44] Why were a rising United States in the late nineteenth and early twentieth centuries and a rising China in the twenty-first century not adequately balanced militarily? Is it possible the other great powers did not view the rising power as sufficiently threatening? Moreover, not all balancing is rational: leaders could shift their policies and begin a rapid arms buildup if they perceive that the balance of power is shifting against them, even though it may not be.[45] And some scholars argue that it seems to occur more readily against continental powers such as Germany and Russia than against maritime powers like Britain and the U.S., which tend to favor offshore balancing of their continental adversaries.[46]

Between the two techniques (internal and external) of hard balancing, the more prominent is the latter: the alignment of like-minded countries to oppose a powerful state.[47] States, including great powers, flock together to form coalitions to achieve defensive as well as deterrent strength so as to dissuade the hegemonic power from becoming too strong or threatening. If they do not form such coalitions to check the rise of a hegemon, they may eventually lose their sovereign existence. Weaker states also band together to prevent bullying by stronger powers. From the structural realist perspective, since self-preservation is the primary objective of states, balancing recurs in international politics as an automatic, natural law-like phenomenon.[48]

The Recent Lack of Intense Hard Balancing

Despite realist claims that balancing is almost a natural law-like phenomenon, there have been times when states were reluctant to play the game. One such era was the period between 1991 and approximately 2010, the aftermath of the Cold War. For at least two decades, despite the massively increasing power capabilities and warlike behavior of the United States, no credible balancing coalition emerged against it. U.S. power capabilities rapidly improved relative to other great powers, giving it the wherewithal to become overwhelmingly dominant. According to traditional balance-of-power theory, the American power position should have been balanced by other states out of fear that their security and status would be curtailed if the U.S. power were not contained before it became overwhelmingly superior.[49] But no such balancing occurred.

The solution to this mystery may lie in the changes that have taken place in world politics since World War II, and more importantly since 1991. These created the necessary and facilitating conditions for soft balancing as a dominant security strategy. The intensified globalization that emerged after the Cold War brought the economies of all rising and established powers to an unprecedented level of interconnectedness. In terms of trade and investment, these economies are linked, and developing an autarkic economy has become very difficult for any rising power. One school of thought, belonging to the economic interdependence theory, tells us that such deeply interconnected economies would be reluctant to escalate rivalries to the military level by pursuing intense hard-balancing strategies. Granted, this is a contested argument, since there was conflict among interdependent economies in the early nineteenth century. Great Britain fiercely defended the gold standard because it facilitated free trade, which favored Britain because it was able to import raw materials and profitably export manufactured goods.[50] Although some scholars, such as Dani Rodrik, have argued that the global economy was also highly integrated before World War I, others—such as Michael Bordo, Barry Eichengreen, and Douglas Irwin—have pointed out that trade in the pre-1914 world was largely between imperial centers and their colonies, and that trade between empires was relatively slight.

Today's integration is "deeper" and "broader" than a century ago.[51] More important, as Stephen Brooks argues, the biggest difference today to the pre–World War I era is that multinational corporations (MNCs) manufacture goods across the world. The unprecedented geographical dispersion of complex supply chains makes interdependence much deeper while making conquest a much less viable means of economic advancement.[52] For instance, the 2017 *World Investment Report* stated that there were approximately 100,000 multinational enterprises, which also owned some 860,000 foreign affiliates, including many state-owned enterprises.[53] Globalization of production and international subcontracting make contemporary interdependence much thicker than in previous eras.[54] The fact that all rising powers benefit from deepened globalization is a positive feature of the current system.

As early as the 1970s, Richard Rosecrance and Arthur Stein wrote that although foreign investment as a percentage of national income had decreased since 1913, the type of investment gave MNCs a larger stake in the foreign sector. Foreign investment was no longer simple credit but partial ownership and transfer of technology. These make it difficult for the country receiving the investment to threaten closure. And even as the costs of breaking off trade and investment relationships have increased, governments have become more responsive to foreign investment than they were in the nineteenth century. Moreover, "under the gold standard of 1880–1913, short-term capital movements were neither as extensive nor as disruptive" as they have become in recent times.[55] These factors have only increased in magnitude since the end of the Cold War. Scholars now argue that the level of interdependence makes intense military balancing very costly in economic terms. Steve Chan, for instance, contends that "balancing policies would entail forfeiting possible gains that could accrue from cooperation, gains that states are wary of foregoing in the absence of demonstrable hostility from a stronger neighbor."[56]

Economic interdependence alone may not be sufficient to produce the rise of soft balancing. Other factors have been just as crucial. The technological innovations of warfare are yet another development that restrains direct conquest. Nuclear weapons come to mind first, of course, but a whole array of weaponry today supports defense and deterrence as opposed to offense, leading to a more secure international environment.[57] Leaders' perceptions of the balance between defensive and offensive capabilities are an important aspect of this, and so psychological factors also play a role—the "cult of the offensive" (in which all major European powers believed in the value of offensive military doctrines that extolled striking first) shares some blame for the start of World War I.[58] Such technological factors are important in constraining rising powers, since expansion is more difficult when offensive capabilities are at a disadvantage. Of course, asymmetric strategies can also be used offensively, as evident in Russia's and China's use of cyber weaponry today. Moreover, there is no guarantee that future revolutions in military affairs will not produce new weapons that might favor offensive over defensive strategies.

A further critical condition is the widespread availability of international institutions that allow great powers and other states to engage and constrain one another as an alternative to hard balancing. Institutions furnish a field for soft balancing and engagement, and their proliferation at the global and regional levels provides many arenas for a rising power to assert itself and acquire status. China, for instance, is a member of key multilateral institutions such as the United Nations and the World Trade Organization as well as financial institutions such as the World Bank and the International Monetary Fund, where it is increasingly demanding and being granted a greater voice. The rising powers themselves have been creating new institutions such as the BRICS Development Bank and the Asian Infrastructure Bank and have also had some success in modifying institutional structures like the G-20.

The third factor explaining the absence of intense hard balancing is the norms of territorial integrity that grew out of the Cold War era and were strengthened by decolonization.[59] These offer a level of assurance against blatant territorial expansion. It remains to be seen whether they will extend their disapproval in the next few decades to indirect control of foreign states, or will continue to prohibit only direct acquisition of territories. China may not be following the norms fully when it challenges the territorial orders in the South and East China Seas and along its border with India. Its pursuit of land acquisition and control of oil and natural gas fields in Africa, Central Asia, and Latin America may also generate problems if norms of territorial integrity are understood to prevent indirect control of other states' territories. Russia's support for separatists in eastern Ukraine since 2014 and its reannexation of Crimea in March 2014 also pose significant challenges to the territorial integrity norm—as did U.S. interventions in Iraq, Libya, and Syria. Still, there is little chance the outside world will recognize Chinese and Russian territorial claims even if there is no direct military response. The territorial integrity norm, despite some key violations, has been functional for much of the post–Cold War era.

Finally, the absence of expansionist ideologies such as Fascism, Nazism, and Marxism-Leninism offers some comfort that rising powers may not succumb, as their earlier counterparts did, to the temptation to become highly revisionist.[60] Expansionist ideologies generate uncertainty for nonadherents and neighboring states, both of which may become targets of predation. Germany and Japan succumbed to Fascism in the 1930s even though they had recently been quasi-democracies. Militaristic elites found the international climate so intolerable that they took control of their states and began occupying other countries and territories, and their populations appear to have supported this idea. The established powers' attitudes did not help. For instance, the racist immigration policies of the United States might have aggravated the Japanese public's hostility toward it. The established powers' grand strategies held little room for the peaceful accommodation of the revisionist powers.

These variables, taken together, are crucial for understanding the modern turn toward soft balancing and limited hard-balancing strategies, especially among great powers. Three decades before World War I, economic interdependence was high, but the other conditions were absent. Weapons technologies such as the Maxim machine gun favored offense over defense, great powers embraced an expansionist ideology in the form of imperialism, and norms of territorial integrity and international institutions were both absent. The threat environment is heavily determined by the combination or predominance of these key elements of international order.

The absence of intense bipolar or multipolar rivalry also encourages soft balancing. When rivalry is intense, states tend to resort to hard balancing. They may occasionally augment these efforts with soft balancing and paint their opponents' military or security strategies as illegitimate, but intense bipolar or multipolar systems are not conducive to soft balancing. A near unipolar system such as existed in the post–Cold War era offers favorable conditions for soft balancing to be applied more regularly, especially when the hegemonic power is perceived, as the United States was at least briefly, as benign and legitimate. This perception was rattled by the policies of the Bush and Trump administrations and to some extent by Obama-era interventions and drone attacks as well.

In most parts of the world, America's actions as a unipolar power reassured small and large countries alike that their sovereign existence and territorial integrity were reasonably secure. A counterfactual exercise might be useful here. If these conditions had been present during the early part of the twentieth century, could Europe have avoided the intense balance-of-power competition that led to the First World War? Although economic interdependence was high among some key states, other factors were not favorable. Today, countries seem less prone to hard balancing against power and are more often using nontraditional instruments.[61] Traditional balancing has given way to complex patterns and strategies among great powers and others. I argue that in this transition era, states are increasingly resorting to soft balancing along with diplomatic engagement, supplemented with limited hard balancing. These instruments reflect an overarching hedging strategy in a period of uncertainty. In this new era, balancing is a complex art that can no longer be seen as an automatic consequence of the distribution of material power in the international system. Instead it a manual outcome, a policy consciously implemented by leaders.

This does not mean that soft balancing has no relevance in eras when hard balancing dominates. Great powers in such times can use soft balancing as a secondary instrument. It can be employed even in periods of intense rivalry in order to delegitimize an opponent's aggressive moves or as a first step toward tougher hard-balancing strategies. The two are often used in conjunction.

Restraint by Other Means

Traditional balance-of-power politics does not fully capture great-power behavior in our era. Since the end of the Cold War, second-tier states have balanced the threatening behavior of the United States, and to some extent that of China, with limited, tacit, or indirect balancing strategies, largely through coalition building and diplomatic bargaining within international institutions. They have not formed formal bilateral and multilateral military alliances but have resorted largely to soft-balancing strategies. I define soft balancing as *restraining the power or aggressive policies of a state through international institutions, concerted diplomacy via limited, informal ententes, and economic sanctions in order to make its aggressive actions less legitimate in the eyes of the world and hence its strategic goals more difficult to obtain.*[1]

I should clarify the differences between soft and hard balancing. Hard-balancing alliances are formal arrangements, often with combined command structures, operational plans, bureaucratic frameworks, and military forces permanently stationed and ready to fight. NATO and the Warsaw Pact are prominent examples.[2] As Henry Kissinger describes it, an alliance "creates a formal obligation to act in a precise way in defined contingencies. It brings about a strategic obligation fulfillable in an agreed manner. It arises out of a consciousness of shared interests, and the more parallel those interests are, the more cohesive the alliance will be."³ Another scholar defines an alliance as a "formal agreement that pledges states to cooperate in using their military resources against a specific state or states and usually obligates one or more of the signatories to use force, or to consider (unilaterally or in consultation with allies) the use of force, in specified circumstances."⁴ By their nature, formal alliances obligate members to commit to using force to defend their partners or to advance their offensive goals. This reciprocity makes formal alliances different from other forms of security cooperation.

Soft-balancing coalitions tend to lack these elements. Second-tier states pursuing soft-balancing strategies often develop limited diplomatic coalitions, or *ententes,* to balance a powerful, rising, or threatening state. An entente is an informal or friendly understanding between two or more states on security matters without a formal commitment to military action.⁵ These coalitions do not have official structures, permanent institutions, or coordinated military planning beyond a minimal level.⁶ Consultation can be intense during crises, but otherwise it may remain limited and episodic.

International institutions offer themselves as venues where contestation for legitimacy, a key tool of soft balancing, takes place. Hard balancing presupposes intense rivalry or expected rivalry—sometimes of a zero-sum nature—among the balancing states, whereas soft-balancing coalitions tend to be ad hoc. The intentions of the parties engaged in soft balancing are also important: the purpose of their tacit strategies should be directly related to reducing the effects of the target state's threatening behavior. Soft-balancing strategies are usually directed against specific threats, whereas hard balancing can be developed against both specific threats or the fact of power alone, on the assumption that a powerful state will eventually threaten the security of the weaker side.⁷

An in-between category is *limited hard balancing,* which relies on limited arms buildup and semiformal alliances such as strategic partnerships. In the past few years, some of the ASEAN (Association of Southeast Asian Nations) countries, such as Vietnam and India, have formed limited hard-balancing coalitions with the U.S. in response to threatening behavior from China. These arrangements allow joint efforts and sharing of resources but not offensive warfare or operational coordination. They include the agreements Washington makes with many countries, with no formal alliance, to allow the use of base facilities for the U.S. Navy. India's limited hard balancing involves such a coordination with Washington as well as targeted spending meant to offset China's military capabilities, without any intention of putting India's military on an equal footing with China's. In recent years, China and Russia have also formed a limited hard-balancing coalition in which both states have engaged in limited arms buildup aimed at balancing U.S. power, again without the intent of reaching parity soon. The strategic goal of these efforts is to make a potential attack costly and frustrate efforts at coercion.

Table 1 shows the different types of balancing behavior. Hard balancing generally occurs among rivals or potential rivals. Rivals compete in multiple areas, including territory, ideology, and spheres of influence,

Table 1 Types of balancing

Type	Mechanisms	Objectives	Examples
Hard balancing	Formal alliances Matching arms buildups	Confront/balance powerful/ threatening state	Triple Alliance vs. Triple Entente Allied vs. Axis Powers NATO vs. Warsaw Pact
Limited hard balancing	Coordinated military activity, short of formal alliances Limited, asymmetrical arms buildups	Restrain power/ threatening behavior	China vs. U.S. India and U.S. vs. China (2010–)
Soft balancing	Limited institutional alignments Informal ententes	Restrain power/ threatening behavior	Concert of Europe (1815–53) Russia and China vs. U.S. (1996–) India and Japan vs. China (2014–)

and they may have a history of militarized conflicts.[8] The security dilemma among rivals is a large problem.

Limited hard balancing also assumes limited or partial rivalry. It may occur during a pre-rivalry phase when states expect a rivalry to emerge in the near term, as a form of hedging against anticipated threats. Semiformal alignments and arms buildups not matching the strength of the powerful actor are characteristic of this form of balancing. Unlike hard balancing, soft balancing can occur among allies and adversaries alike. Soft-balancing strategies are limited, institution-based, noncooperative attempts to make the powerful threatening state relent in its behavior and return to normal friendly attitudes and postures.

I should clarify that both soft balancing and hard balancing are *coercive* strategies intended to alter the target state's cost-benefit calculations. Whereas hard balancing seeks to aggregate material capabilities in an effort to diminish, deter, or if necessary defeat a powerful or aggressive opponent, soft balancing seeks to accomplish one or more of the following:

- To impede the target's ability to profit from bad behavior (for example, through the imposition of economic sanctions);
- To increase the marginal cost to the target state of carrying out its plans (for example, access denial via institutional frameworks);
- To delegitimate the target's behavior in the eyes of third parties;
- To signal that continued noncompliance by the target may trigger hard balancing.

In adopting these approaches, states make a number of cost-benefit calculations. First, the target state is more likely to alter its policies in a benign manner in response to this approach, whereas it could react with heavy reprisal if the states attempted military balancing. Second, the powerful actor is prone to reform its policies if they make its leaders suffer a loss of legitimacy. In some instances, the targeted state may be a key contributor of public goods, including an export market that it is likely to continue to provide. The states in a soft-balancing coalition are calculating that the costs of their actions are tolerable and can be shared among the participants if the target engages in punitive actions.[9] The aim of a soft-balancing strategy is to deny legitimacy to actions that challenge the international or regional order. The expectation is that the target will return to cooperation and that the parties can reach an equitable bargain.[10] Through soft balancing, states are also attempting to influence domestic opinion within the target state, perhaps anticipating that powerful coalitions within that state will seek to stop behavior that is adversely affecting its reputation and legitimacy.

Why would a great power use soft balancing as opposed to limited hard balancing or full-fledged hard balancing? The key determinant is the threat level posed by the target state. If a rising state is revolutionary and has proclaimed its intention to fundamentally alter international or regional order, especially territorial order, that could trigger hard balancing. But if the balancing state perceives that the threatening state has only limited aims and can be persuaded to alter its policies through institutional or limited coercive mechanisms, soft balancing or limited hard balancing may be the most cost-effective option. The strategy may be to give the target an opportunity to alter its policies. A revisionist state that fundamentally challenges the sovereignty of several states requires large-scale hard balancing. Sometimes the status quo states do not grasp the revisionist states' goals at an early enough stage to prevent war, as happened with the intentions of Germany, Italy, and Japan during the 1930s.

International Institutions and Balancing

International institutions have been a key component in restraining great powers since the nineteenth century and have been particularly important in the post–Cold War era. Yet the role of institutions in discouraging great powers from pursuing aggressive policies has received relatively little attention from scholars. The dominant realist discourse downplays the importance of international institutions, while liberal and constructivist scholars often pay little attention to the power dynamics inherent in international institutions. The literature on international institutions generally concentrates on their role in international cooperation, especially economic cooperation. Liberal institutionalist theorists have demonstrated how institutions facilitate transactions and cooperation between states, help overcome coordination dilemmas, and act as vehicles of transnational participation and as catalysts for coalitions among states.[11] But these functionalist discussions seldom explore how great and non-great powers use institutions to reduce the aggressive behavior of others while avoiding the necessity of military balancing. Soft balancing is an effort to limit the utility of military strength. States resort to it when they face constraints in balancing a power by military means, for instance, if they are smaller states vulnerable to military counteractions by a powerful target.

Liberal scholars such as John Ikenberry have explored the use of institutions by the U.S. after victory in major wars to bind secondary states.[12] The converse, however—how secondary states use institutions to bind the U.S. or other great powers—has yet to draw much scholarly attention. Moreover, it remains a weakness of liberal theories of institutions that we do not know when and how institutions promote changes in policies, and when they instead generate intense nationalism and confrontational responses in the targeted power.

This oversight is somewhat surprising given that the use of international institutions as a component of soft balancing, which today is a prominent feature of international politics, is not an especially recent one. Great powers have been using institutions to curtail each other's aggressive behavior for a long time. In some historical eras, such as the first decade of the Concert of Europe or the two decades since the end of the Cold War, soft balancing was an important complement to the hard-balancing instruments of arms buildups and formal alliances.

The Congress of Vienna, which inaugurated the Concert of Europe, largely depended on an institutional mechanism to restrain great powers, and institutional means have been a key part of the European powers' overall balancing strategy ever since. In the aftermath of World War I, the Allied powers attempted to blunt the aggressive behavior of Germany and Italy as well as Japan through the League of Nations. They were simultaneously building their military capabilities, although initially at a slower pace. During the Cold War, the U.S. and USSR used

the UN system—especially their veto power in the Security Council—
to restrain one another, although hard-balancing approaches dominated the Cold War era. Today, the U.S., its European allies, and smaller
states in Asia use institutions and sanctions to constrain the aggressive
behavior of Russia and China while also employing hard balancing and
limited hard-balancing strategies. For instance, the main vehicle of hard
balancing by the West against Russia—NATO and its military buildup—is supplemented by economic sanctions against Russian banks and
individuals involved in activities of which the West does not approve.

Limited Alignments and Informal Ententes

A second technique of soft balancing is the use of informal alliances
or ententes, sometimes called "strategic partnerships." Through these
mechanisms, countries engage in periodic meetings, joint exercises, and
other limited activities without entering a formal military alliance. They
need not make a mutual pledge to come to each other's rescue or participate in one another's conflicts. Often these partial alignments are
signaling devices and means of reassurance. The U.S., for instance, has
many states as strategic partners, including India, Indonesia, Vietnam,
Malaysia, and New Zealand. These are not strictly military alliances
and entail a lesser commitment than that enjoyed by a NATO ally or
a "Major Non-NATO Ally," a formal classification the U.S. gives to
countries like Israel. These looser alliances are meant to coordinate diplomatic positions on security issues and allow a certain amount of cooperation, especially in weapon and technology transfers.[13] The level of
commitment varies. India has agreements with many countries that are
little more than rhetorical statements.[14] I include strategic partnership
as a soft-balancing tool only if it has a security component and
is explicitly aimed at balancing the power or threatening behavior of
another state but is below the level of a formal alliance. Limited joint
military exercises can be a soft-balancing signaling device, but if the
relationship develops into anything more significant, such as allowing
the use of base facilities, then such an alignment counts as limited hard
balancing.

Economic Sanctions

A third key mechanism of soft balancing has been economic sanctions on target states. Such an action is an alternative to doing nothing, and it registers displeasure through economic punishment—and, should the behavior be modified, through rewards. Historically, sanctions have been used for containment and coercion of weaker states. Woodrow Wilson called them the "economic, peaceful, silent, deadly remedy"; he considered them a substitute for war in dealing with any state that broke its promises to the League of Nations.[15]

Sanctions can be unilateral, multilateral, or sector specific. Multilateral sanctions imposed through international and regional institutions appear to have more legitimacy and higher chances of success than unilateral sanctions, unless the target is fully dependent on the sanctioning state for the sanctioned products or services. Over the years, the major powers have found sanctions increasingly attractive as the costs of military intervention—in money, lives, and public opinion—have risen.[16] One important objective of economic sanctions has been to signal to national and international audiences one's displeasure at the target state's behavior or policy choices. But they require international support if they are to work.[17]

Whether sanctions are more likely to be used, or are more effective, in an era of globalization is a contentious question. Some argue that globalization has increased interdependence, and sanctions could end up hurting both the states imposing them and the target state. But military conflict would be worse. Short of war, antagonistic alliances formed through hard balancing could also hurt interdependent economies. Although sanctions have limitations, they may be more effective if they follow international institutional or treaty guidelines such as those of the World Trade Organization. Their impact can quickly fade away if the target finds alternate sources for the goods being denied.[18] This is why the backing of international institutions and near unanimity among great powers have been critical for sanctions to work. The recent sanctions against Iran, for instance, were effective because the U.S., Europe, Russia, and China all joined in opposing Tehran's nuclear weapons program.

As part of a soft-balancing strategy, sanctions can be a way to send a strong signal to a threatening state without engaging in violence or a costly arms buildup. Economic sanctions and denial were very much part of the U.S. and Western containment efforts during the Cold War era. Containment is often a strategy of the powerful against a threatening state or coalition, sometimes alongside an overall hard-balancing strategy. Economic sanctions under soft balancing may be episodic and issue specific, and weaker actors can also attempt to apply them against stronger targets.

It should be noted that some of these same instruments can be used for other strategic objectives. Sanctions are good ways to signal disapproval in response to behavior that is not necessarily threatening but is still seen as unacceptable. More important, they can be used to weaken the target's military power or its leadership's legitimacy, both of which reduce its hard-balancing capabilities. American economic containment during the Cold War era, for example, relied on a strategic embargo to weaken the Soviet Bloc's ability to build weapons, and thus to reduce the national strength that Moscow could have used against the West.[19]

Legitimacy Denial

A common thread runs through all of these soft-balancing mechanisms: the denial of legitimacy to the threatening power. Great powers have used institutions to legitimate their policies or to delegitimize those of their opponents for two centuries. As a key tool of soft balancing, economic sanctions have often performed the same functions. Legitimacy rises for the sanctioning state if sanctions are multilateral and have the authority of an international institution such as the United Nations. Denying the aggressor international legitimacy, the thinking goes, makes aggressive behavior costlier. In the past, even when great powers did not succeed in curtailing an aggressor's behavior militarily, they periodically used economic sanctions to constrain threatening behavior. They believed legitimacy could be an instrument of persuasion. Implicit in this is the acknowledgment that a state's durability as a great power is based on the authority and respect it is accorded within the international system, in particular by its great-power peers. Weaker states, if they are united, can also use institutions to diminish the legitimacy of great powers.

According to Robert Jackman, legitimacy is a foundational idea for power relations in the political realm "because it reflects the degree to which those who seek to rule (i.e. to exercise power) are accepted by the ruled."[20] Martha Finnemore defines legitimacy as the "tacit acceptance of social structure in which power is exercised."[21] It is conferred by others, even though one can debate its source. According to some scholars, legitimacy in modern times has been determined largely by a great power's actions, especially the degree to which they are consistent with international legal norms. To Ian Hurd, legitimacy is "the normative belief by an actor that a rule or institution ought to be obeyed."[22] It implies "lawfulness by virtue of being authorized or in accordance with law."[23] Legitimate power involves not just the "capacity but also a right to act, with both capacity and right being seen to rest on the consent of those over whom the power is exercised."[24] There are relational, ideational, and intersubjective elements to legitimate power: actors gain it only "within relationships," it is "constituted in social institutions," and it exists within the "shared communicative realm between individual actors."[25] For English School scholars, legitimacy is a foundational idea in international relations. Adam Watson defines it as "the acceptance of authority, the right of a rule or a ruler to be obeyed, as distinguished from the power to coerce." Martin Wight puts it more broadly: legitimacy is "the collective judgment of international society about the rightful membership of the family of nations; how sovereignty may be transferred; and how state succession is to be regulated, when large states break up into smaller, or several states combine into one."[26] For both large and small states, legitimacy lowers the cost of exerting power, and states make considerable efforts to obtain, maintain, and prolong their power position through legitimacy. International institutions as well as legal instruments such as treaties are key arenas where legitimacy is achieved and maintained. The quest for legitimacy has both rational and emotive aspects: it is a fact of international politics that people wish, often fervently, for their nations to have the world's respect. This gives leverage to institutions that can confer legitimacy.

Hegemonic powers especially need legitimacy to acquire and maintain supremacy. The goal of soft balancing for second-ranking powers is to deprive the powerful actor of the legitimacy it needs to maintain its authority, especially in the institutions it uses to justify co-ercive military actions.[27] A great power whose legitimacy is challenged can engage in a counter-legitimacy push or else change the rules of the legitimacy game. Christian Reus-Smit argues that in 2003, when the UN Security Council would not approve the Bush administration's offensive on Iraq, Washington attempted to argue that compliance with its posi-tion was a test of the UN's legitimacy, not of the American decision to wage war. But this self-legitimation effort failed.[28]

Classical balance of power has been partly based on this legitimacy principle, as alliances themselves cannot be sustained if the leading power lacks authority. But the neorealist conception of balancing, as at-tributed to Kenneth Waltz, does not include legitimacy as a key aspect of balancing. The theory relies solely on material capabilities, operating in a somewhat mechanistic fashion. Maintaining and sustaining one's alli-ance leadership and obtaining new allies require legitimacy, and while crude military power is useful, coalitions based only on that do not nec-essarily last. The assumption of neorealists is that legitimacy itself is determined by material power. But second-ranking states always try to create normative boundaries for great-power behavior, and transgress-ing these boundaries can be costly.

Much international relations scholarship of the realist variety as-sumes that great powers are largely restrained through military power and alliances. Nonmilitary instruments for balancing power are seen as ineffective or epiphenomenal to power, and efforts to use them are even taken as signs of weakness.[29] An exception is Christopher Layne, who found soft balancing using diplomatic methods a valuable "component of counterbalancing strategies," arguing also that it lays the groundwork for hard balancing in the future.[30] The realist position arises from a se-lective reading of history. In the modern world, great powers have re-sorted as often to softer diplomatic instruments as to military ones to restrain their opponents. Great powers use these instruments particu-larly in response to the aggressive behavior of rising powers when it threatens their interests. Moreover, while nonmilitary instruments are sometimes dismissed as ineffective, military instruments have also failed, and the resulting breakdowns in the balance of power have led to disastrous wars.

Facilitating Conditions

Scholars who ask whether soft balancing works—whether it actually modifies any state's behavior—are implicitly comparing it to hard balancing through military instruments. The assumption is that military balancing works more effectively. But this should not be assumed away; it requires careful analysis. The debate over soft balancing resembles the one over economic sanctions, to which some scholars and practitioners assign little value as a tool of statecraft. But as Jonathan Kirshner reminds us, military force has often failed to produce positive results, and all techniques of statecraft must be weighed in terms of their political costs and benefits. No strategy offers a guarantee of success. All one can do is to develop an optimal policy that takes costs and benefits into account.[31] This being said, I can suggest some general insights about the ideal conditions for favorable soft-balancing outcomes. These conditions have normative, material, and technological dimensions.

A number of facilitating conditions should exist for soft balancing to succeed or even to be seriously attempted. First is the threat environment: it should not be existential or even severe, and rivalry among the target and balancing states should be limited. The rise of a powerful actor with the perceived intent and capabilities to alter states' independent existence could encourage them to resort to hard balancing, even though they could gain more legitimacy for their efforts by combining it with soft balancing.

Second, the success of soft balancing depends on how much importance the great powers assign to international legitimacy as a basis of their power. The more important it is that their power be seen as legitimate, the higher the chances that soft-balancing efforts will be effective. The legitimacy of the international order is also important, as power and legitimacy are certainly related. States, especially powerful states, use institutions to reinforce what they perceive as legitimate behavior. This affects the success of soft balancing because if targeted great powers perceive the international order as illegitimate, they may disregard the norms inherent in its institutions. If institutions are seen as illegitimate, their use as part of soft balancing may even trigger nationalism and aggressive behavior by the targeted power. When great powers are driven by ultra-nationalism or perceived grievance against dominant powers, soft balancing is unlikely to work.

Third, the immediate aftermath of a major conflict is more conducive to soft balancing than two or more decades later. Great powers conspicuously turn to institutions following a large war or a major conflict like the Cold War. We saw short-lived "golden periods" of institutions immediately after the Napoleonic Wars, after World War I and World War II, and again at the end of the Cold War. The creation of institutions in immediate postwar settlement periods may be the result of war fatigue among the great powers. It seems, however, that war fatigue has a limited life span, and postwar institutions become weaker or extinct as the institutions prove increasingly unable to address major issues. The importance accorded to institutions by major powers after a conflict temporarily facilitates soft balancing.

Fourth, broad participation by all key states in institutions is a factor in the success of soft balancing. After a war, the winning and losing sides should both have a significant role to play in international affairs. The success of the Concert System is attributable in part to its continued incorporation of victors and defeated powers. The same has been true of the post–World War II multilateral system. The post–World War I institutional system was less representative and less permanent. John Ikenberry has argued that the U.S. designed and developed institutions in the post–World War II era to constrain the behavior of its allies.[32] Yet not only the U.S. but all great powers have on occasion used the post–World War II multilateral institutions to further their strategic goals and to constrain their opponents. Only when great powers were excluded from the dominant institutions have they failed to play a role. Broad participation in international institutions especially facilitates soft balancing if it enables states to benefit from economic integration and growth. The immediate post–Cold War era, when economic globalization encouraged leading powers to support welfare-enhancing institutions, was one such opportunity.

Fifth, soft balancing works better when defensive and deterrent systems dominate the day's military weapons. Offensive weaponry can be correlated with offensive doctrines, aggressive warfare, and a rising power's desire to use force to alter the status quo. Soft balancing has also failed when technology and ideology led states to see an advantage in conquest. When aggressive states could (or thought they could) achieve their goals easily through offensive military means, institutions were often perceived as perpetuating an unjust order.

Sixth, the success of soft-balancing techniques could depend on the target state's relative dependence on limited sources for its economic well-being and the absence of alternate trading partners or sources of national income. This is one reason economic globalization and high levels of interdependence favor soft balancing, but this variable alone may not be sufficient to prevent hard-balancing coalitions from emerging. The effectiveness of soft balancing may also depend on the degree of international support for the sanction regimes. If other sources are available, the target state could ignore the sanctions and continue its aggressive behavior.

Finally, the success of a soft-balancing strategy will depend on how much domestic support the state resorting to it has to sustain the strategy, and how much its actions can influence domestic political opinion in the target state. A state may attempt soft balancing if dominant coalitions within the ruling structure demand and support it. While this may explain one side of the story, the target state's public opinion matters too if the strategy is to succeed. If soft balancing by other states makes the target's public more nationalistic, then the strategy could backfire, as happened with Italy and Japan prior to World War II. The target state must contain powerful factions that can push it to modify its behavior toward a nonthreatening posture.

These conditions are ideals, and not all of them need to be present for soft balancing to succeed.

Critics of Soft Balancing

During the past decade, the soft-balancing literature has drawn much criticism, chiefly from realist scholars. The main criticisms can be summarized as follows. First, these scholars contend that there is little empirical support for the phenomenon of soft balancing, and that the limited number of cases makes it difficult to produce a valid theory. Second, soft balancing is more like simple "diplomatic friction" than a concerted policy, and therefore it lacks coherence. Third, it is best understood as a rhetorical device rather than an active policy instrument. Fourth, as a policy instrument, its value is questionable because success is not guaranteed. Finally, soft balancing is relevant only under conditions of unipolarity and hence has limited value for situations where power is not concentrated in one state.[33] I will take up these criticisms in order.

First, soft balancing makes many appearances in the historical record, going back well beyond the post–Cold War era. States have relied on it as a complement to hard balancing since at least the Concert of Europe. A number of scholars have noticed its regional operation in places ranging from Africa to Latin America to Central Asia.[34] Others have examined its validity in different historical eras and international systems.[35] Second, soft balancing is more than diplomatic friction. It implies active use of institutions, limited coalitions, and coordinated actions for an extended period, all employing specific strategies aimed at restraining a threatening power and changing its behavior. States that engage in soft balancing are intentionally targeting a powerful actor. The definition of soft balancing I use focuses on three key strategies. Not every diplomatic activity meant to frustrate a great power's threatening behavior qualifies as soft balancing. The actions need to be consistent and applied systematically for a period of time. As the case studies in subsequent chapters demonstrate, great powers have used institutions on a coordinated and consistent basis to restrain the power and aggressive policies of targeted states. Non-great-power states have also consistently used these mechanisms as conscious policy instruments.

Third, soft balancing is a rational and calculated response to threatening behavior, employed when other options, such as alliances and arms buildups, are not easily available. It is not a mere rhetorical device but a consistent strategic approach relying on mechanisms such as institutions and economic sanctions. It differs from routine diplomacy and may be more a matter of necessity than choice. The case studies suggest that other options may not be seen as viable when the target state is too powerful or the balancing state is too reliant on the other's markets and protection. This seems particularly important when small and medium powers opt for soft-balancing strategies. They can be attractive because hard balancing, almost by definition, is directed at adversaries, while soft balancing can also be directed at friends when a specific policy is found to be objectionable. Moreover, hard balancing is more rigid and thus more difficult to embed in a hedging strategy, whereas soft balancing fits easily within a hedging strategy and permits flexibility in state policies.

Fourth, there is no dispute that soft balancing does not always work, just as there is no guarantee that hard balancing can create permanent or even temporary peace. A balance in material power is seldom permanent but always subject to changes in technology and in economic fortunes. Revisionist powers feel a strong temptation to break the military balance and may use asymmetric strategies to gain an advantage over militarily superior opponents. Often defeating such a determined adversary requires overwhelming preponderance in capabilities, not just equilibrium.

Finally, soft balancing is not irrelevant outside a unipolar era. As I show in the next chapter, it was practiced by European great powers during multipolar eras as well. Soft balancing appears to be a viable strategy under all systems in world politics, be they multipolar, bipolar, or unipolar. It may be used along with hard balancing, although its application may be limited, and could well become a key approach in the emerging international order, given the constraints on hard balancing imposed by intensified globalization and nuclear deterrence.

The discipline of international relations can learn much about softer approaches from other disciplines. For instance, soft law is a well-established, powerful branch of international law that supplements hard laws—those that create precise obligations and have proper authority to interpret and implement them. Soft laws have weaker arrangements, obligations, and implementation as well as more fluid interpretations. Many countries prefer soft laws because they are less threatening to sovereignty and because soft law is more flexible and adaptable to compromise among different actors.[36] Soft balancing has some of the same advantages. It can also avoid the entrapment problem inherent in hard-balancing alliances: that allies are obliged by treaty obligations to fight unwanted wars.

Similarly, soft power has in recent years been recognized as an important component of national power. As defined by its leading theorist,

Joseph Nye, soft power is "the ability to get what you want through attraction rather than coercion or payments. It arises from the attractiveness of a country's culture, political ideals, and policies."[37] Scholars of international relations now accept the existence of soft law and soft power—although they are uncertain how to measure their effects. Nothing should prevent us, therefore, from recognizing and theorizing softer approaches to balancing power. The instruments of soft balancing can be observed and measured through careful empirical work. These three approaches—soft law, soft power, and soft balancing—are united by their focus on loose conceptual definitions and an absence of hard instruments or mechanisms.

Skeptics of institutional means to restraining power often argue that institutions do not bring lasting peace. John Mearsheimer contends that their impact on world politics is minimal. They simply reflect the preferences of powerful actors, and their creation and maintenance depend on those actors' influence. Cooperation is difficult, as states have a powerful incentive to take advantage of each other and to cheat if an opportunity arises. War prevention comes largely through hard balancing, not through institutions.[38]

This criticism of institutions reflects an apolitical understanding of their value. If they are worthless enterprises, why do great powers participate in so many of them and sometimes allow themselves to adhere to institutional norms? Why would great powers agree to be bound by them? These critical perspectives also ignore the classical realist attention to diplomacy, international law, and the legitimacy of power. As Robert Keohane points out, classical realists such as E. H. Carr and Hans Morgenthau, as well as some contemporary realists like Joseph Grieco, recognized the importance of international institutions in the context of power-based bargaining between states.[39] Morgenthau, in his later writings, even saw supranational institutions as a means of controlling nuclear weapons. He felt that broad membership in institutions and concession by all members of some amount of national sovereignty were very much in every nation's interest.[40] Great powers often have had little choice but to use institutions when war and military balancing were not readily available options.

The objection that institutional balancing is fleeting might also be applied to balancing through weaponry and alliances. These can also be fleeting, if they work at all. The cost of arms races is often justified by the argument that if a state does not balance, it will face even higher costs in the future. But these costs can sometimes be reduced through soft balancing. For instance, if the U.S. gets into a severe balance of power competition with China, it will generate a costly arms race. China's participation in international institutions and the globalized world economy offers an opportunity to restrain it while facilitating a peaceful and legitimate rise to power. Though the dynamics of military competition remains implicit, interdependent economies can use institutions to restrain each other. Against China, this form of restraint may be more effective than a military strategy alone, as China is likely to respond militarily, creating a self-fulfilling prophecy of costly arms buildups and potential crises. This does not mean that limited hard balancing is not a feasible means to restrain a rising power—but it may often work better alongside soft-balancing techniques.

Similarly, China could use its membership in international institutions—or create new ones, as it has been attempting to do—to attain its goals as a rising power while maintaining its legitimacy. Its practice of escalating territorial disputes will simply alienate neighboring states that could otherwise give China a certain legitimacy and status. Nationalism and sovereignty are powerful forces in Asia, and countries are likely to resist efforts at forceful territorial change. Given that China may eventually have to resort to diplomacy and institutions to obtain its strategic goals, it would be better off preventing the emergence of a hard-balancing coalition against it by adopting softer instruments now. The alternative of creating new institutions as well as legal norms to legitimize its power would certainly be more costly than working within or reforming existing institutions as well as legal and social norms.

Likewise, a resurgent Russia cannot easily be contained through hard balancing alone. The effort by the NATO alliance to expand into Eastern Europe has not prevented Moscow from engaging in limited military aggression toward its neighbors. In fact, the expansion of NATO quite likely provoked Russian moves against Georgia and Ukraine and the country's efforts to undermine democratic norms in Europe and the U.S. Nor were soft-balancing strategies properly attempted: institutions such as the Organization for Security and Cooperation in Europe (OSCE) and NATO Partnerships for Peace have not effectively integrated Russia into their organizations. Sanctions are not easy to apply given

Europe's dependence on Russian oil and gas. One must imagine that these softer instruments might eventually succeed by slowly weakening the Russian economy. But they require legitimacy and a willingness on the part of the Western powers to abide by collective decisions. Great powers need to realize that the alternative is a costly arms race that offers no guarantee of peace and may in fact escalate into crises and wars.

Other Strategies

The three balancing strategies I have identified—hard balancing, limited hard balancing, and soft balancing—are only part of the larger set of strategic choices a state may have. Other options include *bandwagoning, binding* or *enmeshing, buck-passing, appeasement,* and mixed strategies combining two or more of these. Bandwagoning is the opposite of balancing: a bandwagoning state joins the state or alliance that is becoming more powerful and threatening because it expects to reap rewards for doing so. Binding or enmeshing is the closest to soft balancing. Binding is often used by friendly states in alliances or institutional settings to make all of the members abide by institutional norms. The idea is to restrain them from defecting to the opposition camp. Soft balancing could include binding, but it is different in the sense that soft-balancing mechanisms are used against a threatening state and are ad hoc. As John Ikenberry notes, the U.S. adopted a binding strategy early in the Cold War to enmesh new allies like Germany and Japan through institutional arrangements.[41] The American idea was to lock in other key states by offering constitutional-style arrangements that would restrain them all. Soft balancing is thus related to Ikenberry's institutional model, but different in the sense that it targets a state's adversaries, and at times, non-adversaries. Institutions in both cases serve to keep states bound by norms.[42]

Buck-passing is when a state free-rides on another state's balancing effort without contributing its own efforts. The buck-passer hopes to obtain security through the accident of being in the right geographical location or political context. Appeasement is making concessions to an opponent in the hope that its aggression will end, sparing the appeaser a costly conflict.[43] Paul Schroeder has argued that besides bandwagoning, small states have also attempted to secure themselves by "hiding from threats" and "transcending" conflicts.[44] Even allies use different strategies such as "leveraging" (getting concessions in exchange for support), "hedging" (avoiding costly decisions), and "compensating" (with some other commitment) to avoid costly wars.[45] Today, in response to China's rise, some ASEAN states are attempting to use mixed strategies, which may involve partial bandwagoning with a threatening state while using institutions to soft-balance Beijing.

The key point is that states adopt a variety of strategies to deal with a powerful or threatening actor. Soft balancing needs to be examined as part of this mix of choices.

Soft Balancing in Historical Perspective

In today's world, deepened economic globalization and other normative and material constraints on offensive warfare have made softer instruments more important than is often recognized. Balancing is much more nuanced and less straightforward than in previous eras of great-power politics. More than ever before, great powers and their allies rely on international institutions and economic instruments to balance power and restrain the threatening behavior of their opponents. The proliferation of international institutions creates multiple avenues to engage in this strategy. Since 1991, these instruments have been used more often to restrain great powers, especially the U.S. and increasingly China and Russia. Will these instruments become more successful in the emerging international order?

Answering this question requires examining the long-term relationship between hard and soft balancing in order to understand which conditions lead states to hard balance, which lead them to use softer instruments, and which lead them to pursue both strategies simultaneously. During immediate postwar periods, institutions led by the victors can be prominent instruments in international politics. But as the war's losers become increasingly restive or new actors come on the scene, the institutions will grow less effective unless there is adequate status adjustment of these states. The great powers committed to the status quo can still keep using the institutions they created to restrain the power or threatening behavior of newcomers, but if they are too inflexible they may actually provoke the rising power or revisionist state to engage in aggression. Table 2 shows the application of soft-balancing techniques since the early nineteenth century.

Looking back at Europe, the most prominent theater for traditional balance-of-power politics, we can see that balancing has often included nonmilitary coercive mechanisms. In chapter 3 I will explore in detail the Concert of Europe and the period leading up to World War II. The Concert was a successful institutional arrangement that restrained the behavior of Europe's major states in order to preserve international order. Some of the threats to international order emanated from these states' volatile domestic politics, in particular their revolutionary movements. Post-Napoleonic Europe witnessed the greatest experiment in institutionalized restraint of great powers, a soft-balancing effort in which Concert diplomacy was systematically used to legitimize or delegitimize their behavior and restrain their aggression toward each other.[46] The collapse of the Concert in 1853 and the ensuing intense hard balancing produced violent military conflicts that began with the Crimean War and culminated with World War I.

Following the Great War of 1914–18, European states once again resorted to soft balancing through the League of Nations, although they simultaneously relied on hard-balancing strategies. The League was called into action on many occasions: to address Germany's territorial conquests, Italy's invasion of Ethiopia, and Japan's aggression in China, among other events. Facing the threatening rise of Germany, Japan, and Italy, the Allied powers engaged in soft balancing as well as haphazard hard-balancing efforts. The former included asymmetric arms-control agreements, condemning resolutions at the League of Nations, and economic sanctions. These soft-balancing measures, meant to delegitimize the positions and claims of the revisionist powers, only stoked the virulent nationalism of their populations and enabled their leaders' aggressive behavior. Yet hard-balancing efforts also failed, and from 1939 to 1945 the world witnessed the most violent conflict in its entire history. Despite claims that hard balancing was not tried until too late, the arms buildup and alliance activities were intense, and we cannot know if more balancing would have prevented the war.

Table 2 Historical soft balancing, limited hard balancing, and hard balancing

Period	Main states	Instruments	
		Hard Balancing	Soft Balancing
Concert Era (1815–1853)	Austria, Prussia, Russia, France, UK	—	Concert System
Post–World War I (1919–1939)	Allied vs. Axis powers	Alliances/arms buildup	League of Nations/ economic sanctions
Cold War Era (1949–1991)	U.S. vs. USSR Blocs	Alliances/arms buildup	United Nations
	NAM vs. Superpowers	—	United Nations/ Non-Aligned Movement
Immediate Post–Cold War Era (1991–2010)	Russia & China vs. U.S.	Limited arms buildup	UN Security Council
	Other second ranking states	—	ASEAN/UN Security Council
Rising Power Era (2010–)	U.S. vs. Russia	NATO/arms buildup	Sanctions/limited alignments
	U.S. vs. China	Arms buildup/alliances	Limited alignments
	Europe vs. Russia	NATO/limited arms buildup	Sanctions
	India vs. China	Limited arms buildup	Limited alignments
	ASEAN	—	ARF/Law of the Sea Tribunal

In the aftermath of World War II, the great powers helped to create the UN system and resurrected some principles of collective security. Although the postwar peace quickly evolved into the Cold War, both superpowers used the UN and its institutions as restraining devices in order to legitimize their own stances and delegitimize their opponent's. It is generally assumed that hard balancing was the chief instrument of Cold War politics, but the Conference on Security and Cooperation in Europe (CSCE) arising from the Helsinki process, which began in 1973 as a series of talks and agreements between Eastern and Western countries on a basket of issues ranging from arms control to human rights, was used as a diplomatic forum by European states to institutionally restrain the Soviet Union and its allies. Moscow participated in these forums to gain legitimacy for its positions as well as to restrain Western behavior, using the UN and other channels for the same purpose. Western countries and the Soviet Bloc states also practiced economic sanctions toward one another and used arms control as an instrumental mechanism for restraining each other's power. But these soft-balancing instruments were all secondary to the intense hard-balancing strategies pursued by the superpowers and their respective alliances. The newly emerging states attempted limited soft balancing through the Non-Aligned Movement and at the UN. While their concrete impact was not immediately visible, they played a cushioning role as norm entrepreneurs in the areas of decolonization and nuclear disarmament. Independent-minded Western countries such as France under de Gaulle also attempted limited soft balancing by refusing to join NATO and making efforts to restrain American power in Europe.

The near-unipolar world that emerged at the end of the Cold War witnessed a proliferation of institutions at the global and regional levels. American efforts to use U.S. power coercively, especially toward regional challengers, generated important instances of soft-balancing attempts, in particular by Russia, China, and a few U.S. allies such as Germany and France. As I will show in chapter 5, two cases stand out: the 1999 Kosovo intervention and the 2003 Iraq invasion.

Especially during the George W. Bush administration, soft balancing through multiple institutional avenues became the key strategy to constrain U.S. power. These efforts often involved the formation of limited diplomatic coalitions or ententes intended to delegitimize America's coercive behavior.[47] American interventions became more difficult when the U.S. ignored or sidestepped the UN, in part because of their lack of legitimacy. The case study I will present in chapter 5 concludes that soft balancing did not prevent American interventions, but it did play a role in the U.S. decision to withdraw from Iraq. The Obama administration made a strong argument for withdrawal based on the lack of international legitimacy for the U.S. intervention and continued presence in Iraq. In short, soft balancing was partially successful in restraining U.S. behavior, even though it failed to stop the initial intervention. To a great extent, the Obama administration's reluctance to become more involved in Libya and Syria could be a result of the soft balancing in Iraq by key states.

Soft Balancing in the Emerging World

Beyond the case of the United States, the rise of China has also engendered low levels of balancing during the two decades since the end of the Cold War. China's rise is historically unprecedented: it accrued substantial economic wealth through an export-driven strategy that undermined the economic power of the dominant state. Beijing's new wealth has fueled a steady but focused increase in military spending, expansion of naval power, acquisition and use of asymmetric strategies such as cyber warfare, and the increasing escalation of territorial disputes with neighboring states. China has slowly sought to build a blue-water navy that will include aircraft carriers and submarines. These limited hard-balancing activities are yet to constitute a major affront to the existing order, but they may do so in coming years as Chinese capabilities begin to balance or even replace American hegemony in the region. In response, regional states and the United States have resorted to a mixed strategy comprising soft balancing, limited hard balancing, and diplomatic engagement.

Russia's not-so-peaceful resurgence has drawn responses that have elements of both hard and soft balancing. The hard-balancing efforts have included NATO's increased unity and its stationing of additional troops in Eastern Europe and the Baltic states. The soft-balancing efforts include Russia's expulsion from the G-8, with the offer of return if Moscow modified its behavior. Following Russia's involvement in Ukraine, the Western nations imposed economic and political sanctions on Russian companies and individuals. Russia responded with its own sanctions and formed limited balancing efforts with China and friendly states in the former Soviet Union. It has attempted to create its own economic union in Central Asia. Moscow and Beijing have also been making soft-balancing and limited hard-balancing efforts, although these have yet to produce meaningful gains.

These three post–Cold War soft-balancing efforts—against the U.S., China, and Russia—have yielded mixed results. One area in which soft balancing has been effective is in ensuring that the three powers' aggressive behavior has cost them international legitimacy. The U.S. invasion and occupation of Iraq failed to garner international approval, Russia's behavior in the Ukraine has been roundly condemned and generated sanctions, and China has received little international support for its claims to South China Sea islets or for its island-building activities. The tribunal of the Law of the Sea declared in 2016 that Chinese island-building activity had no legal basis at all. Russia's behavior also produced hard balancing, though not rising to the Cold War levels.

What is interesting is that the target states themselves are developing counter strategies to achieve their goals. A prime example is the willingness of China's friends in Southeast Asia (especially Cambodia) to prevent the necessary consensus for ASEAN to act on several issues. Southeast Asia's consensus-based diplomatic norms make a divisive strategy relatively easy to execute, and in this respect the design of institutions becomes an important element in the efficacy of soft-balancing measures. The UN Security Council veto power of the Permanent 5 is another clear example of an institutional structure that can both inhibit and promote soft balancing, depending on the context.

The story of balancing continues. U.S. president Donald Trump has accused American allies of free-riding and has promised to revamp NATO and other alliances in order to reduce this problem. He also explicitly wanted to improve U.S. relations with Russia, which were badly bruised in the aftermath of the Putin regime's annexation of Crimea and support for insurgencies in eastern Ukraine. But the most likely balance-of-power relationship will be with China if the Trump administration's jingoistic rhetoric against North Korea compels Beijing to step up its own military buildup. Hard balancing is likely to emerge, at least in this relationship, breaking away from the softer and limited balancing approaches that the U.S. has employed since the Nixon era.

Soft-balancing approaches occupy an important space in foreign policy in that they give threatened states a set of options that fall between costly arms races and wars on the one hand, and doing nothing on the other. They can assuage the balancing state's domestic public opinion and also influence public opinion in the threatening state. The latter effect may or may not be positive, as the target state's leaders can use soft-balancing efforts against it to justify further aggression. Still, in a complex world such as the one we live in, soft-balancing approaches must be part of a mix of strategies to prevent aggressive policies.

Soft Balancing from Concert
to the Cold War

Two prominent historical examples of soft balancing through institutions are the Concert of Europe (1815–53) and the League of Nations (1920–39). Both were created by the great powers of the day to restrain their adversaries from engaging in aggressive policies. Neither institution paid much attention to the interests of smaller states—the Concert practically none. The League made these states partial beneficiaries when it was convenient to do so. While neither the Concert nor the League survived for long, they left behind ideas and strategies great powers have practiced ever since.

The Concert of Europe

The Concert of Europe consisted of the five great powers that emerged from the Napoleonic Wars of 1799 to 1815—the UK, Austria, Prussia, Russia, and France—and existed as an active international institution between 1815 and 1823. It then continued in weaker form until 1853. The concept of conference diplomacy, one of its key innovations, continued until the early twentieth century. The Concert system is largely credited for the absence of great-power wars in Europe between 1815 and 1853 as leaders employed diplomacy to manage crises that, if not for the Concert, could have led to major armed conflicts.[1]

The Concert system was the product of the Congress of Vienna, which met at the Austrian capital from September 1814 through June 1815 amid much pomp and splendor. It was premised on several foundations. First, the great powers were responsible for monitoring and managing the peace settlement of Vienna, which ended the Napoleonic Wars. Second, changes in territorial boundaries would be made only with the approval of all great powers. Third, the interests of all great-power members of the European state system must be protected. Fourth, the great powers should not make unilateral changes to their foreign-policy positions, especially those that would disadvantage another power, but must obtain a consensus among all powers. Finally, no great power should be humiliated by any other power.[2] This last measure recognized great-power status as a key ingredient of the Concert system. Even the considerably weakened Ottoman Empire had to be kept alive to avoid a great-power scramble over its territorial possessions.[3]

The Concert was a bold experiment in combining hard- and soft-balancing approaches. As Kal Holsti states, the Concert system and balance of power were "not opposites, but [were] complementary. In the minds of the peacemakers in 1814–15, the Concert could not work unless there was a balance, defined in territorial terms."[4] The Concert system even affected alliance patterns. The Quadruple Alliance among Austria, Prussia, Russia, and Britain, signed in Paris on November 20, 1815, was not a typical military alliance. It was meant to prevent any expansionist power from once again threatening the European order and the independence of states as France had done under Napoleon. But its mechanisms included periodic conferences of the leaders of the great powers, including France, to settle disputes and prevent the use of military power to change the balance. Most meetings were held on an ad hoc basis as the Concert never created a formal institutional mechanism.[5] This elastic institutional dimension is what differentiated the Concert system from simple hard balancing. Most realist scholarship pays little attention to this nonmilitary institutional dimension of balance of power. Liberal scholars would highlight the liberal dimensions of institutions, while constructivists pay special attention to the normative aspects of the Concert experience.[6] While both approaches have their strengths, I contend that the Concert's dual nature—the material dimensions of the experiment along with the normative dimensions—demands an eclectic approach.

The Concert system was largely based on self-binding institutional and normative restraints by Europe's great powers that were meant to strengthen their hard- and soft-balancing efforts against each other. As far as the great powers were concerned, it was perhaps the most successful experiment in creating institutional restraint to that point. It included political arrangements at the domestic and regional levels as well as monitoring, regulating, and sanctioning bodies. It also established procedures, rules, and norms to govern the behavior of states.[7] The British foreign secretary, Viscount Castlereagh; the chief minister of Austria, Prince Clemens von Metternich; French ambassador Charles Maurice de Talleyrand-Périgold (popularly known as Talleyrand); Russia's Tsar Alexander I; and the Prussian diplomatic representative had, in other words, found a way to self-bind. As Holsti puts it, they had created a mechanism to "check or regulate their own ambitions."[8] Diplomatic historian Paul Schroeder correctly points out that this institutionalized balance-of-power system broke with eighteenth-century precedents of interstate balancing as well as with other political practices of the period.[9] As John Ikenberry explains, the Vienna Treaty made use of earlier mechanisms—limits on power, the redistribution of territory and power, counterbalancing, and reinforcement of state autonomy—but the institutional aspects were new. The result was a unique arrangement that "exhibited characteristics of a 'pactum de Controhendo,' a pact of restraint."[10]

The Concert system was based on the principle of legitimacy among great powers, and wide acceptance of this legitimacy was apparent in the stable relationships that characterized the system. As Henry Kissinger points out, having accepted the premise of the system, states were more inclined to seek adjustments rather than try to overthrow it.[11] Where these efforts at improvement did not succeed, we often see the hand of Britain, which believed in hard balancing and preferred a situation in which alignments could be made and remade as needed.[12] It saw itself as Europe's balancer, changing alliances as necessary to maintain the continent's equilibrium. The temporary but crucial success of the Concert system suggests that hard balancing is not automatic but man-

ual, and that it can be complemented with soft balancing. Britain's opposition to aspects of the Concert also suggests that one power may
upset an institutional order for its own political gain.

The legitimacy that the conservative great powers wanted to create
was based on international law as they established it. Their ideal, however, was not grounded in a great sense of justice, equality, or the will of
the people but in Machiavellian realpolitik. The realist roots of this enterprise thus cannot be excluded from any honest appraisal of the Concert system. Except for revolutionary states, the system they devised paid
no attention to any state's political character and gave a handful of great
powers and their rulers the right to determine the nature of the international order.[13] Henry Kissinger acknowledges that the Concert was not
based on principles of justice, and that the principle of relative security
meant diminishing the security of some for the larger good.[14] The great
powers paid no attention to smaller states, which were expected to "rat-
ify *ex-post facto* the authoritative decisions" made by the great powers.
Even though nominal equality was maintained, great powers made virtually all the crucial decisions.[15] They pursued hard balancing as well—
with limitations—but this was supposed to be aided by soft-balancing
techniques relying on institutions and normative restrictions. They did
not, however, always preserve the balance of power in the same way they
had done before the Concert or as they would after its demise.

Although the powers were united in their desire to preserve international order, their motives for supporting the Concert system differed. Britain wanted a general equilibrium to prevent a continental war,
and as an island nation with a powerful navy, it was confident of its own
security. Austria's Metternich, who saw himself as the legitimate custo-
dian of the balance-of-power system, sought to prevent revolutionary
upheavals in Europe and claimed the right to intervene to defeat social
unrest throughout his multiethnic empire.[16]

It is often asked how the Concert system succeeded in helping to
prevent major wars between European powers. From 1815 until the end
of the nineteenth century, only four wars occurred in Europe, and they
were limited in objectives, scale, and duration. None of these conflicts
challenged the survival of a major power. Even in its weakened state, the
Concert helped to prevent direct great-power war in Europe for more

than half a century. To be sure, the long peace had little impact on the periphery, where conflict continued unabated—often pitting one European colonial power against another or against local forces. But in Europe itself there was a definite reduction in conflict. As Kal Holsti reports, during the ninety-nine years following the Congress of Vienna, from 1815 until 1914, conflict and armed intervention occurred at a 13 percent lower rate than in the previous century.[17]

Holsti describes the Concert's successes as often the result of self-abnegation at the cost of domestic opposition: "the British relinquishment of colonial conquests for the sake of constructing the overall balance in the Treaty of Vienna; Guizot's moderate policies and abandonment of the French revisionist cause, Alexander's feelings of loyalty toward the unity of the powers, and his and Nicholas I's sacrifice or tempering of Russian ambitions in Greece and elsewhere in the Balkans for the greater good of Europe, all despite immense pressure to take aggrandizing actions from nationalist and military elements in the Tsar's court."[18]

In a broader sense, what accounts for the Concert's success? The relative peace that prevailed under the Concert system reflected a number of factors: the inclusion of all great powers; the decision by the leaders to see the institution not as a means of exacting punishment on the vanquished and permanently fixing a particular distribution of power but as a mechanism to prevent future abuses of power; the respect (within limits) of states' status aspirations; institutional mechanisms that encouraged regular contact—and thus socialization—among great powers; a flexible approach to institutionalization; and the fact that no great power was looking for absolute conquest in Europe. Holsti identifies two further factors: the absence of armament-making technology that would have made quick land grabs possible, and the generally conservative nature of great powers, which precluded the highly expansionist ideologies that would take hold in the twentieth century.[19]

One dimension of the Concert's success was that it embodied an effort by the winners of the Napoleonic Wars to prevent such hegemonic conquests by creating an institutional and normative mechanism to resolve conflict. It was not created to punish the vanquished. The May 1814 Treaty of Paris did not impose huge indemnities on the restored French monarch, Louis XVIII. Although France lost some over-seas territories, it was permitted to keep the areas it had possessed in January 1792 and was even given some new enclaves. British and German efforts to obtain indemnities from France did not succeed; Louis XVIII made clear his unwillingness to pay any financial impositions, and the powers ultimately even let the French keep art treasures looted by Napoleon's forces.[20] The victorious powers also included France in their deliberations about territory. Although they initially wanted to keep those decisions to themselves, they feared Paris would organize smaller states against them. The point is that the victorious powers resisted the impulse to exact revenge and retribution in deference to the larger goal of preserving international order. This included avoiding making France too weak to play a meaningful role as a great power.[21]

In contrast to the previous century's practice, European great powers after 1815 did not seek to destroy or diminish the status of other great powers while giving themselves special rights and duties to preserve the system. Instead, they sought to maintain the territory, status, and vital interests of their peers. They accomplished this through a series of interlocking treaties and diplomatic practices and a commitment not to intervene in one another's internal affairs. The willingness to observe legal restraints on territorial expansion contributed to the general preservation of peace.[22] For instance, during the Seven Weeks' War between Prussia and Austria in 1866, Otto von Bismarck, the advisor to King William I of Prussia, insisted on not humiliating the Austrians. No victory parades were held in Vienna, and the war was ended as soon as Prussia's limited objectives were obtained.[23]

Institutional mechanisms grounded in legitimacy were a further aspect of the Concert system. The Vienna settlement of 1814–15 that followed the Paris Treaty had three core principles: "compensation for the victors, legitimacy and balance of power."[24] The concept of balance of power was strongly supported by Metternich, Castlereagh, and Talleyrand, although Talleyrand thought a perfect equilibrium was not possible. The former two believed that an equilibrium of territory, population, and resources would reduce the incidence of war to a minimum.[25] Despite Talleyrand's skepticism, institutional arrangements became critical to maintaining the balance of power.

The leaders of the great powers also wanted to create an executive body to deal with threats to balance of power as and when they occurred. The March 1814 Treaty of Chaumont stipulated such an arrangement, and the Quadruple Alliance of November 1815 called for periodic meetings of foreign ministers to deal with matters of peace. Under pressure from monarchs, the Quadruple Alliance intervened in countries threatened by liberal revolutions, despite British objections, but this disagreement did not cause the collapse of the Concert system. The British attended every foreign minister meeting where international crises were discussed.[26] The inclusion of all the great powers and the model of joint decision making contributed to cooperation by imposing reputational costs on any nation that reneged on its commitments.[27] Although institutionalized, the system was flexible; it prevented the formation of rigid formal alliances. It was decentralized and self-regulating, and its management was considered the responsibility of all great powers. In part, reduced conflict on the European continent came at the expense of peripheral states. The availability of colonial theaters for expansion made the competition less zero-sum, and it was not until the territories for colonial conquest were largely occupied that statesmen once again began to view competition in zero-sum terms.[28]

Soft- and hard-balancing techniques were often combined to prevent war. The mechanism of conference diplomacy facilitated bargaining among the great powers and may have helped to bring diplomats' views into alignment, as Matthew Rendall notes.[29] For instance, in the early 1830s, when the Belgians rebelled against Dutch rule, instead of interfering unilaterally in the conflict for their individual gain, the five great powers met four times during 1831 to discuss armed intervention. They ultimately managed to resolve the conflict before it spread to other areas.[30] Other observers agree with Rendall that by acting as a security regime, the Concert helped the great powers to agree on issues like this.[31] This does not mean that it faced no crises or that the great powers were able to avoid all unilateral interventions. In many more instances, they were unable to agree—Rendall cites the French intervention in Spain and Russian intervention in Turkey in the 1820s, the imposition of a treaty settlement on the Dutch by Britain and France in 1832, and the decision by Russia (over France's opposition) to send troops to the

Bosporus in 1833. He notes that "Austria's and Britain's 1840 intervention to drive Mehemet Ali Pasha out of Syria so infuriated Paris that many feared a European war," although it did not materialize.[32]

The Concert system also motivated great powers to adopt policies that were not only popular at home but also defensible to other states. The Concert gets credit for Russia's restraint in this period. During the Greek revolution of 1821–29, Russia waited seven years before intervening, and when it did, it ultimately brokered a peace treaty with the Ottoman Empire that, in Rendall's words, "essentially restored the European status quo." Far from pressing its clear material advantage to gain hegemony, Russia under Alexander I demonstrated restraint that Paul Schroeder attributes to "moral principle."[33] He argues that it was not hard balancing that mellowed Russia but its need to satisfy friends and allies Austria and Prussia, whose help it wanted with the problems it faced in Poland and Turkey.[34] While keen to pursue its interests, during this period, Russia treated legitimacy as a key principle of international relations.

The Concert system lasted in its strong form for less than a decade, although it survived in limited manifestations for a subsequent three decades. Yet the hard-balancing politics that followed the Concert had a far worse record of preserving peace. The European balance of power did not deter Britain's Lord Palmerston or France's Napoleon III from participating in the Crimean War (1853–56), Count Camillo Cavour of Piedmont from waging war with Austria in 1859, or Bismarck from launching the German unification wars (1864–71). Britain also sought to prevent Russia from enlarging its territory as the Ottoman Empire declined. Hard balancing by the great powers in the post-Concert era was more a catalyst for war than a means of preventing it.

The Crimean War stands out as a failure of both hard and soft balancing. The French emperor Napoleon III's decision to isolate Russia from the Holy Alliance of Britain, Prussia, Austria, and Russia was a major catalyst for the crisis that preceded the war. The French successfully demanded that the Ottoman Empire replace the Orthodox clergy in charge of Christian holy places around Jerusalem with Catholic monks, infuriating Russia. In February 1853, Tsar Nicholas sent Prince Menshikov on a special mission to Istanbul demanding the dismissal of the minister who had put Catholics in control in Jerusalem and insisting on the protection of Orthodox citizens of Turkey. When this mission failed, Russia took over the Turkish provinces of Moldavia and Walachia.[35]

Britain, Austria, and Prussia all feared that Russia had ambitions to gain control over the Ottoman Empire's strategic territories. A conference in Vienna in July 1853, where Russian interpretations of Turkish concessions were vehemently opposed by Britain and France, failed to reach agreement. The Turks declared war on Russia that October, and the Russians responded by destroying a Turkish fleet at Sinope. This put pressure on Britain and France to send expeditionary forces to Sevastopol, the Russian Black Sea Fleet's base on the Crimean Peninsula, in September 1854. Although London was interested in fighting a limited war to protect the European order, Paris sought a revision of that order. Russia was ultimately defeated by Prussia's and Austria's refusal to take its side; instead they joined the Anglo-French alliance.[36] The further weakening of Turkish territorial control would bring major territorial revisions.

Why did the Concert system fail to prevent the Crimean War? Soft balancing was no longer working well. Neither France nor Russia feared that it would damage its reputation by violating the Concert principle that no great power should suffer at the expense of another. France was also playing an intense hard-balancing game by trying to divide European alliances in the hope of remaking them in its favor. Thus, even as soft balancing was failing, hard-balancing calculations were not creating peace. In a sense, the Crimean War was inevitable, as it arose from the long-term decline of the Ottoman Empire and the other powers' ambitions to capture as much of the Turks' land and influence as possible. Neither Nicholas I nor Napoleon III nor the British government could retreat in the conflict for prestige once it was launched. As A. J. P. Taylor puts it, "Nicholas needed a subservient Turkey for the sake of Russian security; Napoleon needed success for the sake of his domestic position; the British government needed an independent Turkey for the security of the Eastern Mediterranean. . . . Mutual fear, not mutual aggression, caused the Crimean war."[37] The changed international and domestic environments, the availability of new weapons like Enfield rifle-muskets, logistical and transportation innovations involving telegraph, railways, and steamships, and the temptation, especially on the Russian side, to go for unilateral gains had brought a general loss of the Vienna spirit among the great powers. The gradual decline of soft-balancing mechanisms and the failure of hard balancing left the European great powers sliding toward a major war.

The conditions that enabled the successes of the Concert system largely match the conditions that favor a soft-balancing strategy. Coalitions in the period following the Napoleonic Wars were defensive and status quo oriented, not meant for mastery over Europe. Russia, for example, was relatively contented with the territorial status quo. Although it tried to dominate Turkish politics, it did so for defensive reasons.[38] Fearing no existential threats, the great powers recognized their security interdependence and "consciously self-disciplined to avoid undermining the system overall."[39] The times when the Concert system succeeded in averting conflict also suggest that institutional mechanisms work better when alliances are flexible and the great powers' goals are not extreme. If great powers are gaining from the system in both material and status dimensions, they are more likely to preserve it. Schroeder suggests that great-power competition in the nineteenth century was "like the competition for shares of the market in an oligopolistic industry."[40] Collectively, great powers had much to gain from maintaining the system.

By the same token, if a great power feels it has no further room to expand its sphere of influence and gain economically, it may challenge the order militarily. Hard balancing did not prevent war during the twentieth century (or even reduce its severity), nor was it a source of peace prior to the Concert system. Both supporters and opponents of balance of power saw it as unsatisfactory. As early as 1711, Alexander Pope warned: "Now Europe's balanc'd, neither Side prevails, For nothing's left in either of the Scales."[41] Or as Elrod put it more prosaically, "Balance-of-power politics—the politics of confrontation—generated intolerable international tensions, produced increasingly serious armed conflicts, and inspired progressively extravagant plans of aggression. It neither maintained peace nor preserved the independence of sovereign states; by the time of the French Revolution, the international system had broken down altogether."[42] Far from stabilizing the system, as realist theorists of international relations would contend, hard-balancing efforts often increased tensions and aggressiveness. Despite these shortcomings, statesmen are often tempted by hard balancing as it gives them some recourse against a threatening power.

The End of the Long Nineteenth-Century Peace

The Concert system was not permanent, and after it fell, the great powers returned to hard balancing. Crises and wars upset the European order, and the peace of the long nineteenth century came to an end in July 1914. For some, the First World War reflected a collapse of the balance-of-power system. For others, the war's causes lay more in great powers' neglect of the institutions they had created for war prevention, and their return to zero-sum competition based on miscalculation and misreading of their adversaries' capabilities and intentions.

The chief culprit in upsetting the European order was Germany, which rose as a world power relatively quickly. After reunification in 1871, Germany under Bismarck embarked upon a massive program to achieve global power by military and nonmilitary means. Bismarck began establishing military alliances in 1879 with the conclusion of the Austro-German alliance against Russia. In 1882, Germany concluded a treaty with Italy against a French offensive and a secret agreement with Romania against a possible Russian attack, both of which threatened the security interests of France and Russia. By 1894 there were two alliances: the Triple Alliance of Germany, Austria-Hungary, and Italy, and the Dual Alliance of France and Russia—with each coalition offering its members military support in the event of an attack.[43] These two hard-balancing alliances may have created an ephemeral semblance of stability, but they also showed the risks of relying on tight military alliances. By the early 1880s, European great powers were competing intensely for new territories in Africa, Asia, and the Pacific.[44]

Bismarck's strategy was successful until German nationalism became virulent as a result of Kaiser Wilhelm II's policy of aggressively asserting Germany's global power ambitions. Austria-Hungary's decision to join Germany in this pursuit created a bipolar alliance system in

Europe. The resulting intense hard-balancing competition by France, the UK, and Russia against the German led-coalition made the German leaders even more belligerent. The alliances grew more rigid, and crises such as the one in 1911 in Morocco increased the distrust among the major powers.[45] Balance-of-power theory tells us that these well-established military coalitions should have been sufficient to preserve peace, but they did not. As Bernadotte Schmitt states: "It was the schism of Europe in Triple Alliance and Triple Entente which fused the various quarrels and forces into one gigantic struggle for the balance of power; and the war came in 1914 because then, for the first time, the lines were sharply drawn between the two rival groups, and neither could yield on the Serbian issue without seeing the balance passed definitely to the other side."[46]

The war was triggered by the assassination of Archduke Ferdinand of Austria in the Bosnian city of Sarajevo. But the preparations for war had been going on for three decades. The powers risked war in 1914 because they feared their positions were being weakened by their adversaries' growth.[47] According to the military theory of the day, advances in technology and transportation had made offensive weaponry and doctrines a necessity, giving a major advantage to those who could make the first strike and creating a "cult of the offensive" among the European powers.[48] This made the balance of power a fleeting condition in their eyes, and the pressure to take advantage of strategic openings moved them toward catastrophic conflict.

World War I produced some 37 million casualties and reshaped the map of Europe.[49] But the "war to end to all wars" did not produce the expected peace. The great powers ignored many of the lessons from the Vienna settlement of 1815 and the Concert system, meting out a punishment to Germany that bore no resemblance to the one applied to post-Napoleonic France by the statesmen in Paris and Vienna a century before. The Treaty of Versailles made onerous demands for retribution, while the victors made little effort to integrate Germany into the European order. They thus failed to create a peace, and the bitter war, even after its end, divided them more than ever. Germany was named the sole aggressor, made to bear all financial burdens of reparation, and a number of new, ethnically fragmented states were created between Germany

and Russia, which also faced intervention by the Allied forces.[50] Prudent
and visionary statecraft was missing on all sides.

The League of Nations

While the peace settlement following World War I bore no resemblance
to that of 1815, the war's aftermath did see the creation of a new institution intended to establish a collective security system among states. The
League of Nations grew out of the 1919 Paris conference deliberations
and was formed in January 1920. It was one of the fourteen points presented by U.S. president Woodrow Wilson, although the United States
never joined the institution because of Republican opposition in the
U.S. Senate.[51] Despite Wilson's attempts to steer clear of European balance-of-power notions, the League's founders derived some ideas from
the Concert of Europe, including the great powers' role as the keepers of
global security. The League Covenant comprised several articles dealing
with war avoidance, peaceful settlement of disputes, and diplomatic, legal, economic, and military sanctions against aggressors.[52]

The victors were far from united in their vision of the postwar
settlement. French prime minister Georges Clemenceau, who disliked
Wilson's proposal for the League, demanded the resurrection of an alli-
ance-based balance-of-power system and a permanent reduction in
German military power. British prime minister David Lloyd George
eventually sided with Clemenceau, although he had initially supported
a more moderate approach.[53] Despite this opposition, the League was
established, with the major powers holding veto power on key decisions. The idea of collective security was enshrined in article 10 of
the Covenant: "Members of the League undertake to respect and preserve as against external aggression the territorial integrity and existing
political independence of all Members of the League. In case of any such
aggression, or in case of any threat or danger of such aggression, the
Council shall advise upon the means by which this obligation shall be
fulfilled."[54]

The League principles of collective security created an obligation
on its members but had no strong legal force with which to enforce this
obligation. Although the League principles proposed sanctions in the

event of territorial aggression, members made no formal commitment to come to one another's aid. This effectively nullified the collective security provisions. It also reflected Wilson's position that "legal and moral institutions are not easily imposed on society, domestic or international. Institutional constraints and obligations must grow and evolve."[55]

Wilson vehemently criticized balance-of-power ideas, arguing that the Allied soldiers "fought to do away with an order and to establish a new one, and the center and characteristic of the old order was that venerable thing which we used to call the 'balance of power'—a thing in which the balance was determined ... by the unstable equilibrium of competitive interests; a balance which was maintained by jealous watchfulness and an antagonism of interests, which, though it was generally latent, was always deep-seated."[56] He wanted to replace balance of power with a "community of power," meaning that any aggressor would confront the preponderant power of all states, whereas in a balance-of-power system an aggressive power "faces only the contingent and inferior deterrent created by a coalition made up of those states whose immediate interests are threatened."[57] He was convinced that article 10 of the Covenant would deter conquests, with diplomatic and economic boycotts as the chief enforcement tools.

While campaigning for the ratification of the Versailles Treaty and the League, Wilson told a crowd at Indianapolis: "The most terrible thing is outlawry. The most formidable thing is to be absolutely isolated." Military action was "on the outskirts. War is a secondary threat."[58] In September 1919, he made some forty speeches across the United States in just twenty-two days, putting great strain on his already failing health. The next month, he suffered a debilitating stroke that prevented any further campaigning.[59] The legislation ratifying American entry failed in the Senate the following March, keeping the U.S. out of the League throughout its existence. What Wilson envisioned certainly qualifies as soft balancing: he favored collective security and legitimacy denial through the League as a response to aggressive actions, and he vehemently repudiated the European powers' hard-balancing strategies. The aim was to prevent war by using an international institution to restrain the great powers' behavior.

THE RESURGENCE OF GERMANY AND BALANCING EFFORTS

Germany initiated an ill-conceived war in 1914 and after considerable loss to itself and its allies surrendered through the armistice agreement of November 1918. The measures then imposed on Germany by the Allies further alienated both the German people and the elite. Hitler's rise and Germany's swift rearming were responses to this humiliation. The Allies answered with both hard-balancing and soft-balancing strategies. International relations scholars often argue that since the prevailing balance-of-power system in the 1930s failed to prevent the war, what was needed was a greater balancing effort by the status quo powers.[60] It is seldom appreciated that the Allies tried to restrain German power and threatening behavior by both hard and soft means. The soft-balancing efforts, though haphazard, came largely via the League of Nations. Such efforts directed at Germany's ally Japan included economic sanctions and the conclusion of unequal arms-control agreements. Ultimately, both types of balancing failed. The revisionist powers were bent on altering the international power structure and saw the status quo powers as only trying to maintain their control and deprive the rising powers of the wealth, status, and power that were their due.

The League of Nations served as the key institutional instrument to balance and prevent German resurgence. The victors of World War I believed that through the League they could impose punitive sanctions on Germany and collect the indemnities mandated by the 1919 settlement. Yet they disagreed over whether the League should be a means for achieving peace or a means of imposing peace terms on the vanquished. The British leaders believed the League Covenant offered a constitution-like instrument for creating a moral community. Britain was keen to reintegrate Germany, as France had been reintegrated after the Napoleonic Wars through the Concert system, and thus develop a dual approach toward the use of institutions for achieving balance of power.[61] The British leaders' expectation was that Hitler could be accommodated without war, just as previous great powers had been.[62] The French, on the other hand, saw the League as a defensive alliance to make the 1919 settlement permanent.[63] Intending to use both hard and soft balancing to keep Germany from returning as a major power, they sought British cooperation in balancing Germany and supported the Little Entente alliance of Yugoslavia, Czechoslovakia, and Romania.

Germany was badly hurt by the war-guilt clause of the Treaty of Versailles and the French occupation of the Ruhr industrial area until Berlin paid reparations. Democratic rule in Germany was the most significant casualty.[64] The Rhineland clause of the Versailles Treaty was meant to cripple Germany's military capabilities and create a permanently asymmetric relationship between Germany and the war victors. Articles 42 and 43 of the treaty took the Rhineland from Germany's sovereign control and denied Germany the right to maintain military capability—troops or fortifications—west of the Rhine or along the river's east bank.[65]

The initial French idea of creating a Franco-British alliance to punish Germany and enforce the Versailles Treaty ultimately gave way to greater reliance on multilateral means, especially the League, as the enforcement mechanism. By adopting the League's framework, Germany was legally and politically constrained within a rule-based multilateral system that ensured that revisions to Versailles would take into account French security concerns.[66] When the French found themselves unable to form the necessary military coalition to restrain Germany, they sought balancing through institutional means. But where French concerns were primarily security based, Britain's were largely economic. It was interested in enmeshing Germany through institutions and quickly restoring what had been its second-largest export market. The British public also had developed a strong aversion to war and did not welcome the idea that a full-blown alliance with France could drag them into yet another European conflict.[67]

Thus the League was viewed as an alternative to traditional balance-of-power politics, and it played a key role in the grand strategies of both France and Britain in the 1920s and early 1930s. The French used it to restrain German remilitarization and to obtain security guarantees from Britain, while the British used the disarmament negotiations under the League to contain German resurgence without having to rearm themselves.[68] Understandably, however, Italy, Japan, and Germany, the three revisionist powers, sought to undercut the League's coercive powers and interference in their expansionist policies. Germany in particular sought relief from reparations and the removal of restrictions on armaments and territorial expansion.[69] The League was further constrained by the self-imposed isolation of the U.S., the seclusion of the Soviet Union, and the initial distancing of defeated powers, especially Germany.[70] The unsettled territorial issues of Eastern Europe applied further pressure as the League could not cope with repeated crises involving smaller powers.

The League had some minor successes in placing institutional checks on states. In 1924, it concluded a protocol for peaceful settlements of disputes, and the 1925 Treaty of Locarno allowed Germany to enter the League with a seat on the Council. It negotiated settlements of minor disputes such as those between Greece and Bulgaria, and facilitated the follow-up meeting of the 1922 Washington Naval Disarmament Treaty.[71] Later, the League would play an important role in soft balancing directed toward Italy, the other member of the Axis alliance and a power, like Germany, determined to upset the European order.

SOFT BALANCING AGAINST ITALY

In October 1935, Italy under Benito Mussolini invaded and occupied Abyssinia (contemporary Ethiopia), an independent state that had been ruled by Emperor Haile Selassie and his predecessors since 1855. The crisis had been brewing since the Wal-Wal incident of December 1934, in which some thirty Italian and ninety Ethiopian soldiers were killed in clashes on the border of Italian Somaliland and Abyssinia's Ogaden province. Mussolini demanded compensation and rejected Ethiopia's offer of arbitration. As Italy made plans for an invasion, Britain and France attempted to de-escalate the crisis by conceding to many of the Italian demands. In January 1935, Abyssinia approached the League to request arbitration, to which Italy reluctantly agreed in May. The League found neither side culpable, a ruling that apparently incited Mussolini to further action.

The October Italian invasion of Abyssinia was swiftly condemned by the League Council. A special conference attended by some fifty states decided to impose economic sanctions under article 16 of the League Covenant, and the Council used a procedural device to avoid an Italian veto. The sanctions included an embargo on the export, reexport, and transit of all arms and munitions to Italy; the cutting off of loans and credits; a ban on importing goods grown or produced in Italy; and a ban on the sale to Italy of strategic war materials like rubber, bauxite, iron ore, chromium, and tin.[72] Italy was not prohibited from purchasing oil, steel, and coal; no country broke off diplomatic relations; and the Suez Canal was not closed to Italian troops and warships.[73]

The British were initially lenient toward Italy because they wanted to prevent Mussolini from joining Hitler's coalition. They saw balance of power as more important than either the League or Abyssinia's territorial integrity. Mussolini got hold of a British memorandum that stated: "No vital British interests exist in Abyssinia or in adjoining countries sufficient to oblige His Majesty's Government to resist a conquest of Abyssinia by Italy."[74] In addition to allowing Italy to move troops through the Suez Canal, the British let Italian planes refuel at their bases in Somaliland, British-controlled Sudanese granaries were used to feed Italian soldiers, and the Anglo-Iranian oil company continued to supply Italy with oil. An oil embargo would have probably persuaded Mussolini to withdraw from Ethiopia, as Mussolini himself acknowledged.[75] Britain even opposed efforts by two of Italy's oil suppliers, Romania and Russia, to impose sanctions. As Samuel Hoare, the new British foreign secretary, explained to the cabinet, he feared that an oil embargo would only encourage Mussolini to undertake the "mad dog" action of attacking France.[76] Hoare and French foreign minister Pierre Laval agreed on a dual approach: to engage in "most patient and cautious negotiations that would keep [Mussolini] on the Allied side" and to create "a united front in Geneva [the League of Nations] as a necessary deterrent against German aggression."[77]

The leaking of a secret British-French plan to allow Italy to take two-thirds of Abyssinia, some sixty thousand square miles, in return for which Abyssinia would be allowed to keep enough of its own former lands to preserve a three-thousand-square-mile outlet to the sea, created an uproar in Britain and Hoare was forced to resign.[78] It has also been alleged that Britain and France tried to slow down the League action on Italy and that London was not keen on implementing the sanctions.[79] Chamberlain eventually signed the Anglo-Italian Easter Accords in April

1938, approving Mussolini's conquests in Ethiopia and supporting Italy's contribution of some eighty thousand troops to fight for Francisco Franco's right-wing party in the Spanish Civil War.[80]

Both Britain and France wished to prevent Italy from siding with Germany and at different points hoped Mussolini would join their alliance. After Hitler abandoned the League in 1933, renounced the Versailles agreement, and began to remilitarize, many French leaders, as well as the French Navy, hoped for a Franco-Italian alliance. Foreign Minister Pierre Laval—who would become prime minister twice, in 1931 and 1935—wanted to use Italy as a second front as well as a route to supply weapons and materials to Eastern Europe. Laval hoped that by ending its rivalry with Italy, France would free some seventeen divisions from the Italian border to be redeployed in the "lightly protected north above the Maginot Line."[81] This hope reduced the French appetite for taking serious measures against Italy. Some even suspected that Britain and France had tacitly agreed to Italian expansion in East Africa at the 1934 Stresa conference.[82] The Franco-Italian agreement of January 1935, for instance, gave Italy a free hand in Ethiopia in return for Italy's support of Austrian sovereignty. But the British decision to support sanctions against Italy forced France to side with London, ending the prospect of an Italian coalition with France. In October 1936, Mussolini and Hitler signed the Axis alliance.[83]

Meanwhile, Italian occupation forces and Abyssinian forces continued to clash. The Italians took Addis Ababa in May 1936 and Mussolini declared himself emperor of Abyssinia. Emperor Haile Selassie's plea to the League Council to defend his country's independence fell on deaf ears. Nor did Italy's use of chemical weapons in Abyssinia during the war evoke a response from the League, showing the institution's weakness.

The Allied powers' response to Fascist Italy during the Abyssinian conflict largely involved soft balancing: economic sanctions and other measures taken through the League's collective security provisions. No hard-balancing coalition emerged to thwart Italian aggression. It was not a case of bandwagoning either, as the League did approve some sanctions—the first of their kind it had ever imposed. Those measures, League members believed, would restrain Mussolini, encourage him to withdraw, and dissuade him from further aggression. They had some limited impact, causing a one-third reduction in Italian exports, the decline of the Italian lira, and a reduction of Italy's gold reserves.[84]

Several factors, however, nullified these measures: the League's lack of an enforcement mechanism for collective security, internal politics among the Allied powers, and the Great Depression. France and England differed on the usefulness of sanctions. The French were worried that they would anger pro-Fascist leagues inside France and also weaken the French franc, while the British were concerned that an unchecked Mussolini might attack Italy's neighbors militarily. Those anxieties were astutely exploited by Mussolini, who made gestures that both threatened war and hinted at a willingness to compromise. The League-led sanctions generated intense nationalism in Italy and increased domestic support for Mussolini's absolute rule. The war in Ethiopia became highly popular among the Italian masses, who increasingly demanded autarkic policies and further state control over the economy. Italy grew more xenophobic and aggressively nationalist.[85]

By failing to stop the Italian conquest of Abyssinia or to impose collective security provisions, the League undermined its credibility as an instrument of soft balancing. Far from preventing Italian aggression, the limited sanctions the League did enact pushed Italy into the arms of Germany, which would replace Britain as Italy's chief coal supplier. This alliance, formalized in the "Pact of Steel" of 1939, increased Germany's influence in Italy while limiting the restrictions on Berlin under the Versailles Treaty.[86] According to some scholars, Fascist Italy showed only limited appetite for revisionist policies from 1922 until the Ethiopian War of 1935–36. The shift occurred with that war, and by February 1939 Italy had adopted a full-fledged revisionist strategy. Mussolini's domestic insecurity was part of the reason, but he was also influenced by Hitler's support of Italy's revisionist goals and his own perception that Britain and France lacked the ability or will to resist his territorial moves.[87] As George W. Baer put it, by "winning in Africa, winning against the League, Mussolini also won at home. Sanctions and world disapproval were used to make the war popular in Italy. Mussolini's proclamation of a new Roman empire was a great moment for Italians."[88]

Hard-balancing strategies also scuttled the key soft-balancing strategy of economic sanctions. The British were concerned that Hitler might attack Austria, and the Allies thought for a time that they could persuade Mussolini to join them to deter this move. Hitler's denunciation of the Locarno Treaty in 1936 and his occupation of Rhineland changed the European balance of power. In May of that year, Italy completed its occupation of Ethiopia, and the League removed the sanctions in July.[89] Having failed to deter Italy, the League would fail again during the Munich Crisis of 1938, when its short-lived resolution would prompt British prime minister Neville Chamberlain to declare "peace in our time." Five months later, in 1939, the League and its collective security provisions collapsed for good.[90]

This case shows that the fear of a targeted state forming a hard-balancing coalition with another adversary can affect soft-balancing efforts. Unfortunately, however, hard balancing also failed: the Allies could not get Mussolini to join their coalition against Germany. They had no stomach to fight Italy in an African country, and many of the Allied powers themselves would soon fall before Hitler's continued onslaught. The case also shows that soft balancing, which relies on institutional mechanisms and sanctions, can backfire and cause more aggressive nationalist behavior in the target state. The nature of the regime, its ideology, and its strategic goals all affect the success of soft balancing. Finally, the Italian case shows the importance of effective coordination. The sanctioning states' inability to coordinate their actions clearly limited their effect, and Mussolini adroitly took advantage of divisions among the Allies. Thus several facilitating conditions necessary to soft balancing were not present. The absence of a territorial integrity norm, the presence of an expansionist ideology, military capacity for offensive operations, and the weak legitimacy of institutions in the eyes of Italian leadership all limited soft balancing's effectiveness.

SOFT BALANCING AGAINST JAPAN

The League of Nations was also the key arena for the Allied powers' soft balancing against a rising Japan, which had engaged in aggressive expansion into China. A second institutional arena was the arms-control regime imposed on Japan by the Western powers in order to limit its naval buildup. Following World War I, Japan failed in its efforts to gain recognition as a great power within its own sphere of influence in Asia. Its friction with China over its continued presence in Manchuria deepened throughout the 1920s. The Allies' major initiative at soft balancing through the League occurred after the Manchurian episode of September 1931.

Following the 1905 Portsmouth Treaty, Japan had limited rights in a railway yard in Mukden, Manchuria. On September 18, 1931, an explosion took place there and the Japanese Kwantung Army quickly occupied the town, provoking a crisis with China, ruled by the Kuomintang Party under Chiang Kai-shek. The Japanese occupation army had acted on its own, without orders from Tokyo, specifically to prevent Japan's civilian leaders from reconciling with China.[91] Peking duly complained to the League of Nations, and the Council accordingly passed a resolution that included assurances from both Japan and China. Japan stated that it had "no territorial designs on Manchuria" and would withdraw its troops to the railway zone, while the Chinese government guaranteed the safety of Japanese nationals outside the zone.[92] Under the ruse of the Mukden incident, the Japanese military resorted to a full invasion of Manchuria, which would eventually lead to the establishment of a puppet regime there. On October 24, with a sole dissenting vote from Japan, the Council passed a resolution instructing the Japanese forces to withdraw within three weeks—an injunction Japan simply disregarded.[93]

On December 10, the Council appointed Lord Victor Bulwer-Lytton of Britain to conduct an investigation. But while the Council was adjudicating the dispute, the Japanese Army was entrenching its position, and in March 1932 Japan created a puppet state in occupied Manchuria called Manchukuo, with the last emperor of China, Pu Yi, as its nominal head. The Lytton Report, submitted to the League that September, rejected Japan's justification for the invasion. Noting that a large majority of Manchuria's population refused to recognize the Manchukuo regime, the report called for the establishment of Manchuria as an autonomous region of China.[94] A committee of the League approved the Lytton Report and issued a second report calling for Japan to withdraw its troops to the railway zone and recognize Chinese sovereignty over Manchuria. It also called upon League members not to recognize the new state of Manchukuo. Yet the great powers' unwillingness to undertake any precipitous action led the committee to omit any recommendations for economic or military measures against Japan.[95] In February 1933, the League General Assembly approved both reports by a 42 to 1 vote, with Japan again the sole dissenter. On March 11, the General Assembly reaffirmed article 10 of the Covenant respecting territorial integrity and political independence of member states, the ending of hostilities, and the withdrawal of armed forces.[96] On March 27, Japan withdrew from the League.[97]

This soft-balancing effort through the League's collective security provisions failed because Japan, already suffering an economic crisis and with its military poised to take effective control of the government, would not accept the legitimacy of the League or the limited efforts by the Western Allies to constrain its expansion. The appropriate conditions for the success of soft balancing and collective security were not present. The Japanese Army that engaged in the Mukden incidents was apparently acting on its own in an effort to weaken the civilian government in Tokyo. Japan was heavily dependent on the U.S. for natural resources, especially oil, and while an embargo would certainly have gotten Japan's attention, the U.S. and other leading members feared that such a strong action would produce a military coup in Tokyo.[98]

Between 1924 and 1936, Japan was ruled by civilian governments (Kensei Jodo) that were generally internationalist and wanted to improve Japan's international image. The "Taishō democracy school" believed that participation in international institutions would facilitate internal reforms and a reduction in defense spending. Its adherents supported Japan's active membership in the League of Nations, despite feeling that the League was overly focused on European affairs.[99] But in the early 1930s the military faction began to gain control of the Japanese power structure. Factions within the General Staff supported an unsuccessful coup in March 1931. The Manchurian incident that September and the assassination of liberal prime minister Inukai Tsuyoshi the following May were the beginnings of the army faction's gaining full control of Japanese domestic politics.[100]

In the wake of the Manchurian incident, Premier Koki Hirota accepted the military's demand that only active-duty officers be appointed as war and navy ministers. This ensured that the state's military policies followed the army's position.[101] Hisaichi Terauchi, a strong proponent of military expansion, became the war minister and persuaded Hirota to step up the arms buildup. The Hirota government launched a new naval buildup program and concluded the Anti-Comintern Pact with Germany in November 1936.[102] Other military initiatives included the withdrawal from the League of Nations and the renunciation of the Washington Naval Treaty when it expired on December 31, 1936. Several cabinets came and went while the military reinforced its position. By 1936, the Japanese government castigated the concepts of collective security and internationalism as "criminal."[103]

The League's inability to enforce collective security provisions against Japan dealt a fatal blow to its credibility, especially among smaller states.[104] As in Europe, in many respects the League's soft-balancing efforts had the opposite effect from what was intended. Its attempt at sanctions increased Japan's determination to occupy Manchuria and strengthen its foothold on Chinese territory while generating intense nationalism and xenophobia within Japan and accelerating the army's overthrow of the civilian regime.

U.S. SANCTIONS: SOFT BALANCING THROUGH ECONOMIC STRANGULATION

While the Allies made limited efforts at hard balancing and deterrence, the Roosevelt administration's primary strategic approach toward the Japanese threat was soft balancing.[105] Ilai Saltzman notes that the United States considered the European theater the primary security threat.[106] He contends that the soft-balancing efforts were deliberate policy postures to constrain Japan's aggressive policies, not random acts of policy friction. The constraints the Roosevelt administration faced in adopting an active hard-balancing strategy against Japan included not only Japan's domestic situation but also the various neutrality acts, worries about a two-front war, and American concerns about military unpreparedness in the face of the aggressive and disciplined Japanese Army and Navy.[107] The naval arms-control regime was viewed as the best institutional means to prevent Japan from building its military capability even further. Before the League and the U.S. imposed their sanctions, during the 1920s and 1930s, the Allied powers had attempted to institutionally balance Japan through unequal arms-control measures. At the Washington Naval Conference of 1921–22, the largest naval powers, including Japan, signed three major arms-control agreements to restrain each other, especially in the area of naval arms buildup. These included the Five-Power Treaty, in which Japan agreed to a 5:5:3 ratio of ship tonnage for the UK, the U.S., and Japan, respectively. The Four-Power Treaty among the U.S., the UK, France, and Japan called on the parties to consult one another before undertaking military action in East Asia, while the Nine-Power Treaty (the U.S., the UK, Japan, France, Italy, Belgium, the Netherlands, Portugal, and China) called for all nations to respect China's territorial integrity while recognizing partial Japanese hegemony over Manchuria.[108] The first London Naval Treaty of 1930, a serious effort to restrain Japanese military buildup, was a follow-up to the Washington treaties. The parties—the U.S., the UK, Japan, France, and Italy—agreed to limit their submarine arsenals, heavy and light cruisers, and destroyers.[109] Japan later withdrew from all of these treaties and did not participate in the second London Treaty of 1936.

The U.S. and its allies assumed that a weaker Japanese Navy would not engage in offensive action. But nationalists in Tokyo resented the arms-control treaties, which they perceived as adding insult to their injury following their military difficulties in China. Balancing by institutional means, especially the arms-control treaties, thus helped fuel the rise of ultra-nationalist factions within Japan. By the time it formally renounced the treaties in 1936, Japan had already built more weapons than it was permitted, including three aircraft carriers, and had started the construction of a fourth. It had also acquired seventeen naval aircraft squadrons and 284 naval aircraft, a formidable force in the Pacific during that period.[110] The navy had embarked on six different rearmament programs to build additional aircraft carriers, cruisers, destroyers, and submarines so as to achieve parity with the U.S., as well as three super battleships of seventy-two thousand tons each.[111]

The Japanese decision makers realized that time was not on their side. If they waited too long, the U.S. and the UK would build more and better warships. The best Japan could hope for was to quickly build a short-term offensive capability that would give it a bargaining advantage in diplomatic dealings with the Western powers.[112]

For the rest of the 1930s and early 1940s, the United States played the pivotal role in balancing and containing Japan. To this end, the U.S. adopted both hard and soft strategies. As the "Rising Sun of Asia," Japan sought economic and political autarky by conquering vast areas of China and Indochina. In 1938, it was still heavily dependent on American raw materials: the U.S. supplied 75 percent of Japan's scrap iron, 93 percent of its copper, over 60 percent of its machine tools, and 90 percent of its oil.[113] This economic dependence offered the U.S. a second soft-balancing mechanism with which to stem Japanese expansionism: it could impose economic sanctions, and it did so multiple times in the late 1930s and early 1940s. These actions included the termination of the 1911 commercial treaty in 1939 and the Export Control Act of 1940, which authorized the U.S. president to prohibit export to Japan of defense materials. In July, shortly after the act was passed, Roosevelt used it to prohibit the export of aviation fuel and lubricants; in October 1940, he banned scrap iron and steel export; and in July 1941 he froze Japanese assets in the U.S. and stopped the export of oil. U.S. allies, the UK, and the Netherlands followed suit.[114] Unfortunately, the sanctions had the opposite effect to what was intended. Japanese leaders realized that the United States' immediate defensive and deterrent capabilities in the Pacific were limited and that Japan enjoyed a window of opportunity. Its desperate need for oil propelled Tokyo to aggressive policies toward Southeast Asia, while Germany's stunning military successes in Europe during 1939–41 left the British, French, and Dutch colonies in the region relatively undefended. The Japanese leadership seized the opportunity to expand.

This case study points to the difficulty of implementing balancing strategies, either hard or soft, against a determined revisionist state whose elites are willing to take huge risks. Japan's minister of war, General Hideki Tojo, told Prime Minister Fumimaro Konoye in September 1941 that "at some point during a man's lifetime, he might find it necessary to jump, with eyes closed, from the temple Kiyomizu-dera on the heights of Kyoto into the ravine below."[115] The strength of the U.S. and the mobilization then under way under Roosevelt did not deter Japan from offensive action in 1942. Japan calculated that in the short run it could wage a fait accompli war and achieve its objectives before the U.S. completed its formidable mobilization, and then the global alliance structure would assure its victory. War prevention based on hard balancing was unlikely to work in such a situation unless it was backed by an overwhelming military force and credible retaliatory threat in the theater of operations. Additionally, the Allies offered no reassurance that Japan's territorial and economic interests would be accommodated; essentially the only option they gave the aggressor was that of backing down. Partly because its domestic politics precluded a more accommodating stance, the United States all along pursued coercive diplomacy in the expectation that its aggregate power capability would compel Japan to give in. Soft balancing failed when Japan attacked Pearl Harbor on December 7, 1941, bringing the U.S. into a devastating war with Japan in the Pacific, culminating in the August 1945 atomic attacks on Hiroshima and Nagasaki and Japan's eventual surrender.

Two-plus decades of great-power politics after 1919 produced serious efforts at soft and hard balancing, but none succeeded in preventing war in either Europe or Asia. On the contrary, soft-balancing efforts only inflamed aggressive nationalism in the three principal revisionist powers, Germany, Italy, and Japan, and helped bring down the Weimar and Taishō democratic regimes in Germany and Japan. Henry Kissinger has claimed that balance of power is meant to limit aggression but not prevent it.[116] But the severity of the two world wars in the first half of the twentieth century suggests that it did not even accomplish that, despite many efforts to maintain an equilibrium in power. In the face of these efforts, the Axis powers sought instead to break the Allied powers' superiority through strategies such as blitzkrieg and surprise attacks. Japan, for instance, calculated that it could win a short war against the U.S. but not a long one, and planned accordingly. These historical examples show a problem with hard balancing: it may produce more wars than it prevents as leaders may either misinterpret balance of power or else disregard its ultimately pacific intentions. One leader's calculations on equilibrium may be different from another's.

The Mixed Legacy of Soft Balancing

Since 1815, great powers have often used institutions to restrain one another, and especially to restrain threatening states. The Concert system
was the first major attempt at this, and although it did not last long, the
ideas it generated still linger. It was more successful than the League of
Nations in restraining aggression through a combination of hard and
soft balancing. Legitimacy was a crucial principle of the Concert, and the
equal treatment of all great powers—both winners and losers of the
Napoleonic Wars—produced a period of general restraint. The League,
on the other hand, was viewed by the rising revisionist powers of Germany, Italy, and Japan as retributive, and they sought to undermine it.
The limited efforts at soft balancing created intense nationalism, which
was all too easily exploited by these countries' political and military
elites.

Except for limited economic interdependence, the facilitating conditions I described in chapter 2 were absent in the League era. But this
interdependence was not deep enough to generate favorable conditions
for soft balancing. Other conditions encouraged revisionist states to try
to refashion the international order by military force. Hard balancing
through arms buildups and alliances did not prevent a devastating
war—it made that war wider and more destructive. The weapons of the
day, including tanks, aircraft, aircraft carriers, and submarines, all allowed expansionist strategies. Ideologies were expansionist, national-
isms were virulent, the territorial integrity norm was nonexistent, and
international institutions, especially the League, were far too weak to
restrain revisionist great powers. Gaining legitimacy was not an issue for
the challengers as they had no concern for the institutions built by the
victors of World War I, which they saw as unjust and massively favorable
to the Allies.

F · O · U · R

Balancing during the Cold War

The United Nations was created in 1945 to provide security and peace through institutional means. It was aimed at denying legitimacy to aggressive behavior by any state, including the great powers. The main institutional mechanism, the collective security provisions of the UN Charter, consisted of improved versions of similar provisions in the League of Nations Charter. Chapter VII and articles 39–51 of the UN Charter call for the Security Council to determine "the existence of any threat to the peace, breach of the peace, or act of aggression," make appropriate recommendations, and in the event of noncompliance by parties, authorize the use of force to restore international peace and security.[1] The founders' expectation was that the threat of collective intervention would prevent or deter a state from military aggression. Although this goes beyond balancing in a traditional sense, the logic of collective deterrence is relevant to institutional balancing as it is aimed at giving the UN, as an international institution, the means to restrain aggressive states.[2]

While the motives for creating postwar institutions were embedded in liberal logic, these institutions offered the Soviet Union and its allies a chance to be accepted as legitimate states in the postwar order. Different categories of states—strong and weak alike—found the institutional set-up useful to pursue their strategic aims, even when they accepted sovereign equality through the General Assembly and inequality through the Security Council. The P-5—the Security Council's five permanent members, the U.S., USSR, China, Britain, and France—were each given the power to block any resolution they disapproved of. This veto power would become a soft-balancing tool for the superpowers, allowing them to block one another's military interventions and deny UN approval—that is, legitimacy—to another's unfriendly actions. Still, superpower behavior during the Cold War was dominated by hard balancing, with soft balancing serving mainly to make hard balancing more palatable to the superpowers' allies, enemies, and nonaligned states.

The prominent characteristic of postwar international security relations was the onset of the Cold War in the early 1950s. This became the archetypical era of hard balancing, with two power blocs relying on alliances and arms buildups and engaging in intense balance-of-power behavior. Surprisingly, the superpowers also used soft-balancing mechanisms, albeit less frequently and less intensely. Institutional soft balancing was noticeable in the actions and policies of the new African and Asian states, especially following their Bandung conference of 1955 and with the formation of the Non-Aligned Movement in 1961. Larger emerging countries such as India attempted limited soft balancing through the UN system, while a smaller country, Tito's Yugoslavia, practiced soft balancing against the Soviet Union by opposing Stalin's policies through institutional means. Yugoslavia refused to join the Warsaw Pact and got itself expelled from the Communist Information Bureau (Cominform). The Non-Aligned Movement had only limited impact on the superpowers' behavior, but its normative influence was seen in areas such as decolonization, the creation of a new international economic order, and nuclear disarmament. The nonaligned countries played a limited cushioning role, helping to avoid escalating the Cold War conflict by not offering material assistance and base facilities to the superpowers in most cases, and they also acted as norm entrepreneurs in such areas as global disarmament, the nuclear test ban, and nuclear nonproliferation. The European countries also practiced a form of institutional balancing through the Helsinki process and the Conference on Cooperation and Security in Europe (CSCE), co-founded with the Soviet Bloc countries, that began in the mid-1970s. These mechanisms created

opportunities for institutional engagement and restraint on several issue areas such as arms control, human rights, minority rights, and democratic freedoms. France under Charles de Gaulle attempted a form of
limited soft balancing vis-à-vis the United States while also practicing
hard balancing against the Soviet Union. These efforts, however, do not
fully fit the definition of soft balancing I offered in chapter 2.

The superpowers' use of institutional mechanisms was more pronounced in the first few years after the UN's founding. But the onset of
the Cold War in 1949 severely impeded the UN's capacity to act as an
arena for restraint and great-power peace. The creation of the competing NATO and Warsaw Pact alliances and the beginning of the superpower arms race made hard balancing the dominant approach to
security. Yet the great powers continued to use the United Nations to
deny legitimacy to one another's policies. These efforts largely supplemented rather than supplanted their hard-balancing strategies. The
superpower-led conflict was largely zero-sum, despite some occasional
efforts at cooperation, and few of the facilitating conditions for soft
balancing were present.

The Superpowers and Balancing

Throughout the Cold War, the superpowers used the UN to increase
their legitimacy and delegitimize their opponents' behavior. Sometimes
they cooperated, especially on nuclear arms control, nonproliferation,
and regional crisis management, but barring a few successes against
smaller states in areas like conflict prevention, de-escalation, and peacekeeping, the UN could not restrain the superpowers' competitive behavior.[3] Many of the facilitating conditions needed for successful soft
balancing were not present during the Cold War era. The greatest challenge was the ideological contestation between the two power blocs. The
United States and its allies feared that the Soviet Union was an expansionist power bent on world domination, while the Soviet Union wanted to guarantee that capitalism failed so that imperialism would be
replaced by a Socialist world order. Hence a key facilitating condition
for soft balancing—the absence of intense rivalry between great powers
with expansionist ideologies—was lacking.

More important, as part of their containment strategies, the two power blocs closed off economic interactions with each other. The U.S. adopted a general strategic embargo to deny the Soviet Union items that would strengthen its war-making capabilities, and also used tactics like economic embargos in an effort to change particular Soviet foreign-policy behaviors.[4] The Western export controls under the Coordinating Committee (COCOM), which became operational in 1950, were primarily intended to weaken the Soviet Union's ability to wage war on the West. The Soviets viewed the formation of the General Agreement on Tariffs and Trade (GATT) in October 1947 as a way to enhance trade among liberal states or those supporting liberal rules of trade, and they generally abstained from it. This meant there was little economic interdependence, an important prerequisite for soft balancing, between the two groups. The Marshall Plan in particular was seen by the Soviets as a highly threatening plot by the Americans to consolidate their preponderance in Europe, and Moscow forbade its allies to take part in it, even though they were invited to do so. The Berlin blockade of 1948 can be attributed to Soviet opposition to the Marshall Plan (1948) and the efforts by the Western allies to prop up the economy in the sections of Berlin they occupied. The Soviets also created the Council for Mutual Economic Assistance (COMECON) in January 1949 to promote exclusive economic cooperation among Eastern European states.

The founding of NATO the same year fundamentally altered Stalin's calculations and led him to act in a way that killed any possibility of détente.[5] His policies in Eastern Europe had already created what Winston Churchill called an "Iron Curtain," a line that separated Eastern Europe by placing it under Soviet control and making it all but closed to the West.[6] George Kennan, an official at the U.S. embassy in Moscow, first proposed a strong containment strategy in his famous Long Telegram, which later became a *Foreign Affairs* article, published under the pseudonym "X." He called for "a long-term, patient but firm and vigilant containment of Russian expansive tendencies" and argued that Soviet behavior had little to do with external antagonism but was instead aimed at "the maintenance of dictatorial authority at home."[7] This argument was compelling to U.S. policy makers who considered the Soviet Union an expansionist power bent on dominating the world and spreading Communism by force.

Founding NATO was their core external balancing act. The Greek civil war of 1946–49, in which the U.S. and Britain supported the Greek government against Communist insurgents, was in the background of the Cold War, and the Marshall Plan and Truman Doctrine were part of the Western answer to perceived Soviet expansionism. The Truman Doctrine, proclaimed in March 1947 in response to Soviet pressures on Turkey for naval rights through the Bosporus Straits, was a pledge by the United States "to support free people who are resisting attempted subjugation" by Soviet-backed forces.[8] This was the beginning of the Cold War: the Soviets viewed the economic and security assistance to Turkey and Greece as directly challenging their strategic position in the region.

What is most significant from a hard-balancing perspective is that U.S. efforts during this period were meant to consolidate its dominant status in Europe, bring forth a separate peace among its allies, and prevent the Soviets from receiving equal status as the victor and liberator of Eastern Europe. America wanted preponderance, an ambition that was thwarted by Soviet control of more than half of Europe. Soviet behavior followed the classic balance-of-power dictums, with ideology as a cover. The question is, would history have been different had the victors after World War II adopted an institutional mechanism, similar to the Concert of Europe in the nineteenth century? The policy choices of the Western and Eastern elites helped to produce these balance-of-power coalitions and balancing outcomes.[9] The U.S. National Security Council document, NSC-68, of April 1950 made worldwide balance of power a key goal of the U.S. through a perimeter defense, massive increases in the defense budget, and a major boost to military aid to allies. The document asserted that "any substantial further extension of the area under the domination of the Kremlin would raise the possibility that no coalition adequate to confront the Kremlin with greater strength could be assembled."[10] The Korean War encouraged the Truman administration to implement many of the recommendations of NSC-68, including the acquisition of a hydrogen bomb. Under the Eisenhower administration, massive retaliation emerged as the major component of the so-called New Look security policy, giving nuclear weapons the extraordinary role of preventing limited wars like the one in Korea. The Kennedy administration, finding this approach too extreme, adopted a Flexible Response strategy that gave the president multiple options for responding to a crisis with the Communist countries.[11]

Other regional and bilateral groupings followed, such as the Southeast Asia Collective Defense Treaty (SEATO), the Central Treaty Organization (CENTO), and U.S. bilateral security treaties with Japan, Korea, and Taiwan. The SEATO pact was signed in September 1954 by the U.S., Australia, New Zealand, the UK, France, the Philippines, Thailand, and Pakistan, and CENTO was concluded in 1955 among Iraq, Turkey, the UK, Pakistan, and Iran for the Middle East, but neither survived.[12] SEATO was dissolved in June 1977, and CENTO met the same fate two years later, in 1979, after the Iranian Revolution, because of lack of interest and political differences among key participants. The AN-ZUS (Australia, New Zealand, United States Security) Treaty of September 1951 was yet another Cold War defense treaty that bound member states to one another's collective security.[13] The U.S.-Japan Mutual Cooperation and Security Treaty was originally signed in 1952 but amended in 1960, and the 1953 U.S.-Korea mutual defense treaty further solidified America's position in the Far East.[14]

The Soviets concluded the Warsaw Pact in May 1955 with Albania, Bulgaria, Czechoslovakia, East Germany, Hungary, Poland, and Romania. They also formed bilateral alliances with China, Egypt, Syria, and Cuba. The treaties with China, Egypt, and Syria would not survive, but the Warsaw Pact and Cuban alliance were not dissolved until the end of the Cold War. Limited friendship treaties, with arms supply as their core feature, were also signed with Egypt and Syria in 1955, India in 1971, and Iraq in 1972. Soviet support for Cuba after the Bay of Pigs invasion of 1961 would lead to major arms supplies and the deployment of nuclear missiles that produced the Cuban Missile Crisis of 1962. The USSR was also a key supporter of North Korea during the Korean War. The Sino-Soviet friendship treaty of February 1950 did not formally expire until 1979, but by then it had far outlived any actual friendship. The bitter rupture between the USSR and China in the 1960s led to a warming of relations between China and the U.S. a decade later, a rapprochement with major implications for the balance of power. The USSR also, from 1949 to 1991, led COMECON, an economic union comprising most Eastern European states and other Communist countries, except China.[15]

Both of the superpowers engaged in internal balancing through the buildup and deployment of military capabilities worldwide, including nuclear weapons. Each time one of the superpowers developed a weapon system, it was matched by the other, and by the end of the 1960s they had reached strategic parity or mutual assured destruction (MAD). The nuclear arms race was a textbook example of internal balancing, especially the development of the hydrogen bomb; the nuclear triad consisting of aircraft-based bombs, intercontinental ballistic missiles (ICBMs), and submarine-launched ballistic missiles (SLBMs); multiple independently targetable reentry vehicles (MIRVs); and other systems to retain nuclear prominence.[16] The result was a huge number of weapons in both states' arsenals, reaching some fifty-eight thousand warheads by 1990, far beyond what was necessary for minimum deterrence and balance of power.[17]

Containment, a step more advanced than a simple hard-balancing strategy, was the key operational strategy adopted by both power blocs against each other. Western containment included, among other things, export controls on strategic goods sold to Soviet Bloc countries.[18] The founding of NATO transformed U.S. strategy in Europe from rebuilding based on the Marshall Plan to containment. The Truman administration's NSC-68 was pivotal in this transition.[19]

Moscow's balancing reaction was equally strong. Along with eight Eastern European states, it created the Warsaw Pact in May 1955 and began to catch up with the West in nuclear and conventional forces, attaining superiority in the latter in Eastern Europe. Ideological support for the Soviet side in the Cold War came from figures like Andrei Zhadnov, who in September 1947 formulated the doctrine of "two camps" at the founding congress of the Cominform in Poland. (The Communist International, Comintern, which had been closed down in 1943, was reestablished as Cominform with headquarters in Belgrade in September 1947. But the Yugoslav leader, Marshal Tito, not an obedient follower of Stalin, saw his term as the host of Cominform cut short, and it was dissolved in April 1956.[20] Notably, Tito's Yugoslavia was the only Eastern European state not liberated by Russia and hence not occupied by the USSR.)

Yet the superpowers relied on international institutions to legitimate their policies and delegitimize their opponent's. The Baruch Plan and the Soviet counterproposal, the Gromyko Plan, were perhaps the first arms-control proposals to reduce the threat of nuclear weapons acquisitions by states. The 1946 Baruch Plan, based on earlier proposals by Dean Acheson and David Lilienthal, called for international control of the atom by a veto-proof system of "swift and assured penalties" for violators. But it was premised on America's retaining its nuclear monopoly until all other countries agreed to the plan and a proper international mechanism was created.[21] The 1946 Gromyko Plan recommended an international convention prohibiting the production, stockpiling, and use of nuclear weapons by all states. Within three months of the convention's coming into force, all nuclear stockpiles were to be destroyed. Given that the U.S. was the only state with nuclear weapons at the time, it was not hard to see where the plan was aimed.[22] These proposals by the U.S. and the USSR relied on institutions and legal treaties to curtail each other's nuclear ambitions.

The first test of the UN collective security provisions came during the Korean War in October 1950. In response to a North Korean attack on South Korea, the UN authorized a U.S.-led coalition under the command of General Douglas MacArthur to undertake military action under the collective security provisions. Beyond this intervention, the U.S. hoped to use the UN to delegitimize aggressive actions by Communist states, in particular North Korea. The U.S. considered North Korea a surrogate of the Soviet and Chinese Communists, whom it believed had encouraged the war.

In addition to the Korean War (1950–53) and later the Vietnam War (1955–75), the Cold War produced a long succession of crises. Among the more prominent were the Taiwan Strait Crisis (1954–55); the Quemoy Crisis (1958); the two Berlin Crises (1958–59 and 1961); the Cuban Missile Crisis (1962); several Middle East crises beginning with Suez (1956) and continuing with the 1967 and 1971 wars; and the Soviet actions in Hungary (1956) and Czechoslovakia (1968). Deterrence and balance of power between the East and the West did not reduce the number of crises, although the two powers did avoid a major war. But the balance-of-power competition may have helped create and intensify these smaller crises.

The Suez War stands out as an example of soft balancing. The war began in October 1956 with the Israeli invasion of the Egyptian Sinai.

The UK and France joined Israel in the offensive, which was intended to prevent Egypt's Gamal Abdel Nasser from nationalizing the Suez Canal and also to remove him from power. The U.S. opposed the war and, despite being allies, threatened the UK with selling off U.S.-held pound-sterling bonds, an action that would have severely damaged the British financial system. American and Soviet pressure at the UN forced the three states to declare a ceasefire and withdraw their forces, allowing Nasser to nationalize the Suez Canal. The U.S. denied Britain IMF loans and worked with emerging countries such as India to obtain the deployment of UN peacekeeping forces in the Sinai. The U.S., irked by its allies' lack of consultation over the invasion plans, was concerned about Soviet intrusion in the Middle East and was hoping to establish its dominant role in the region. The technique of soft balancing against its own NATO allies was a success.[23] Britain, the nation most affected by U.S. economic sanctions, responded quickly to pressure. Although France had reasons to worry about the sanctions' impact on the franc, the French were less easily coerced due to their strong desire to see Nasser lose power. While Israel did not rely on the United States for economic aid at the time of the crisis, Tel Aviv relented as it could not risk losing the U.S. as an ally.[24]

The nuclear arms race of the 1950s and 1960s was driven by the balance-of-power competition. The Soviets wanted to obtain parity, which they achieved by the late 1960s. Soviet missile capabilities following the Sputnik launch in October 1957 generated fears in the U.S. of an imbalance and later of a "missile gap." By the early 1960s, the U.S. had caught up with this perceived deficiency and the missile gap was shown to be a myth.[25] More important, the nuclear arms–control treaties of 1970s and 1980s allowed both sides to retain equilibrium without pointlessly increasing their massive stockpiles.

Hard balancing by the two superpowers was credited by realists for the long peace in Europe. According to John Mearsheimer, the early Cold War saw several crises in Europe, but none after the 1974 Cyprus War involving Turkey and Greece. He attributes the forty-five-year peace to a bipolar distribution of power, parity in military capability between the two blocs, and the presence of nuclear weapons.[26] While there was relative stability in Europe, we may reasonably ask whether it could have been obtained with less threatening instruments. How sustainable was it, given that power dynamics change under any balance-of-power system? I would also note that it came at a steep price: the key weakness of this balance-of-power system was apparent in the violent proxy wars the superpowers waged in the Third World.[27] The superpowers magnified these conflicts and occasionally even came to the brink of using nuclear weapons. Of the twenty known cases of nuclear alert by the U.S. and one by the Soviets, sixteen were in the context of conflict in the developing world—seven of them in the Middle East.[28]

In the newly emerging countries of the Third World, the superpowers vied for local support by seeking military bases and providing arms and ammunition to competing states.[29] Many of these proxy wars were engaged alongside ideologically sympathetic groups fighting within and outside the new states. The United Nations was a key theater for these contestations for influence. The UN was also the chief arena where new states attempted to restrain the superpowers from their excessively competitive behavior, especially in nuclear and conventional arms races.

Balance of power was once again challenged when the Soviets began to talk about the "correlation of forces" favoring them in the 1960s and 1970s—by which they meant the world order was shifting in favor of the Socialist countries, resulting in a corresponding weakness of the Western-led order and alliances. This idea prompted Soviet interventions in Africa and Latin America. The "correlation of forces" theme had been part of Soviet strategic thinking since the days of Stalin, and it was revived under Khrushchev as the Soviet advancements in science, technology, the economy, and, more significantly, nuclear capability were projected as delivering a long-term advantage to the USSR. Soviet-supported activism in Southern Africa, especially in the civil war theaters of Angola and Mozambique, prompted the U.S. to support anti-Soviet groups there and elsewhere. Brezhnev believed that the détente process with the U.S. happened because the correlation of forces favored Moscow.[30]

The perception of correlation of forces advancing Moscow's interests probably inspired the ill-fated invasion of Afghanistan in December 1979, ordered by Leonid Brezhnev. Soviet forces found themselves pitted against a U.S.-led coalition comprising Pakistan, Saudi Arabia, and the mujahideen forces, the latter trained and funded by the U.S. Central

Intelligence Agency.[31] In many respects, the desire to tilt the global balance of power to one's favor and to preclude bandwagoning of emerging states with the enemy were key parts of the superpowers' strategic calculations. The violent conflicts in the developing world show how balance-of-power competition among great powers can spiral out of control.

The U.S. decision in the 1970s to create a limited alliance with China was even more significant for the global balance-of-power competition. The U.S. rapprochement with China created a major realignment in the international system. Between 1971 and 1979, the U.S. agreed to allow the People's Republic of China to take over China's UN Security Council seat from the Republic of China, enabling Beijing to transform itself into a nonrevisionist state. Later, under Deng Xiaoping, China liberalized its economy and became a trading state of immense economic capabilities. President Richard Nixon and his national security advisor, Henry Kissinger, used the rapprochement with China first as a means to exit the Vietnam War, and then to form a formidable coalition against the Soviet Union, although the latter goal was achieved during the presidency of Jimmy Carter. China's support for the American side in Afghanistan was also a crucial hard-balancing event that helped end the Cold War.[32] During the 1970s, while developing links with China, the U.S. also engaged in a détente process with the Soviets, with the idea of encouraging Moscow to accept "a code of conduct" or "rules of the game for political competition."[33] This policy had some brief success but came to an end after the Soviet invasion of Afghanistan in 1979.

The Ronald Reagan era (1981–89) saw the balance of power tilt in favor of the U.S. Some believe Reagan's tough approach to the Soviet Union was largely responsible for Soviet reforms and for Mikhail Gorbachev's efforts to change Soviet policy.[34] From a balance-of-power perspective, however, this argument has problems: it challenges the theory's basic axioms, as change in this case was induced by an anticipated preponderance of one competing state over the other. It is unclear why the Soviets abandoned the symmetry approach and chose conciliation when they still retained considerable military power. The end of the Cold War and the way it ended pose serious intellectual challenges to balance-of-power theory. Why would one of the competing powers abandon the competition peacefully, even though it could have—and, according to the theory, should have—maintained the balance? Is it possible that Gorbachev realized that the intense competition with the U.S. was destroying the Soviet economy and society, and concluded that the existential challenges were better ameliorated through rapprochement? This case also shows that balancing can end through leaders' strategic choices.

The Nonaligned Countries and Soft Balancing

The newly emerging countries, including many of the states where the superpowers vied for influence, practiced a limited form of soft balancing under the rubric of the Non-Aligned Movement. The decolonization process that began with India's independence from Britain in August 1947 added many new states into the international system, first in Asia and later in Africa. While these states had limited military and economic power, they nevertheless attempted to use international institutions to create a soft-balancing coalition against the superpowers, achieving only limited success. But the simple fact that they tried and sustained this informal institutional structure for three decades suggests that soft balancing can be developed as a strategy by secondary states.

The intellectual foundations of the Non-Aligned Movement were very much a counterstrategy directed against balance-of-power politics. In September 1946, Jawaharlal Nehru, as vice president of the interim government of pre-independent India, stated: "We propose, as far as possible, to keep away from the power politics of groups, aligned against one another, which have led in the past to World Wars and which may again lead to disasters on an even larger scale."[35] Nehru believed balance-of-power politics allowed the European powers to maintain their domination over much of the world and that renewed balance-of-power competition would produce a new round of great-power dominance over weaker states. Nonparticipation in power blocs would allow India to act as a mediator of conflicts rather than an active participant.[36]

The Non-Aligned Movement's antecedent was the 1955 Bandung meeting of Afro-Asian states organized by Prime Minister Nehru, Sukarno of Indonesia, and Gamal Abdel Nasser of Egypt. The meeting was held at a time when the Cold War was beginning to intensify and the leaders of newly emerging states were increasing their efforts to remain separate from any military alliances. The Bandung conference and the Bandung spirit were important to the extent that materially weak states were making efforts to stay away from the key mechanism of hard balancing among the superpowers. This was unique in the modern international system. Never before had weaker states gathered together and made strong policy statements against the dominant powers of the day.

The conference, held in the Indonesian city of Bandung, April 18–24, 1955, thus assumes special importance in the efforts by newly emerging states to obtain a voice in international affairs. The conference developed what it called the "Pancasila," or "five principles of coexistence" as a counter to hard balancing and alliance politics as well as to the ideological schisms dividing the Asia-Pacific nations. The principles—"mutual respect for each other's territorial integrity and sovereignty; mutual non-aggression; mutual non-interference in each other's internal affairs: equality and cooperation for mutual benefit; peaceful co-existence"—presented a clear counternarrative to hard balancing. The movement enjoyed some success in encouraging newly emerging countries to refrain from joining either of the blocs. For instance, Nehru successfully persuaded Laos and Cambodia to at least temporarily refrain from joining a U.S.-led military alliance.[37] The conference achieved a few additional objectives as well: while accepting collective defense, it exposed SEATO as an alliance of low legitimacy; established the principle of avoiding entangling great-power alliances; and declared that large states such as India and China would not dominate Asia.[38]

The conference also demanded independence for the remaining French and Dutch colonies. Its final communiqué contended that the full realization of fundamental human rights required the self-determination of all colonial societies.[39] "Colonialism in all its manifestations," it read, "is an evil which should speedily be brought to an end. . . . The subjection of peoples to alien subjugation, domination and exploitation constitutes a denial of fundamental human rights, is contrary to the Charter of the United Nations and is an impediment to the promotion of world peace and cooperation."[40] Still, the institutional mechanism created at Bandung did not result in the Non-Aligned Movement immediately, partly because China tried to steer the movement in its direction. Nehru in particular was worried that China would hijack the movement. Although he had invited Premier Zhou Enlai and also introduced him at the conference, Nehru apparently was concerned over the warmth with which the Chinese leader was received.[41]

Why was the Non-Aligned Movement akin to a limited soft-balancing effort? One of the key objectives of its leaders was not to allow newly emerging states to join military alliances and divide the world vertically. Many of them had fought long struggles for their freedom from the colonial powers, and they saw the Cold War as another form of colonial control by the superpowers. They resorted to institutional and normative mechanisms as a way of questioning the legitimacy of the Cold War alliance systems, and thereby questioning hard balancing itself.

The name NAM (Non-Aligned Movement) was adopted at the 1961 Belgrade meeting, and one of the key points at NAM meetings after that was opposition to Cold War alliances and the arms race, both characteristic elements of the superpower-led blocs' hard-balancing strategies. The Indian scholar M. S. Rajan sums up the foundational principles and objectives of the Non-Aligned Movement as: (1) substantial freedom in foreign-policy choices on the basis of an issue's merit, as opposed to the option of joining either of the two power blocs; (2) a forum for making ad hoc decisions; and (3) the coexistence of ideologically different states each respecting sovereign equality, seeking to remove discriminatory international relations, and committed to abstinence from military blocs or the provision of military bases to the competing power blocs.[42]

The NAM reiterated these principles at its second summit meeting, in Cairo in 1964.[43] However, the goals of nonalignment generated contention at these meetings, where the final resolutions often revealed minimal agreement among the participating states. The New Delhi declaration of the foreign ministers of nonaligned countries in February 1981 reiterated the principles as "the struggle against imperialism, colonialism, neocolonialism, Apartheid, racism, including Zionism and all forms of foreign aggression, occupation, domination, interference or hegemony as well as against great power or bloc policies."[44]

The nonaligned states refused to define themselves as neutral in the manner of Switzerland, Austria, Ireland, or Finland as they wanted the freedom to make policy pronouncements and play an active role in international politics through institutional means. The key difference between neutrality and nonalignment is the legal sanctification of the former; neutral states formally agree to refrain from either giving military aid or bases to others or participating in power politics. Permanent neutrality obligates a state not to initiate a war or participate in a war by others, and during peacetime not to accept any military obligations to come to the aid of other states.[45] Nonaligned countries do not have such legal sanctification, and although they were not supposed to provide support to either superpower, they did not want to give up the right to side with Cold War rivals on specific matters. They wanted to take "positions on the basis of the merits of each issue as they see it," and as a result, "sometimes they took parallel positions of either of the blocs, depending on which side has greater merit."[46] Thus, "nonalignment represent[s] less formal types of self-neutralization, expressed as statements of policy rather than as constitutional or legislative acts."[47] The nonaligned states, unlike neutral states, sought to give opinions and make proposals for peace and change in international relations.[48] This position predictably generated criticism, as some NAM positions favored the Soviet Bloc, largely because—at least outwardly—the Socialist states were more sympathetic to core nonaligned positions on colonialism and racism. Many of the nonaligned leaders also tried to implement Socialist economic ideas, often haphazardly, even as they maintained democratic political systems and mixed economies. These countries also adopted nonalignment for domestic reasons: they feared that strictly following either of the two competing political and economic models would adversely affect their domestic economic development.[49] In some countries the adoption of either model would have aroused fervent opposition from powerful domestic interests and thus carried huge political costs.

The United Nations was a key arena where the nonaligned states proposed measures, including those promoting decolonization, a new international economic order, nuclear disarmament, and a nuclear test ban treaty. Diplomatic opposition to many superpower-led interventions in the developing world was part of their strategy. They resisted attempts to institutionalize the movement other than through the summit meetings and the Bureau of the Non-Aligned at the UN headquarters, where they coordinated their day-to-day activities.[50]

Nuclear disarmament emerged as a key topic on which nonaligned countries used UN mechanisms to pressure the superpowers. The 1961 Belgrade declaration contained three documents calling on the superpowers to conclude a treaty on general and complete disarmament, engage in disarmament negotiations through the UN, and agree on a nuclear test ban treaty. Subsequent meetings incorporated these and other proposals, such as the dismantlement of foreign bases, the creation of a zone of peace in the Indian Ocean, and chemical and biological disarmament. The nonaligned states also made several attempts to link disarmament with development.[51]

These diplomatic efforts can be understood as limited efforts at soft balancing, given that during the 1950s and 1960s the nuclear threat was viewed as one of the most pressing security threats to all nations, including the developing countries. Nuclear disarmament would emerge as a key theme for the group and its founding leaders, especially Nehru and Tito, who actively threw their governments' support into peace movements. These states made major contributions at the UN disarmament forums, especially the Eighteen Nation Disarmament Committee (ENDC); the negotiations leading to the 1963 Partial Test Ban Treaty (PTBT), which banned nuclear testing in the atmosphere, outer space, and under water; and the negotiations for the Non-Proliferation Treaty (NPT) and subsequent review conferences.[52] The PTBT was an effort by the nuclear states to mollify the Afro-Asian states' demands for a complete ban on testing following the accelerated atmospheric testing in the 1950s. It was Nehru who first proposed, in April 1954, a standstill agreement on nuclear testing.[53]

The non-nuclear nonaligned countries played a major role in the negotiations leading to the NPT in 1968, its several review conferences, and the 1995 review meeting that extended the treaty in perpetuity. More important, they initiated the 1994 UN referral to the International Court of Justice (ICJ) on the legality of nuclear use. Although the ICJ did not prohibit nuclear use outright, it ruled that most use of nuclear weapons would be prohibited under international laws on armed conflicts. The only instance where the court could not reach a definite conclusion was on the lawfulness of nuclear use for self-defense in an extreme circumstance involving a state's survival.[54] The nonaligned non-nuclear states also played crucial roles in the creation of nuclear weapon–free zones in Latin America, Southeast Asia, and Africa. They acted as norm intermediaries in creating the tradition of the nonuse of nuclear weapons.[55] One of the key initiatives on nuclear disarmament came during the waning days of the Cold War in 1986, when India's prime minister Rajiv Gandhi led six national delegations to produce the Delhi Declaration on the Principles of a Nuclear Weapon–Free and Non-Violent World. Soviet leader Mikhail Gorbachev responded favorably to this initiative and supported the call for a meeting of experts from the U.S. and USSR to work on a comprehensive test ban treaty.[56] However, these efforts had little impact in the U.S., despite the fact that President Reagan was personally interested in nuclear disarmament.

Another area where nonaligned states attempted to make a difference was in calling for a zone of peace in the Indian Ocean. This idea was first proposed at the 1970 Lusaka summit and was adopted by the UN General Assembly in 1971. Subsequent nonaligned summits at Colombo (1976) and Havana (1979) gave more clarity to the idea, leading the UN General Assembly to host an international conference on the subject.[57] The Soviet Union showed much interest, largely because the U.S. had active military bases in Diego Garcia and in many countries around the Persian Gulf.

Testing Soft Balancing during Crises

The key tests of the emerging states' soft-balancing efforts occurred during the Korean War (1950–53), the Hungarian uprising (1956), the Suez Crisis (1956), the Vietnam War (1955–75), the Soviet invasion of Afghanistan (1979–89), and several U.S. interventions in Latin America. The attempts by the newly emerging states to intercede and perhaps resolve these crises all failed—although, as we saw, the Suez war ended largely through American soft balancing.[58] During the Korean War, India under Nehru attempted to mediate the conflict and use the UN forum to restrain the behavior of both the U.S. and China. He initially condemned the North Korean attack but would not denounce China's intervention. More pointedly, he opposed the decision to assemble a UN force under the U.S. because he feared an escalation to a superpower war involving the Soviet Union. Yet India did play a limited role as a go-between for Beijing and Washington, helping to bring China to the UN deliberations and playing a part in the truce negotiations over prisoners of war.[59]

Tito engaged in limited soft balancing when he tried to deny the Soviet Union a unified alliance in Eastern and Central Europe. As one observer put it: "Yugoslav resistance to Soviet control interfered with Soviet goals of forming a unified security and military defense block, or buffer zone, in Eastern Europe."[60] The key soft-balancing mechanism that Yugoslavia used was the refusal to join the Soviet-led economic co-operation agreement or the treaty of friendship, assistance, and cooperation.[61] Stalin retaliated by expelling Yugoslavia from Cominform in 1948. Relations between the Soviet Union and Yugoslavia had been tense since 1941, but the strain became more apparent as Tito opposed Soviet strategic goals.

The Hungarian Crisis offered another opportunity for emerging states and their allies to engage in limited soft balancing. Yugoslavia initially provided material and institutional support to the leaders of the Hungarian uprising and attempted to delegitimize Soviet efforts to repress it. The Soviet tanks rolled into Budapest in October 1956 to put down the Hungarian protest movement in support of the ousted reformist prime minister Imre Nagy, whose policies had taken away many controls installed by the one-party state. The crisis was brought on by the return of hardliner Mátyás Rákosi as prime minister in 1955 and his cancellation of all of Nagy's reforms. Mass demonstrations in Budapest caused a few power changes, and the Soviet troops already stationed in Hungary intervened to suppress the movement. Despite a ceasefire and reinstallation of Nagy in October 1956, the unrest continued and Soviet troops returned to Budapest. Nagy's withdrawal from the Warsaw Pact and declaration of neutrality caused Khrushchev to order that he be deposed by the Soviet Army. Some twenty-five hundred Hungarians and seven hundred Soviet troops were killed during the conflict.[62]

Nagy was given asylum in the Yugoslav embassy and the Soviets installed a friendly government under János Kádár and Ferenc Münnich.[63] To the dismay of liberals the world over, however, Yugoslavia supported the Soviet repression in Hungary and allowed Moscow to detain and subsequently execute Nagy. It was very much a move to preclude a

Soviet intervention in Yugoslavia itself, but it generated much doubt about Tito's autonomy. Despite these actions, Khrushchev did somewhat modify Soviet policy. In the de-Stalinization then under way in Moscow, new thinking emerged that took a more conciliatory approach toward the nonaligned and neutral states such as Yugoslavia and Finland, as well as toward emerging states. Leading countries such as India failed to check the behavior of the Soviet Union, and these countries began to be perceived in the West as tilting toward Moscow. India's abstention from the UN Security Council meeting on Hungary was roundly criticized in the West as a deviation from the nonaligned and Pancasila principles, although Nehru did make some diplomatic efforts with Moscow to end the crisis.[64]

As discussed already, the Suez Crisis offered another key opportunity for the newly emerging states, especially India, to apply soft-balancing techniques. The invasion of Egypt by British, French, and Israeli forces was roundly condemned by India and many emerging states. To their surprise, U.S. president Dwight Eisenhower also opposed the invasion, forcing the attacking nations to withdraw from Egypt.

The Non-Aligned Movement was often criticized as less critical of the USSR than of the U.S., as evident in the NAM's divided positions on the Soviet invasion of Afghanistan in 1979 and Soviet interventions in Africa. It is very likely that Soviet support for many causes the NAM supported, such as decolonization and the struggle against racism and apartheid, could have been the key reason for their tilt. Moreover, many nonaligned countries received higher levels of arms aid from Moscow, even though they gained economic aid from the West as well. A Soviet veto at the Security Council helped India by preventing the UN from taking any action against New Delhi's military intervention in East Pakistan in 1971. Soviet support may have also deterred the U.S. under Nixon and Kissinger from intervening militarily on Pakistan's side during this conflict, although Washington sent the USS *Enterprise* to the Bay of Bengal in an effort at coercive diplomacy.[65]

More important, the Soviets used the nonaligned and neutral state meetings as institutional forums to reduce Western influence in member countries and persuade them to deny military facilities to the West. Moscow saw neutral and nonaligned countries as important components of the East-West struggle, and believed the global "correlation of forces" would shift in favor of the "socialist system of states." Moscow did not consider the nonalignment to be static and thought that eventually the nonaligned would join the Socialist camp as natural allies.[66] The Soviets found no difficulty "reconciling their pursuit of détente and peaceful co-existence with the capitalist states and the continuing class struggle in the world."[67] This view, and the Western reactions to it, led both superpowers to intervene in conflict zones from Africa to Latin America, prolonging the conflicts and increasing their violence. In some of these theaters it took the end of the Cold War for peace to break out.

The nonaligned countries were aware of their military and economic dependence on the superpowers, and some of them maintained close military ties with the U.S., the UK, France, or the Soviet Union. In their Cairo meeting in 1964, they tried to make the criteria clearer so that membership could include bilateral defense arrangements but not alliances conceived in the Cold War great-power rivalry. This was done to accommodate several African nonaligned states that were receiving military aid from France.[68] These states' consistent support for anti-colonialism also differentiated them from typical neutral states. They carried "political aspirations, in addition to negative military commitments," something the Soviets understood.[69]

The end of the Cold War challenged the raison d'être of nonalignment, as there was no longer a superpower bloc to oppose. The movement, however, continued as a diplomatic forum for developing countries, especially at the UN. In fact, the founding fathers of the Non-Aligned Movement might have been pleased: the dismantlement of the Cold War was one of their key aims in initiating the movement in the 1960s, and they probably indirectly helped in achieving this aim.

The Non-Aligned Movement can be considered a limited soft-balancing effort in the sense that materially weaker states used their own informal institutions and the UN to delegitimize balance-of-power rivalry as well as the threatening policies of the superpowers, especially in the area of nuclear arms. By refusing to join formal alliances or Cold War interventions, they offered a third pathway in a world dominated by the hard-balancing coalitions of the East and the West. "Naming and shaming" of imperial powers was nonaligned modus operandi. It was not perfect and it was often ineffective, but the fact that so many states engaged in such a posture was important at a time of intense systemic competition. During crises, they could not muster enough unity or strength to strongly condemn the superpowers' aggressive policies, especially those of the Soviet Union, partly because they depended on the superpowers for arms and economic assistance. Regional rivalries among the new states also contributed to their inability to act, as each of the rival states aligned itself with a superpower to assist it against the other.

The nonaligned case offers several examples of general limited soft-balancing efforts during the bipolar era. Most yielded little: the intensity of hard balancing and superpower rivalry was so high that the nonaligned states' efforts had little direct impact on the U.S., the USSR, or their key allies. Still, although often belittled in the West, the nonaligned states were sought after by both sides, especially at the UN, showing that they carried some soft power.

The European States and Institutional Restraints

Most of the Western European states were part of the hard-balancing coalition led by NATO, yet their relationship with the U.S. was not always cozy. On some occasions, European states attempted to balance American power through limited arms buildup, nuclear acquisition, and institution building. The most prominent case was that of France under Charles de Gaulle, who was determined to retain some independence from American hegemony. De Gaulle's decision to withdraw France from NATO's military command, despite remaining a member; his negotiations with Germany to create a Franco-German alliance; and his challenges to some U.S. policies can be seen as a combination of soft and limited hard balancing. During the 1950s and early 1960s, French moves to create a renationalized security policy, develop a limited nuclear force (called *force de frappe*), and oppose the entry of America's chief ally, the UK, into the Common Market, all had elements of limited hard balancing and soft balancing aimed at both the U.S. and the USSR.[70] The goal was obviously to give France more strategic autonomy and a better bargaining position against the U.S. Germany's nuclear acquisition proposals and reluctance to sign the nonproliferation treaty would also make Washington concerned that Bonn might attempt to create its own strategic autonomy for itself. Bonn's Ostpolitik policy toward the Soviet Union also contained a form of soft balancing, as it was intended to modify Soviet behavior through institutional and diplomatic mechanisms at the same time that Germany was pursuing other balancing and containment policies alongside the U.S. and its allies. Arms control was another area where the allies parted with the U.S. and attempted to soft-balance the USSR using institutions such as mutual and balanced force reductions (MBFR). In the Intermediate-Range Nuclear Forces (INF) Treaty negotiations during 1981–87, intense antinuclear protests in several European states led these nations to try to soft-balance both Russia and the U.S.

Also, like the neutral and nonaligned states, European states often used institutional mechanisms to soft-balance Soviet policies they perceived as threatening. The neutral and nonaligned countries, especially Finland, played a crucial intermediary role in launching the thirty-five-member Conference on Security and Cooperation in Europe, transcending East-West bloc negotiations.[71] The CSCE was explicitly developed to restrain Soviet behavior. Some have argued that the Helsinki process, particularly in such areas as cooperative security; economic, scientific, and environmental cooperation; and the promotion of human rights, encouraged the development of a civil society in the Soviet Union that wished to pursue nonviolent strategies toward dissidents, an outcome that Gorbachev accepted.[72]

Soft Balancing amid Hard Balancing

The Cold War era was dominated by intense hard balancing by the superpowers. The two sides relied on excessive arms buildup, especially in nuclear warheads, and used alignment as the key mechanism to balance, contain, and deter each other. But they also used institutions such as the UN to delegitimize each other.

The facilitating conditions for soft balancing were weak or absent. Amid intense ideological competition, each side saw the other as an existential challenge, even if these fears were exaggerated. Economic interdependence between the two sides was virtually nil: each created its own economic sphere and contained the other's economic and military behavior. Each side perceived the other's ideology as expansionist and made efforts to undercut it with intense propaganda and hard balancing. Despite the presence of norms such as territorial integrity, both superpowers made many direct and indirect interventions in the developing world. Weapons of mass destruction were a helpful deterrent, but they did not stop the development of huge arsenals of offensive conventional weaponry, used in proxy wars throughout the world.

The neutral and nonaligned states offered a sort of buffer zone to allow the superpowers to avoid direct conflict, and they often acted as bridge builders between East and West. The Western side, however, was more suspicious of their efforts, while the Soviets saw these countries as their natural allies. Neither view was completely accurate. Several regional rivalries prompted the nonaligned countries to seek military and economic aid from the superpowers, nullifying the influence they could have had in creating a soft-balancing coalition around the Non-Aligned Movement. Limited soft balancing took place under the movement, but the cushioning effect was more evident than any actual modification of the Cold War rivals' behavior.

It took the end of the Cold War after the collapse of the Berlin Wall in November 1989 for soft balancing to become prominent.

The Post–Cold War Era

Restraining the United States

In an interview in 1993, President Bill Clinton admitted: "Gosh, I miss the Cold War."[1] The world after the collapse of the Soviet Union turned out to be a much more complex place, and the president wistfully recalled the familiar rules of conduct under the Soviet-American bipolar balance-of-power game. Handling post–Cold War challenges was a murkier business. Fortunately for Washington, the end of the Cold War had ushered in a "unipolar moment," with the United States now the world's only hegemon. By any measure, the U.S. was the peerless power in the early post–Cold War era. U.S. national capabilities exceeded all other states by multiples in almost all traditional parameters.[2] And the gap was widening in military expenditure, defense-related research and development, and weapons acquisition.[3]

In the years following Clinton's remark, the U.S. would engage in unilateral military activity, most notably in its 2003 invasion of Iraq. Yet there has been no evidence of a traditional balancing coalition against the hegemonic state in order to check its power or aggressive behavior. Balance-of-power theory would predict balancing against the U.S., but eligible major powers seem to have abandoned such strategies.

What explains this lack of hard balancing? I argue that since the end of the Cold War, eligible states have mostly abandoned traditional hard balancing—based on countervailing alliances and arms buildup—at the systemic level, but they have not been helplessly watching the resurgence of American power. They have forgone active military balancing primarily because they do not fear losing their sovereignty to the hegemon, a necessary condition for traditional hard military balancing to occur at the systemic level. In the past, weaker states joined together against a rising hegemonic state because they feared that such a dominant power would inevitably challenge their sovereign territorial existence. The European experiences of the eighteenth and nineteenth centuries and the Cold War fit this bill. If states do not fear losing their sovereignty, their motivations and strategies toward the dominant state can be less intense.

The American imperial strategy often used indirect methods to assure second-ranking major powers that their territorial integrity was safe from predatory attacks by the U.S. These states have seen America as a *constrained hegemon* whose power is checked by many factors, including internal democratic institutions, domestic politics, and, above all, the other great powers' possession of nuclear weapons. The rise of transnational terrorism has also helped reduce the incentive for forming a balancing coalition, as the eligible states themselves are victims of this elusive common enemy. They have been willing to buck-pass the responsibility for confronting the terrorist threat to the U.S., even when they were not fully convinced that the U.S. has been fighting that war morally or wisely.

Eligible states have, however, been concerned about America's increasing unilateralism and its tendency to intervene militarily in sovereign states and forcibly change regimes. In this new context, concerned states have pursued multiple avenues to constrain American power and maintain their security and influence, adopting a mix of behaviors that, depending on the issue, range from soft balancing to bandwagoning, buck-passing, and free-riding. Rather than eligible states abandoning balancing, as some theorists have proposed, the changing U.S. posture on intervention has led these states to *soft balancing*, largely through international institutions and summit meetings. These strategies are intended to restrain America's interventionist policies against smaller powers. Such strategies involve the formation of limited diplomatic coalitions or ententes at specific times when the United States has threatened world or regional order.

American interventionist policies, whether in the Persian Gulf or in Kosovo, act as catalysts to some extent in determining whether soft-balancing efforts occur. Whenever the U.S. has engaged in aggressive unilateralism, some of the affected great-power states have responded with temporary coalition building at the diplomatic level. But when it was clear that U.S. actions did not constitute a major threat to these states, the soft balancing did not last. We see this in the flurry of visits and friendship treaties signed among Russia, China, and India during and immediately after the U.S. offensive in Kosovo in 1999. We also see it in the active stalling diplomacy of France, Russia, and Germany in the UN Security Council in 2002 and early 2003, prior to the U.S.-led war on Iraq. These soft-balancing efforts occurred precisely because other powers feared the U.S. would upset the sovereignty norm by pursuing unilateral military intervention against independent states without UN approval. Conversely, if and when the U.S. becomes overwhelmingly threatening to the vital interests of other great powers—especially their physical security—traditional hard balancing could reemerge. The adoption of an open-ended imperial strategy by the U.S. would provoke hard balancing, as it would threaten the independent existence of many states and seriously constrain the positions of eligible great powers. The U.S. case shows that the first two decades of the post–Cold War era featured balancing against threat, not against power.

Explanations for Why America Was Not Balanced

Existing explanations for the lack of balancing against the U.S. hinge on the absence of a sufficiently capable rival state or coalition of states; the liberal characteristics of American hegemony; and America's liberal-democratic political system. According to William Wohlforth, eligible nonliberal states such as Russia and China, whether single-handedly or in unison with others, were not capable of balancing American power because they could not find allies to help them.[4] The "larger, more comprehensive, and more entrenched the hegemon's lead, the more formidable the collective action and coordination barriers to balancing, and the higher the likely domestic, autonomy, and opportunity costs of pursuing this strategy."[5] Even so, this does not preclude threatened states from balancing the U.S. in less menacing institutional ways. The absence of powerful nonliberal states that feel threatened by the United States' increasing capabilities partly explains the lack of balancing against it. From a liberal point of view, other liberal states did not perceive the need to counterbalance the U.S. because they did not perceive its growing power as a threat.[6] To John Ikenberry, the constitutional character of the U.S. power relationship with many of its allies, the ability of those allies to penetrate American institutions, and the international institutions that Washington helped to create have all offered increasing benefits to participants in the American-led order. Having the capacity to influence American foreign policy, other states have eschewed balancing behavior.[7] To economic liberals, it is economic interdependence and globalization that prevent eligible states from pursuing balance-of-power politics. As all the major powers, especially China, have become linked by trade, investment, and commercial flows with the U.S., they feared that military competition with Washington would derail their economies.[8] To a certain extent, the massive American trade deficit, usually seen as a liability, in fact protects it from hard balancing as exporting nations cannot afford to lose one of their largest sources of cash and employment.

While the liberal argument is important, it assumes that great powers in general are more interested in wealth than in security. It is less clear, however, whether wealth acquisition would override more acute security concerns. Russia's behavior toward Ukraine since 2013 is an example of traditional security concerns overriding the economic calculations of European states. They depend on Russia for natural gas yet imposed major sanctions on Moscow. Further, if a hegemonic power is left unbalanced, it may deviate from pacific ideals if it believes vital interests are at stake. Liberal states are not immune to empire building or military interventions, for either ideological or economic reasons. In fact, some political philosophers see liberal states as inherently imperialistic in that they seek to remake the world in their own images.[9] Moreover, occasionally liberal states can join with nonliberal powers to form balancing coalitions against other liberal states.[10] American policies under President Trump have in fact led many to question whether American hegemony still relies on liberal principles.

Explaining the dearth of balancing efforts against the U.S. as a product of the absence of capable nonliberal states, as neoclassical realists have done, is also unconvincing. It is precisely because a single state cannot match the powerful actor's capabilities that coalitions are formed. Such a coalition needs only to achieve a rough equilibrium; in the nuclear age especially, absolute parity is not required. Logically, if potential balancers are too strong, they do not need to form coalitions or engage in balancing activity in the first place. It is not clear why the combined strength of China and Russia could not create a meaningful balance of power against the U.S.

Against liberal optimism, some realists contend that the U.S. will ultimately be balanced and that the historical interregnum we are witnessing today is most likely temporary.[11] American power will be balanced when a single challenger or a coalition emerges with matching capabilities.[12] With inevitable changes in the military, economic, and technological capabilities of major power actors, international power structures will change—especially in East Asia and Europe—and the international system will once again become multipolar.[13] The problem with realist perspectives is, of course, that we cannot know when this countervailing power against the hegemon will arrive. Moreover, when faced with a rising or threatening power, secondary states in the past have adopted various strategies, including bandwagoning, buck-passing, transcending the power rivalries, and free-riding.[14] The rise of an active balancing military coalition is thus not automatic, and its timing is not easy to predict using the existing realist frameworks.

A variant of the realist argument is the historical/structural perspective on the rise and fall of great powers. By this logic, some believe the U.S. will eventually decline, due to its own overspending, overstretching, and internal failures.[15] Although the history of past empires supports this argument, one needs to be cautious in applying it to contemporary international affairs. First, none of the previous empires had the benefit of capitalism in its highly developed form as the U.S. enjoys today. Although affected by the financial crises of 2008, the U.S. still is looked upon as the ultimate safe harbor for investment. And the dollar's position as the world's reserve currency may help the U.S. to maintain its position for years or decades. While some retreat from free trade is possible under the Trump administration, it is unclear that a massive withdrawal into protectionism would benefit the U.S., let alone the Western allies whose support it needs for maintaining its leadership position. The U.S. also has major advantages in conventional and nuclear weapon systems, although others like China may eventually catch up.

Second, many empires and great powers persisted, even in a weakened form, contrary to the expectations of automatic structural change. For instance, the Roman Empire lasted over 500 years in its Western manifestation and 1,100 years in its Eastern branch. The Ottoman Empire survived over 400 years, much of that time in perilous condition, while the Mughal Empire in India existed for more than 300 and the British Empire more than 250 years. Similar longevity was true for many Chinese and Mongol empires. Without the two world wars, the British Empire would probably have gone on much longer. These cases suggest that indeterminacy of the timing is a problem for theories that predict the automatic rise and decline of great powers.

Third, most past empires declined following long wars against other imperial powers. In the case of the U.S., the relatively low probability of a global war akin to World War II may help prolong its hegemony. Challengers could nibble at the hegemon's power using asymmetric strategies, but given its technological and organizational superiority, the U.S. could devise countermeasures that would maintain its power position even if it cannot fully contain such challenges. Without war as a system-changing mechanism, and with no prospects of an alternative mechanism emerging, even a weakened hegemon could stay on for a long period. Further, because economic superiority does not automatically bestow military capability, American dominance in this area is unlikely to be challenged for some time, even if China, the most obvious competitor, overtakes the U.S. in gross economic terms in a few years. China has used asymmetrical means to advance its interests in addition to strategies such as building new institutions on its own and resurrecting the silk road in both land and maritime versions.

Yet another argument posits that balance-of-power theory was derived from the land-based powers of Europe and that balancing coalitions rarely emerge against leading maritime powers such as the UK. The threshold of balancing against the U.S., as the world's leading maritime power, should therefore be higher than against land-based pow-ers.[16] This again is a questionable argument, especially today, when geography is no longer a prohibitive barrier for military action by a global power such as the United States, which possesses deep-penetra-tion aircraft, supersonic missiles, and unmanned drones. It also has many overseas bases and aircraft carriers to move large numbers of troops against weaker enemies in faraway regions.

Still, a form of balancing has taken place against aggressive Ameri-can behavior a few times in the post–Cold War era. Many states, includ-ing some U.S. allies, became concerned by the increasing unilateralism of the U.S. and its tendency, especially under the George W. Bush adminis-tration, to intervene militarily in sovereign states and forcibly change regimes that pursued anti-U.S. policies. They tried multiple ways to con-strain U.S. power and to maintain their security and influence, switching between soft balancing, bandwagoning, buck-passing, and free-riding as they confronted specific challenges. While these states have not engaged in *hard* balancing against the U.S., they have adopted strategies of *soft* balancing—largely through international institutions and summit meet-ings—in response to U.S. interventions. These soft-balancing strategies involved the formation of limited diplomatic coalitions or ententes in an effort to delegitimize America's coercive behavior. Moreover, the U.S. also used these instruments to soft-balance rising and resurgent powers, especially China and Russia. Second-ranking powers, especially those in Southeast Asia, also relied on soft balancing through institutions to re-strain potential aggression by China.

At the UN, the veto power the second-tier states hold in the Security Council is pivotal to this strategy. By denying UN approval to U.S.-led interventions, these states attempted to deny legitimacy to policies they perceived as imperial and harmful to the norm of sover-eignty. The U.S. has sought to maintain the legitimacy of its hegemony by seeking UN approval for its interventions, although it has sometimes disregarded the UN. Soft-balancing coalitions among the other major powers were aimed at making the U.S. actions less legitimate while in-creasing its costs of action.[17] It is argued that the U.S. has been only too aware that legitimacy is key to any state's lasting power, especially a hegemon's power. Following established international procedures, pursuing policies that benefit others, and conforming to existing moral norms all serve a hegemonic power's purposes.[18] While the desire for legitimacy sometimes seemed to clash with the imperatives of power politics and domestic American politics, it still remained an objective of U.S. foreign policy. Second-ranking powers realized that as a hegemonic power, the U.S. was not immune to legitimacy concerns.

Why was the immediate post–Cold War era so strongly characterized by soft balancing? There are several reasons. First, while the U.S. power position and military behavior caused growing concern, they did not yet seriously challenge the sovereign existence of other great powers. The U.S. had also been a major source of public goods, both economic and military, and would not be easily replaced. Soft balancing permitted the second-tier states to engage the dominant power while also developing institutional links with it in order to ward off possible retaliatory actions.[19] These states also used institutional mechanisms to increase their bargaining power with the U.S., hedging against uncertainty and causing doubt among the American public about the choices its leaders were making.[20]

Such self-doubt was possible because of the widespread consensus that an international intervention, even for humanitarian purposes, needs the "collective legitimation" of the United Nations or a multilateral regional institution representing all key states.[21] Thus a key purpose of soft balancing has been to make sure that any unilateral U.S. intervention lacks international legitimacy and credibility.

When the U.S. *has* ignored the UN or pushed it aside, its interventions have been made more difficult by their lack of legitimacy. In the case of Iraq, many potential allies balked at supporting the intervention, refusing to contribute troops and materials because of the lack of UN approval. The UN's sanctioning of an intervention has been a major cover for states to transcend the sovereignty norm temporarily, as there is an expectation that sovereignty will be restored once the problem that led to the intervention has been dealt with. The UN is unlikely to approve the indefinite occupation of a country by an intervening power or the permanent removal of its sovereignty.

Two prominent examples of how second-ranking states have used institutions to restrain the U.S., especially its threatening unilateralist behavior, are the Kosovo conflict in 1999 and the Iraq invasion in 2003.

The Kosovo Crisis

The diplomatic efforts of Russia and China prior to and during the U.S./ NATO-led offensive against Yugoslavia in March 1999 offer a clear case of attempted soft balancing. NATO intervened in support of the Kosovar Albanians, who were targeted by Serbian president Slobodan Milošević in a campaign of ethnic cleansing after they had sought independence from Serbia. The events leading up to the intervention demonstrate Russia's attempts at soft balancing.[22] The plans for a NATO-led action in Kosovo greatly upset Russia and China because both worried that it would establish a precedent for interventions in their own countries. Russia was fighting against separatists in Chechnya, while China had not yet persuaded the Tibetans to accept Chinese rule; it also worried about legitimizing separatist movements in Taiwan and Xinjiang.[23] An intervention in Kosovo, they feared, would give carte blanche authority to the U.S. and its allies to interfere in the affairs of other countries in the name of humanitarian intervention. Russia also opposed the intervention because much of its population sided with the Serbs as fellow Slavic people. And it feared that a unilateral action by NATO against an independent state without UN sanction would mark a transformation of the alliance's mission from defending Western European nations to a mandate to deploy forces anywhere the U.S. and its allies felt they had an interest.[24]

In hindsight, these concerns appear exaggerated, but at the time the Russians had strong reasons to compare their situation in Chechnya with that of Yugoslavia in Kosovo. Specifically, they feared that Western support for Albanian Muslim separatists in Kosovo would encourage similar movements by Muslim groups inside Russia and other former Soviet republics. The widespread Russian view was that NATO had instigated the conflict by supporting the Kosovo Liberation Army (KLA), with the goal of expanding its military presence in the Balkans. In the eyes of Russian leaders, both the KLA and the Chechen rebels were instances of local Muslim majorities persecuting a Slav minority; both emerged out of the breakup of multinational federations; and both employed terrorism to wage war against what the Russians saw as the legitimate state. Both movements, the Russians thought, also carried territorial ambitions beyond their provinces.[25]

Other than verbal opposition to stall the intervention, Moscow engaged in active soft-balancing diplomacy at the UN, with China's help, and on its own in European multilateral institutions. While Russia and China succeeded in blocking UN approval, their soft-balancing efforts failed to prevent the intervention, largely because it was actively supported by almost all other European states, including Russia's former Warsaw Pact allies, which saw the Milošević regime as a greater threat to Europe's peace and stability than a U.S./NATO-led intervention and military presence. The European states wanted to preclude another Bosnia-type situation, but this was of no concern to the Russians.

Russian soft-balancing efforts continued even after the NATO bombings began. Moscow suspended its participation in the Russia-NATO Founding Act and the Partnership for Peace Program, withdrew its military mission from Brussels, and suspended talks on setting up a NATO information office in Moscow. It also attempted to improve its military ties with allies among the former Soviet republics, conducting joint military exercises with Armenia, Belarus, Kazakhstan, and Tajikistan.[26] And it put diplomatic pressure on the U.S. and its allies to accept the G-8 as the venue for political discussions on the conflict. This led to a G-8 meeting in Bonn on May 21, 1999, that adopted a protocol for negotiating an end to the conflict.[27]

Despite the rupture in Russian-Western relations, Moscow simultaneously engaged in diplomatic efforts to end the conflict. In fact, the Russian efforts helped persuade Milošević to capitulate. On April 14, 1999, President Yeltsin dispatched former prime minister Viktor Chernomyrdin to serve as special envoy to Yugoslavia, and Chernomyrdin worked with U.S. deputy secretary of state Strobe Talbott and President Martti Ahtisaari of Finland to get Milošević to accept NATO's ceasefire conditions. The Russian defense officials decided to involve themselves in the postwar settlement by sending troops to occupy Kosovo's Pristina airport, resulting in a tense standoff between Russian and NATO forces. However, Defense Minister Igor Sergeyev reached an agreement with NATO officials in Helsinki on June 19 under which nearly thirty-six hundred Russian soldiers were deployed throughout Kosovo as part of the Kosovo Force (KFOR), but under the jurisdiction of Russian commanders.[28] Russia thus played an important role in reaching the final agreement that ended the bombing, even though it got little of what it had sought. According to one analyst, Russia may have been more important in persuading Milošević to capitulate than his fear of a NATO ground invasion.[29] The Russian soft-balancing strategy, involving stalling diplomacy through international institutions, bilateral forums, and simultaneous engagement with the Serbian leader, partially succeeded in maintaining Yugoslavia's sovereign control over Kosovo, although it is not clear that the NATO allies wanted to further dismember the Yugoslav state. In February 2008, Kosovo did declare independence, and despite Serbian and Russian objections, after prolonged negotiations it received a fair amount of autonomy and was recognized by many states, including the U.S. Even today, Russian opposition still prevents Kosovo from achieving full-fledged independence and acceptance by the UN as a member state.[30]

Following the crisis, Russia approved a new national security concept and a new military doctrine that placed high emphasis on nuclear weapons in order to protect Russian sovereignty, territorial integrity, and regional influence. The new doctrine stated that although the threat of direct military aggression toward Russia had declined, there remained several external and internal threats to its military security and that of its allies. These included territorial claims by other countries, intervention in Russia's internal affairs, attempts to ignore Russia's interests in resolving international security problems, the buildup of forces violating the existing balance in the adjacent region, expansion of military blocs, and introduction of foreign troops in violation of the UN charter.[31] The beginnings of a limited hard-balancing effort were apparent, but they would not solidify for another decade.

Like Russia, China also opposed the U.S.-led intervention and engaged in soft-balancing efforts to slow it down. Throughout the crisis, China continually maintained a posture upholding the sovereignty norm, which it described as essential to "counter U.S. hegemony in the post–Cold War era."[32] China's view was that "sovereignty must remain an inviolable principle to protect the weak," and NATO's new strategy of acting for reasons unrelated to the defense of its member states was a violation of the sovereignty principle. China thus opposed the Kosovo action because it was not based on UN sanction or P-5 consensus on intervention in a sovereign state.[33]

China's initial soft-balancing efforts were confined to a threat, issued in conjunction with Russia, to veto any attempt by the U.S. and its
European allies to have the UN Security Council authorize the use of
force. In addition, on March 26, 1999, China and Russia introduced a
Security Council resolution calling for an immediate halt to the bombing. This was rejected by a vote of 12 to 3.[34] After the U.S. bombed the
Chinese embassy in Belgrade on May 8, the Chinese reaction became
louder. Beijing and Washington had been engaged in military exchanges
and human-rights dialogue, but after the bombing, China pulled out of
these. Beijing also stepped up strategic collaboration with Moscow, including the activation of a hotline.[35] But it did not take any concrete
hard-balancing actions during the crisis.

The Chinese and Russian moves against the Kosovo intervention
show that while the U.S. was not hard-balanced in the post–Cold War era,
states have used softer instruments to oppose American power. The soft-
balancing efforts by Russia and China continued after the Kosovo crisis.
Russia also tried to enlist India and the Central Asian states in this pursuit.
In the spring of 1999, Russian prime minister Yevgeny Primakov called for
Russia, China, and India to form a "strategic triangle" against NATO.[36]
President Vladimir Putin visited India in October 2000 and signed a declaration of strategic partnership and other agreements, one of which expressed the two countries' opposition "to the unilateral use or threat of
use of force in violation of the UN charter, and to intervention in the internal affairs of other states, including under the guise of humanitarian
intervention."[37] The proposed Russia-China-India alliance failed to ma-
ture, however, as the principal powers began to perceive that there was
actually little risk of U.S. military interference in their internal conflicts.[38]

Russia's interactions with China were more significant. On July 16,
2001, Moscow and Beijing signed a Treaty of Good Neighborliness,
Friendship, and Cooperation, whose areas of cooperation included
"Joint Actions to offset a perceived U.S. Hegemonism" and the rise of
militant Islam in Asia. The treaty called for demarcation of the disputed
forty-three-hundred-kilometer border, a substantial arms sale, and the
supply of technology, energy, and raw materials by Russia to China.[39] In
June 2001, Russia, China, and four Central Asian states announced the
creation of the Shanghai Cooperation Organization (SCO), a regional

association designed to confront Islamic fundamentalism and promote economic development. This strategic partnership has largely been viewed as an institutional mechanism for keeping the U.S. out of Central Asia.[40] The SCO has conducted joint military exercises purportedly to face common terrorist threats, but the underlying desire to maintain autonomy in the face of American encroachments into Central Asia cannot be ruled out. The SCO has also developed common security norms and practices with concepts like "Shanghai Sprit," "New Outlook on Security," and "Harmonious World," all denoting a desire to build cooperation among Central Asian states and prevent encroachments by outside powers.[41]

Although, strictly speaking, the NATO military intervention against an independent state violated the Westphalian norm of sovereignty, there was initially no intention to further break up the Yugoslav state. In the ceasefire agreement, Yugoslavia retained Kosovo as a semi-autonomous region, at least for the time being. Nor did NATO members plan to occupy Yugoslavia or Kosovo permanently. The temporary peacekeeping mission was largely meant to bring stability to the region. The security of Russia and China, if it was challenged at all, was challenged only indirectly. With no imminent threat from the intervention, a balancing coalition became unnecessary. Kosovo was a limited operation intended to punish a threatening regime in Central Europe. The initial Russian or Chinese fear that NATO would stay in Yugoslavia and permanently alter the European territorial order failed to materialize. The intervention was not intended to alter the state system or threaten the physical security and welfare of the other great powers. Nor did it create a precedent for similar interventions in Chechnya or Xinjiang, despite Russia's and China's initial misgivings that it would encourage secessionist movements there. Further, the intervention did not create a powerful norm in support of secession. In many respects, it was designed to forbid violent secession and suppression of minority rights and to preserve the regional order against major instability. Although the NATO attack partially challenged the territorial integrity norm, especially from the Russian perspective, the intervention did not result in a unilateral American expansion into the Balkans or further military activism in the region—developments that would have most likely prompted Russia to pursue active hard-balancing strategies. With the terrorist strikes of September 11, 2001, the possibility of Western and American support for secession dramatically changed, as the interests of the West, Russia, China, and India coalesced temporarily around defeating terrorism.

The Iraq Invasion

The invasion of Iraq in March 2003 offers an example of soft-balancing efforts by three second-tier powers—France, Russia, and Germany—against unilateral American military intervention. The American intervention was preceded by a six-month effort by Washington to gain the support of the UN Security Council for the attack, against the opposition of a coalition led by France, Russia, and Germany. These states engaged in intense diplomatic balancing at the UN through a threatened veto of any resolution authorizing the use of force. In the end, the U.S. decided to launch the attack without UN backing and thereby without the international legitimacy it had sought.

Several times when the U.S. tried to gain the Security Council's support, the second-ranking great power states blocked it. Finally, on September 12, 2002, President George W. Bush spoke at the General Assembly seeking a resolution to take action against Iraq for its failure to disarm. After several weeks of deliberations, on October 25 the U.S. formally proposed Resolution 1441, which would have found Iraq in "material breach" of earlier resolutions, established a new regime for inspections, and warned of "serious consequences" in the event of Iraqi noncompliance. Three days earlier, France and Russia had strongly opposed this resolution, pointing out that it would implicitly allow the use of force by the U.S.[42] In response to American pressure, however, the Security Council unanimously approved Resolution 1441 on November 7, 2002. The resolution did not explicitly threaten the use of force, and the U.S. agreed to return to the Council for further discussions before taking any military action—a major concession to France, Russia, and Germany. Some supporters of the measure argued that it diminished the chances of war by giving the Security Council the key role in sanctioning the use of force and allowing the inspectors more time to establish the veracity of allegations against Iraq.[43] For the Bush administration, however, the three elements of the resolution, and in particular the threat of "serious consequences," amounted to an endorsement of military action.

The three principal opponents of an invasion, France, Russia, and Germany, joined by China, demanded more time for the inspectors to complete their work. French foreign minister Dominique de Villepin told reporters on January 20, "If war is the only way to resolve this problem, we are going down a dead end." In the Security Council, several officials argued that war "would spawn more acts around the globe," and, in the words of Germany's foreign minister, Joschka Fischer, it would have "disastrous consequences for long-term regional stability."[44] Despite this staunch opposition, U.S. secretary of state Colin Powell addressed the Security Council on January 21 and February 5, 2003, making a case that Iraq was still holding weapons of mass destruction in breach of Resolution 1441 and earlier agreements. France, Germany, and Russia responded on February 10 with a joint statement stressing the need for peaceful disarmament in Iraq. They called for the weapons inspection process to be bolstered with more inspectors and increased surveillance technology.[45]

On February 14, the UN weapons inspectors under Hans Blix reported to the Security Council that they had found no evidence of weapons of mass destruction in Iraq, although many items of concern were unaccounted for. Ten days later, the U.S., the UK, and Spain introduced a resolution in the Security Council declaring that under chapter VII of the UN Charter dealing with threats to peace, Iraq had failed to take the final opportunity given to it in Resolution 1441. France, Germany, and Russia upped their opposition, especially to the new U.S. aim of achieving regime change in Iraq. French president Jacques Chirac and German chancellor Gerhard Schroeder, meeting in Paris on February 24, agreed to oppose the resolution and U.S. plans to impose a deadline on Iraq for compliance. They urged that the inspectors be given at least four more months to complete their work.[46] At a meeting on March 5, the French, German, and Russian foreign ministers stated: "We will not let a proposed resolution pass that would authorize the use of force."[47] China declared the next day that it would take the same position. Meanwhile, the U.S. was building up its forces in the Persian Gulf.[48]

Germany and France also used NATO as an institutional arena for soft balancing, temporarily blocking U.S. attempts to involve NATO in the war. On January 16, 2003, the U.S. deputy of defense secretary Paul Wolfowitz asked NATO members to support the U.S. in the event of war. Washington wanted NATO to send AWACs surveillance planes and Patriot antimissile batteries to defend Turkey's 218-mile border with Iraq. Since Turkey is a NATO member, U.S. officials were planning to use its bases as launching pads for air and land attacks on northern Iraqi targets. The U.S. also wanted to employ NATO naval forces to guard approaches to the Mediterranean Sea, through which U.S. warships and cargo vessels would have to pass on their way to the Persian Gulf, and to enlist NATO troops to help guard bases in Europe and in other areas.[49] Opponents of the U.S. proposals vetoed twice (on January 23 and February 12) a U.S.-backed proposal to support Turkey in the event of war, arguing that the move was premature because the UN Security Council had not yet reviewed the weapons inspectors' report. In their view, support for Turkey would encourage a "rush toward hostilities" and "would invite the conclusion that the alliance has accepted the inevitability of war."[50] Later, however, they relented as NATO's article 5 required support for a member state if it was attacked.

French president Jacques Chirac also used the European Union to mobilize the antiwar coalition. He pushed the EU to endorse a statement advocating more time and resources for Iraq's peaceful disarmament. At the time, however, thirteen Eastern European states were waiting for EU membership, and the French pressure was preventing them from speaking on the issue, leading them to denounce France for treating them as "second class citizens."[51] France pursued its opposition in other forums as well. On February 21 in Paris, the French position was endorsed by a summit of fifty-two African countries, including three members of the UN Security Council: Angola, Cameroon, and Guinea.[52]

Two days after the war started, President Chirac vowed to block any UN resolution authorizing the U.S. and Britain to administer the country.[53] Putin, Chirac, and Schroeder met in St. Petersburg on April 11, 2003, calling for a "broad effort under United Nations control to rebuild the shattered country." The three leaders also "warned that the immediate tasks of quelling anarchy and preventing a civil catastrophe fell on the United States and Britain."[54]

Why, among all the second-tier powers, did the French take the most strident position? Ever since the end of the Cold War, France has championed a multipolar system in which Europe would act as an effective pole alongside the U.S. Given the EU's military weaknesses, France has devoted considerable energy to soft balancing with international institutions—especially the UN Security Council, the EU, and NATO—as forums to constrain the unilateral exercise of American power. Although France's immediate concern was that destabilization of the Middle East would bring an increase of terrorism in the West, the underlying motivation for opposition to the U.S. war in Iraq was its concern to maintain the international order. In President Chirac's view, "The Security Council and the European Union are becoming counterweights to the United States in the post–Cold War, post–September 11 world—and in each of those bodies, France has a say greater than its size or military capability."[55]

Germany also opposed the war, even though it has been more dependent on the U.S. for security and trade than France. Chancellor Schroeder used his opposition to the Iraq intervention in his reelection campaign, and his stance received strong support from the electorate because of deeply held perceptions about the illegitimacy of the unilateral use of force by the U.S. At his rallies, Schroeder criticized Bush's policy as an "adventure."[56] Whereas the Bush administration employed a remarkably unilateralist foreign policy, Germany increasingly preferred a multilateralist approach toward regional challenges. In the case of Iraq, the Germans feared that the American intervention would distract from the fight against global terrorism while radicalizing anti-Western opinion in the Middle East.[57] The German view paralleled Europe's increasing adoption of legal norms, with the use of force only as a last resort, as opposed to the Bush administration's tendency to use decisive force without much regard for international law. The Germans valued the UN Security Council as the legitimate authority to sanction the use of force, preferably police force.[58] The American preference for preemptive strategies without UN sanction, based on anticipatory self-defense, was less than convincing to Germany.

In the eyes of France, Russia, Germany, and most other states, the American intervention challenged the Westphalian norm of sovereignty. Many states saw the Bush administration's claims of Iraq's weapons of mass destruction and of Saddam Hussein's alleged links with al-Qaeda terrorist groups as a pretext for an invasion whose real motive was asserting power in the region and gaining another source of oil. They worried that a U.S. success there would increase the Bush administration's appetite for actions in the region against other states, such as Iran. Third, these states were uneasy about America's undertaking unilateral military action despite such clear opposition from prominent members of international institutions. Unlike the Kosovo operations, which received support from France, Germany, and other NATO members, the invasion of Iraq had no formal regional alliance supporting it. Even without full UN approval, Kosovo had some legitimacy, given that it was a NATO undertaking to reestablish regional order. The intervention in Iraq, on the other hand, although it received support from the UK and a few other American allies such as Spain, Italy, Japan, and Australia, was largely a U.S. operation. Even traditional allies like Canada and Belgium opposed the war and refused to support it with troops or equipment. The second-tier powers, France, Germany, and Russia, were thus not alone in opposing the U.S. France, Russia, and China, which held veto power in the UN Security Council, worried that if the UN supported the U.S. in its attack on Iraq, Washington would then be emboldened to attempt regime change elsewhere. They saw the Bush administration as "making a claim to the sovereign right to intervene to disarm and carry out regime change in other countries, subject to no external restraint."[59] The U.S., on the other hand, had a different idea of legitimacy: it conflated its national interests with the interests of global order. This self-legitimation did not convince many of its allies, or any of its adversaries.[60] According to international law scholar Richard Falk, "The abrasive Bush style" and "earlier record of unilateralism and repudiation of law making treaties . . . contributed to the image of the United States as a global leader of severely diminished legitimacy."[61]

The second-tier powers could not prevent the American offensive, but they helped reduce its legitimacy. They also, by demanding UN approval before other nations could send troops, made it more difficult for the U.S. to gain international help for the invasion. American power was thus partially constrained by the soft-balancing efforts of the major powers and their key allies. The rising insurgency against the U.S. forces in Iraq and the long, bloody, inconclusive progress of the war also impeded similar regime-changing military actions against Iran, another regional challenger pursuing nuclear weapons. President Obama, in concluding his nuclear deal with Iran in March 2015, listed the prevention of war as a reason the American Congress should support it.[62]

Despite French, Russian, and German opposition, the U.S. toppled the regime of Saddam Hussein in a twenty-one-day war that began on March 20, 2003.[63] After the initial phase of the war, the three powers continued their opposition by challenging U.S. efforts to gain UN support for its continued occupation of the country. Their soft-balancing efforts continued and culminated in a partial victory in June 2004, when the U.S. agreed to adopt a UN resolution returning partial sovereignty to the Iraqi government, stripping the U.S. of some of its powers in the day-to-day running of the country, except in security matters. The unanimous approval of this resolution was the result of diplomatic bargaining among the U.S., the UK, France, and Germany. Under its terms, the U.S.-led coalition agreed to end the occupation before June 30, 2004, when an interim government would assume responsibility. A transitional national assembly was envisaged by January 31, 2005, with a permanent constitution and constitutionally mandated government by year's end.[64]

In sum, opposition toward the U.S. invasion of Iraq was not based on hard-balancing efforts by key states, but this does not mean there were no efforts to balance U.S. power. Second-tier powers and their smaller allies instead used *soft-balancing* tools to constrain the U.S. Their tactics consisted primarily of coordinating diplomatic positions at the UN and other forums, such as NATO and the EU, and summit diplomacy where their leaders made every effort to delegitimize American intervention.

OBAMA AND SOFT BALANCING

The arrival of the Barack Obama administration in 2009 gave a major fillip to soft-balancing efforts by the opponents of the Iraq invasion. Even before his election, as a senator from Illinois in 2007, Obama had questioned Bush's use of military force to address political problems. In his words: "It was this tragically misguided view that led us into a war in Iraq that never should have been authorized and never should have been waged. In the wake of Iraq and Abu Ghraib, the world has lost trust in our purposes and our principles. . . . To renew American leadership in the world, we must first bring the Iraq war to a responsible end and refocus our attention on the broader Middle East. . . . To renew American leadership in the world, I intend to rebuild the alliances, partnerships and institutions necessary to confront common threats and enhance common security."[65]

During his election campaign, Obama promised that if elected he would pull out of Iraq and Afghanistan, the latter more slowly than the former. He justified his position by declaring that the illegal invasion and occupation of Iraq undermined U.S. power and legitimacy. Iraq was a "war of choice" while Afghanistan was "a war of necessity." In addition to costing the U.S. thousands of lives and billions of dollars, the Iraq War had produced hostility among allies and adversaries alike. Obama wanted to restore American power and reclaim legitimate leadership. His electoral victory was testament to the American public's support for this position. Public opinion had turned against the Bush administration and the Republican Party, and the Iraq invasion played a major part in the resurgence of support for the Democrats.

Far from creating an island of stability against terrorism, years of war had turned Iraq into a hotbed of insurgency and Sunni-Shia violence.[66] The war gave birth to the Islamic State (ISIS), which then occupied large chunks of Iraqi territory and spread across the Middle East. America's image in the world, as measured by Pew Research Center surveys, declined substantially.[67] Obama's victory reignited European enthusiasm more than any other presidential election in recent memory, and the administration made every effort to bolster Europe's confidence.[68] Secretary of State Hillary Clinton stated in January 2009 that the U.S. had no closer allies than the European countries.[69] In February 2009, less than a month after he took office, President Obama announced his plan to pull troops out of Iraq, with a proposed timeline of eighteen months. The pullout was completed in December 2011, and the Iraqis were given full control of the country.[70] In response to increased violence, U.S. forces returned in 2014. Despite the American presence, as of January 2018, Iraq remains a violent and fractured state, although the central government claims to have defeated the ISIS forces and reoccupied much of the land previously held by the extremists.

Soft-balancing efforts, in particular the campaign to undermine the legitimacy of the invasion, seem to have been partially responsible for America's decision to change its Iraq policy and eventually withdraw its forces from the country, although subsequently some U.S. troops returned to wage war against the ISIS forces occupying some areas of Iraq. U.S. intervention policies under the Obama administration were far more attuned to legitimacy than President Bush's, although the subsequent Trump administration has backtracked to an extent. As David Lake states: "By engaging in preventive war against Iraq, the United States overstepped the limits of the international authority that it had previously earned. . . . Authority rests on an exchange of political order for legitimacy and compliance. To give up some portion of their sovereignty, subordinate states must get something in return—usually international security—that is equally if not more valuable."[71]

Soft balancing increased the war's costs for America and closed off any easy exit strategy. During the invasion of Libya in March 2011, the U.S. took a secondary role, portraying itself as "shaping" and "enabling" operations, and leaving NATO and its European allies, France and Britain, to take the lead. Not until a major humanitarian tragedy ensued there did the U.S. join nine other governments, including some Arab states, in supporting a UN resolution under Responsibility to Protect (R2P). The Security Council approved the resolution; China and Russia abstained.[72] The allies did not directly occupy Libya but supported the Libyan rebels who successfully overthrew the Gadhafi regime in October 2011. The internal conflict there also lingers on. The U.S. took a secondary role in the Arab Spring in 2011 and until 2014 was reluctant to get involved in the civil war that ensued in Syria. Obviously, calculations of economic and military costs factored into these decisions, but the need to restore its international legitimacy appeared equally important.

Soft Balancing America

No hard-balancing coalition emerged to oppose the United States despite its international primacy over more than two and a half decades, but soft balancing seems to have been somewhat successful in restraining

American power and policies. It appears that soft balancing is partially successful when it raises the costs of the offending behavior, and it may discourage the target state from doing more of the same in the future. Russian and Chinese soft balancing drove up the costs of the Kosovo intervention, and soft balancing by traditional allies magnified the costs of the Iraq War. Obama's reluctance to get more involved in Syria is evidence of the success of soft balancing resulting from the Iraq experience.

It is clear that in both the Kosovo action and the invasion of Iraq, the concerned states were not engaging in random diplomatic acts but making consistent policy choices intended to restrain the U.S. and encourage it to follow international rules and norms on the legitimate use of force. Their responses unfolded the way they did because several of the facilitating conditions I described in chapter 2 were present during the first two decades after the Cold War, making soft balancing a preferred strategic approach for allies and adversaries alike. Intensified economic globalization since the early 1990s has made states closely linked, with the United States playing the key role in that globalization. Direct hard balancing in both cases was precluded by the expectation that the U.S. intervention would be short-lived and would not profoundly affect the territorial integrity norm. Second-ranking powers such as Russia and China possessed nuclear weapons, which meant they could be far less worried about a direct U.S. attack.

Interestingly, however, since 2010 some states in the Asia-Pacific region have sought American help with limited hard balancing against Chinese power even while pursuing soft balancing against Beijing.

Rising China and Soft Balancing

If secondary states have used soft balancing to constrain the power of the United States, we should also expect to see both hard and soft balancing used against other states, especially rising powers. And so we do: in the post–Cold War era, soft balancing has been adopted by affected states against both China and a resurgent Russia—both of which are responding with hard- and soft-balancing efforts of their own.

From the 1990s until 2009, soft balancing was the dominant approach of the affected states toward a rising China and its security policies in the Asia-Pacific region. More recently, soft balancing has been supplemented by limited hard balancing and diplomatic engagement. In a limited sign of bandwagoning, some smaller Asian states have also shown a willingness to support China in exchange for economic carrots from Beijing, but there is little evidence they endorse China's policies of territorial expansion in the oceans. China's dramatic rise in the era of intensified economic globalization has created considerable challenges for its neighbors in the Asia-Pacific as well as for the United States. Rarely in history has a major state grown so economically powerful so quickly, and it is rarer still that one would do so with no balancing coalition directed against it. The closest parallel is Germany's meteoric rise in the late nineteenth and early twentieth centuries, but that generated intense hard balancing by other European powers.

China's rise is occurring in the context of several facilitating conditions that seem to affect state behavior: an unprecedented level of economic globalization that has produced significant interdependence both within Asia and between China and other states; the difficulties of exercising coercive military force to arrest or accelerate change in the global system; the primacy of defense and deterrence over offense in military technology, making rapid territorial gains difficult or impossible for an expansionist power; and the exponential rise of nationalism among smaller states, which makes direct territorial conquest costly if not unthinkable. Finally, none of the rising powers currently displays an intense expansionist ideology as previous rising powers such as Germany and Japan did. These constraints mean that a rising power has to devise different strategies, other than military expansion or forming military alliances, to achieve its strategic goals.

In 2017, in the face of possible retrenchment by the United States, China emerged as the foremost defender of globalization and free trade. Drawing a metaphor from an old Chinese poem, President Xi Jinping told the 2017 Davos World Economic Forum: "Honey melons hang on bitter vines; sweet dates grow on thistles and thorns." He explained that "economic globalization has created new problems, but this is no justification to write off economic globalization completely. Rather, we should adapt to and guide economic globalization, cushion its negative impact, and deliver its benefits to all countries and all nations." Of China's own approach, he said: "There was a time when China also had doubts about economic globalization, and was not sure whether it should join the World Trade Organization. But we came to the conclusion that integration into the global economy is a historical trend. To grow its economy, China must have the courage to swim in the vast ocean of the global market."[1]

China has also been reluctant to form military alliances with states other than Pakistan, its traditional ally on the Indian subcontinent. Its weapons acquisition has increased, but many of these weapons are defensive and constitute an asymmetric response to America's overwhelming offensive power. China's relationship with Russia has seen ups and downs, but it remains in the realm of a soft-balancing or, at most, a limited hard-balancing coalition. Weapons transfers from Russia were limited after the turn of the century, following Russia's accusation that China reverse-engineered the SU27/30 fighter aircraft into its own J-11 version. But in November 2016, the two nations signed a big contract, worth U.S.$8 billion, for the sale of twenty-four SU-35 jets and six batteries of S-400 surface-to-air air-defense missiles to China.[2] These transfers are commercial, but they strongly suggest a hard-balancing intent. Still, given that China has proclaimed its commitment to reforming the liberal order, its rise will also depend on soft balancing through existing or new institutions.[3]

While China is constrained from engaging in a great-power expansion of the traditional European sort, its neighbors have also been inhibited in forming outright balance-of-power coalitions against it. One reason is that China's expansion into the global commons, such as the South China Sea, has not yet upset the sovereign existence of states, even though it constitutes a challenge to the territorial integrity norm if we broaden the limits of national territory to the Law of the Sea Treaty's two-hundred-nautical-mile exclusive economic zone. Second, China has used trade and investment to make many states dependent on it for their economic well-being. Both opportunity and willingness to create a powerful balance-of-power coalition against China have thus been missing. These constraints in responding to China's rise have been compounded by the fact that two of the pillars of the "liberal peace"—economic interdependence and membership in international institutions—apply in the Chinese case, but China has rejected the third pillar, democracy. This "democratic deficit" creates uncertainty for Beijing's Asian neighbors and the U.S. because China's intentions are not easy to gauge.

From roughly 1980 until 2009, China rose economically and militarily without precipitating significant hard-balancing efforts by other Asia-Pacific states. Most resorted to an umbrella strategy of hedging with the two key pillars of diplomatic engagement and soft balancing. This began to change, however, around 2009 when some of China's neighbors began to complement diplomatic engagement and soft balancing with limited hard balancing. While soft balancing relies mostly on noncoercive means and is intended to buy time for the affected states, hard balancing relies on military buildup and in some cases preexisting formal alliances. Countries are now mixing their strategies and increasingly resorting to a limited form of hard balancing. They are answering the threatening power of China with a "wait and see" attitude, keeping themselves ready to adapt if and when conditions change.

Hedging against the Future: Strategies toward China's Rise

Hedging is the most prominent umbrella strategy taken by the United States and other Asia-Pacific states concerned with China's ascendance.[4] I contend that soft balancing, diplomatic engagement, and limited hard balancing are the key components of an umbrella hedging strategy toward China. The concept of hedging arises from the business world: "Hedging your bets" implies that the future is unpredictable, and by waiting and watching while making use of present opportunities, one's options are widened. A second purpose of hedging is to maximize leverage with the rising power and other potential challengers. Since the rising power is offering collective and private goods such as trade and investment, it is difficult to abandon a relationship with that power because by doing so, one's own country's economic prosperity may be hurt. Hedging also signals to the rising power that assuming an aggressive posture might generate major consequences.

China's regional neighbors have hedged against Beijing by forming limited hard-balancing military alliances and ententes. Southeast Asian states have practiced limited alignment with the U.S. along with institutional engagement with China as a way to achieve security.[5] Hedging was also the U.S. strategy toward China under President George W. Bush. For instance, the Bush administration's National Security Strategy of 2006 stated: "The United States will welcome the emergence of a China that is peaceful and prosperous and that cooperates with us on common challenges and mutual interest . . . while we hedge against other possibilities."[6] The Obama administration, after an initial enthusiasm for diplomatic engagement, in general pursued the same policy. It was endorsed by analysts like Fareed Zakaria, who argues: "Like many hedge funds, the U.S. strategy should have a 'long bias' meaning it should place greater emphasis on efforts to engage China, since that is by far the preferable (and much less costly) strategy compared with entering into a new, long Cold War with what is also likely to be the world's largest economy."[7] He adds, "if China's rise becomes threatening and destabilizing, America should also have in place strong alliances with other Asian powers such as India and Japan—which Obama's [recent] trip sought to accomplish—as building blocks to balance Chinese expansionism."[8]

Among the three approaches to hedging—diplomatic engagement, soft balancing, and limited hard balancing—employed by other
states toward China, soft balancing was used most extensively until
2009. Diplomatic engagement at both official and unofficial levels has
involved bilateral, trilateral, and multilateral forums aimed at gauging
the rising power's strategies and policy directions. This strategy has also
been geared toward building confidence and trust, as each side gets to
know the other's intentions and capabilities. Engagement assumes that
the rising power is not thoroughly revisionist. If it already has a strategy
of fundamentally upsetting the world order and revising the rules of the
game, it is likely to use engagement only as a tool to justify actions it was
already determined to take. Most states accept China's repeated claim
that it has no ambition to alter the international order but wants to
work within it to reform it, even though China's behavior is sometimes
at odds with this position.[9]

Asian as well as other key states have actively sought diplomatic engagement with China at multilateral and regional forums, at international institutions such as the UN, WTO, World Bank, the International
Monetary Fund, ASEAN Regional Forum, East Asia Summit, APEC, G-20,
BRICS, and at other venues dealing with specific issue areas. These venues
have allowed China and other states to work together and exchange views
on a variety of issues. It is unclear if or how these interactions have helped
to reduce conflict over core security issues that divide China and its regional neighbors. China scholars agree that for a period, Beijing was be-
having constructively in the Asia-Pacific. Thomas Christensen argues
that the purpose of engagement has been to shape China's choice and
behavior, and until the 2008 financial crisis it seemed to succeed.[10] David
Shambaugh also praised China's successful engagement with other Asian
states before dramatically changing his view after 2008.[11] The arrival of Xi
Jinping has brought a more muscular policy of expansion.

Soft-Balancing China

The key feature of the hedging strategy toward China has been soft
balancing. The U.S. and regional states practiced this approach from
early 1990s to around 2009 and since then have combined it with limited

hard balancing. There has been little intense hard balancing through formal alliances, except for the continuing U.S. alliances with Japan and South Korea, which date back to the Cold War. Internal hard balancing through arms buildup has accelerated since 2010. Still, the regional states' military buildup is not enough to balance China, meaning that an active military coalition with the U.S. is required if China becomes aggressive. Why have states preferred to restrain China with soft-balancing instruments rather than using intense hard balancing for almost two decades?

That China could sustain its rise without an active balance-of-power coalition forming against it remains an anomaly in international relations—and somewhat of a challenge to balance-of-power theory.[12] The classical balance-of-power theory is meant to address precisely this situation: an effort to arrest the growth of a rising power that can threaten others. China has been swiftly emerging as the lead economic power and is also rapidly modernizing its military forces. It has stepped up its territorial claims in the South China Sea and on its borders with India and Bhutan, and more recently forayed into the Indian Ocean by acquiring ports and bases from Sri Lanka to Djibouti. Although it has been at pains to emphasize its "peaceful rise" strategy, the reluctance of regional states in Asia-Pacific to form active hard-balancing coalitions against it still needs an explanation. They have instead increased economic interdependence with China and have engaged it in many regional institutional frameworks such as the Asia-Pacific Economic Cooperation, ASEAN Regional Forum (ARF), and the Shanghai Cooperation Organization.[13] They have also joined Chinese-sponsored institutions such as the Asian Infrastructure Development Bank and President Xi's New Silk Road or the Belt and Road initiative (BRI). Even some of the larger affected states, such as India, have pursued a hedging strategy, forming only limited strategic partnerships in response to China's rise.[14] More important, the U.S. response to China's encroachments in the South China Sea has been tepid at best, with only a moderate uptick since 2015. This is quite a contrast to the U.S. response to Russia's expansionist moves in Ukraine, which prompted a NATO buildup in Eastern Europe.

WHY NO ACTIVE HARD BALANCING?

What explains the lack of active hard balancing against China? Eligible states (those that are affected and have the potential to develop balancing coalitions) have responded to its rise with soft balancing and increasingly with limited hard balancing, especially through institutional means such as the ARF. There are several reasons for this. Perhaps most important, China's position and military behavior are of concern, but they do not yet challenge the sovereign existence of other states. China has also been a major source of valuable public goods, for instance, as an export market and, more recently, as a source of foreign investment. Moreover, second-ranking states have not had the political will or military wherewithal to pursue a confrontational hard-balancing strategy. Instead, reliance on soft balancing has enabled them to engage the rising power and at the same time develop institutional links with it, at least for now, so as to ward off possible retaliatory actions without eliciting a reaction from China as these are not overt military challenge to its power position.[15]

Most efforts to explain the lack of balancing coalitions against Beijing have focused on economics. For example, Steve Chan has argued that state elites in East Asia have increasingly bolstered their legitimacy and that of their regimes through their ability to provide steady economic performance, instead of factors such as ideology, nationalism, or military expansion.[16] David Kang has written that South Korea has neither balanced nor bandwagoned China and maintained a low profile on China's radar because it perceives the potential for economic benefits from peaceful relations with Beijing as far outweighing any military threat.[17] Elites in East Asia have pursued commercial and financial integration both as a means of securing economic performance and as a way to credibly commit China to cooperation rather than military conflict— although the prospect of conflict still exists.[18] Figures 1 and 2 show China's level of trade with the potential balancers. Although this is only one measure of interdependence, it still offers an important indicator of the constraints states face in hard balancing when they are engaged economically.

In addition to trade, China and other key states have been major sources of investment for one another. In 2016, China was the third-largest recipient of foreign direct investment (FDI), totaling some $134 billion, and it has maintained that high pace of investment for a decade. Although Hong Kong was the country's most important provider of FDI, Singapore, South Korea, and the U.S. also were key sources. During the same period, FDI outflows from China totaled $183 billion, making it the second-largest source in the world. Prospective investors in 2016 cited China as the most attractive country for FDI, followed by

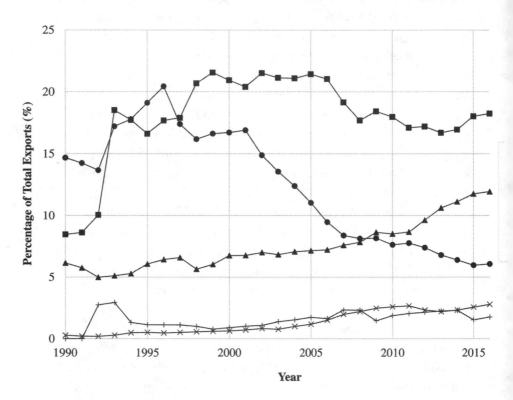

—▲—ASEAN
—✕—India
—●—Japan
—+—Russian Federation
—■—United States

Figure 1. China's Export Dependence on Major Partners (Exports to Partners as Percentage of China's Total Exports): 1990–2016. (*Source: IMF Direction of Trade Dataset, http://data.imf.org/?sk=9D6028D4-F14A-464C-A2F2-59B2CD424B85 &sId=1390030341854. Adapted by Erik Underwood and Daniel Smit.*)

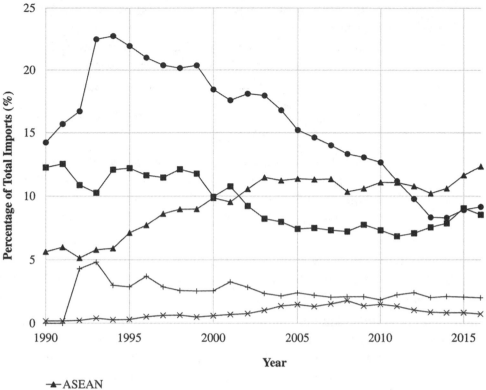

Figure 2. China's Import Dependence on Major Partners (Import from a Partner as the Percentage of Total Imports): 1990–2016. *(Source: IMF Direction of Trade Dataset, http://data.imf.org/?sk=9D6028D4-F14A-464C-A2F2-59B2CD424B85 &sId=1390030341854. Adapted by Erik Underwood and Daniel Smit.)*

the U.S.[19] China's large market and investment-friendly policies are the main reason for this high rate of economic interaction with the rest of the world.

Although economic considerations, especially trade interdependence and FDI flows, are important variables, the tepid balancing response may also have something to do with China's grand strategy. If it pursued a highly expansionist strategy, relying on overt military means, hard-balancing coalitions would have arisen. How a rising state contributes to the threat environment thus needs to be part of any explanation for the relative absence of hard balancing toward China. The presence of many institutions allows regional states to pursue other approaches.

ASEAN

The ASEAN states' strategy toward China has involved institutional engagement through forums such as the ARF, processes such as the ASEAN Plus Three (China, Japan, and South Korea) grouping, and the Chiang Mai initiative. More recently, China has been involved in the Regional Comprehensive Economic Partnership (RCEP), a process to liberalize economic exchange in the wider Asia-Pacific region that includes ASEAN as well as the six third parties with which ASEAN has free-trade agreements: Australia, China, India, Japan, Korea, and New Zealand. ASEAN has also engaged in hedging through what Denny Roy has called "low intensity balancing" by aligning with the U.S. at a modest level.[20] These efforts are aimed at simultaneously engaging China and limiting its expansion into the Pacific and Indian Oceans, as well as limiting aggressive claims over disputed territories. Over the past two decades, ASEAN has made a number of efforts to institutionally restrain China. The 2003 Declaration of Code of Conduct in the South China Sea was chief among them. Beyond this, the following arrangements have been significant in restraining Beijing and other powers:

- China's 2003 signature of the Treaty of Amity and Cooperation (which the Obama administration signed in 2009) was a means to draw major powers into a framework of pacific settlement of regional disputes in accordance with the UN Charter.
- ASEAN's continuing bid to get China and other nuclear weapon states to accede to the protocol for a Southeast Asia Nuclear Weapons Free Zone. Although China and the other P5 have expressed support for the protocol, Beijing is reluctant to follow through because the agreement has im-

plications for its claims to sovereignty in the South China
Sea. The U.S. has not signed because it does not want to
restrict passage of its nuclear vessels.

- The annual Shangri-La Defense Dialogues in Singapore
  have forced Chinese defense ministers to play diplomatic
  defense on the issue of the South China Sea.
- The expansion of the East Asia Summit beyond the ASEAN
  Plus Three to include India, New Zealand, and Australia—
  despite China's opposition.[21]

Territorial disputes between ASEAN states and China have become clear concerns. China claims sovereignty over almost all of the
South China Sea and has created a map that is deeply contested by Vietnam, the Philippines, and Malaysia in particular. These littoral states
argue that under the 1993 UN Law of the Sea Convention they also retain special economic rights to the two-hundred-nautical-mile zone adjacent to the islands they claim. Since 2003, China has increased its
efforts to build man-made islands on atolls and other rock formations
in areas claimed by other states. The Chinese aim appears to be to use
these facilities for economic exploitation of the areas close by or as
future military bases.[22]

The ASEAN states' key response to these encroachments has been
institutional. The creation of the ASEAN Regional Forum in 1994 was
critical to this institutional balancing. Meetings among the twenty-eight
ARF members have emerged as a critical "preventive diplomacy" forum
to discuss key security issues affecting the region, including the South
China Sea.[23] The addition of China as a dialogue partner of ASEAN
since 1996 was meant to encourage Beijing to accept the ASEAN principles on state behavior in the region. Similarly, the formation of ASEAN
Plus Three (APT), involving ASEAN states and China, Japan, and South
Korea, in December 1997 was a response to the Asian financial crisis, and
it was subsequently institutionalized in 1999. The strategy of institutionally binding China had some positive effects in the 1990s. Alastair Iain
Johnston argues that China has been socializing into global norms
through institutions, while Evelyn Goh suggests that ASEAN used an
"enmeshment" strategy to socialize China.[24]

China's membership in multilateral institutions and security regimes, including the nuclear nonproliferation regime, is touted as an example of its changing behavior. In 2011, for instance, it dropped its resistance to extending APT to East Asia Summit countries such as the U.S. and Australia. Amitav Acharya argues that ASEAN's institutional engagement with China produced crucial commitments to ASEAN principles such as noninterference and the avoidance of great-power hegemony or a concert of power.[25] In November 2002, China and ASEAN signed a "declaration of conduct" on the South China Sea that, although not legally binding, nevertheless was viewed as a precursor to China's full-fledged commitment to the ASEAN code of conduct. The key provisions of this code included "parties reaffirming their commitment to the 1982 UN Convention on the Law of the Sea," "respect for and commitment to the freedom of navigation over flight above the South China Sea," and "self-restraint in the conduct of activities that would complicate or escalate disputes and affect peace and stability including, among others, refraining from action of inhabiting on the presently uninhabited islands, reefs, shoals, cays, and other features and to handle their differences in a constructive manner."[26] Still, China has yet to fully sign such a code, although negotiations continue, and Beijing's subsequent behavior in the South China Sea, including building on uninhabited islets and island shoals, violates some of the code's underlying principles.

China has also created new institutions in the Asia-Pacific to further both its own economic goals and its diplomatic engagement with states in the region. These too have soft-balancing implications. These institutional interactions have helped reduce uncertainty and, for now, revealed China's intentions. The New Silk Road is intended to link China with Central Asia and Europe, and its complement, the Maritime Silk Road, would link it with Middle Eastern and African countries through Southeast Asia. The $54-billion China-Pakistan Economic Corridor, linking Xinjiang with Gwadar Port of Pakistan, and the Bangladesh-China-India-Myanmar Economic Corridor are other components of the umbrella project known as One Belt, One Road, or OBOR, now known as the Belt and Road Initiative, which has been received with much enthusiasm by regional states as well as by the UN Security Council. China held a meeting of fifty-seven nations in Beijing in May

2017 when BRI was formally launched. There has been opposition from India and some European states that fear the geopolitical implications of Chinese commercial outreach. The New Development Bank, formerly known as BRICS Development Bank, was launched in July 2015 with its headquarters in Shanghai, and the Asian Infrastructure Investment Bank began in October 2014 with twenty-two member states. By July 2015 it had fifty-seven members, including several U.S. allies: Australia, the UK, South Korea, and Germany. China has also made investments abroad worth some U.S.$1.25 trillion during the past ten years. These investments have increased its stake in the global economy and in globalization in general, and they are expected to exert a tempering effect on high-handed security behavior. Theoretically, regional states with a stake in these institutions will be able to use them for soft-balancing purposes if China threatens them, although they have not done so yet. China could also use these institutions for its own soft balancing against other member states. For now, it has been able to keep security and economic relations compartmentalized, but this may change if BRI is followed by the militarization of the land and seas routes.

Some ASEAN states have attempted soft balancing through legal/institutional means to restrain China. A critical turning point in soft balancing occurred in January 2013 when the Philippines, an ASEAN state, approached the Hague–based International Tribunal for the Law of the Sea for an arbitration ruling on China's claim over much of South China Sea. Manila argued that under chapter XV of the UN Convention on the Law of the Sea, the Chinese buildup, including on the Paracel and Spratly Islands, had violated Philippine rights. Manila was especially contesting the Chinese takeover of the Scarborough Shoal, a submerged area next to one of its islands. In a historic decision in July 2016, the Hague tribunal completely agreed with the Philippine claim and rejected China's position, ruling that China's claim of historic control of the area was unsupported by the evidence.[27] This case can be considered as an institutional and legal means of soft balancing by a smaller state to restrain China. Even if China does not honor the ruling or the Philippines does not pursue the case further, the tribunal dealt a major legal blow to Chinese legitimacy on territorial claims in the global commons.

This is a powerful soft-balancing measure that delegitimized the aggressive behavior of a rising power through legal/institutional means. As China continues its island-building activities, it remains to be seen whether the ruling will influence its behavior over the long term.

Despite these security conflicts, China has emerged as ASEAN's largest trading partner. In 2013 it accounted for 14 percent of ASEAN's trade. This two-way trade grew from U.S.$23.5 billion in 1998 to U.S.$345.76 billion in 2015. The ASEAN-China Free Trade Agreement (ACFTA), which went into force in 2010, has helped the trade volume and is expected to boost it further if the Regional Comprehensive Economic Partnership is concluded among other Asian countries, including China and ASEAN.[28] Many ASEAN companies have created supply-chain networks with Chinese counterparts. Although China is still not a major source of foreign direct investment for ASEAN, this is likely to change when the BRI comes into play. Therein lies the greatest challenge for the regional states that may want to consider forming outright balancing coalitions against China or engaging in an isolationist policy. Yet the weaknesses of soft balancing are also increasingly evident. China has actively courted ASEAN countries, taking advantage of the declining reliability of the U.S. to keep ASEAN from forming a unified position on the South China Sea. At the July 2012 ASEAN Foreign Ministers meeting, Cambodia prevented a consensus declaration on the dispute. As Barry Desker points out, some of the regional states think it is in the interests of Southeast Asia that the U.S.-China rivalry not deteriorate, as "China's rise cannot be blocked," and many states feel the optimal strategy is to strengthen their relationship with China while maintaining ties with Washington. Balance-of-power strategies are used for "increasing the scope and opportunities for political independence, diplomatic engagement and economic interdependence."[29] Countries such as the Philippines and Malaysia have now accepted a less confrontational approach, while more loyal friends of China, such as Cambodia, have supported Beijing's interests at ASEAN meetings. The structural changes taking place in the Asia-Pacific region due to declining U.S. interest and China's increasing economic and military strength make the sustainability of institutional balancing uncertain. The Donald Trump administration has taken a more confrontational approach, threatening to ratchet up

U.S. hard-balancing efforts in the region, in particular toward North Korea and China, but the success of this is yet to be seen. It is also difficult to see regional states joining an aggressive push by the U.S.

The United States' Balancing Response

During much of the post–Cold War era, the U.S. pursued a hedging strategy toward China based on engagement, soft balancing, and hard balancing, with increasing emphasis on the last after 2009. This is not to deny that the long-standing alliances with Japan and Korea have hard-balancing relevance, but they are not exclusively aimed at China. Historically, they were directed toward Russia and North Korea. While the U.S. still remains the leading power in raw military terms, China's position, especially in economic power and naval capability, has grown to the point that it has begun to compromise American superiority. Yet despite this prospect of a relative decline, the American response to China's rise lacks the urgency seen in Europe's response to the rise of Germany in the late nineteenth and early twentieth centuries. It was years, for example, before the U.S. tepidly challenged Chinese islet building in the South China Sea, and even then its main response—sending U.S. ships closer through Chinese self-claimed islands or islets under "freedom of navigation" operations—has done nothing to stop the Chinese activities.[30] The Trump administration has threatened more strident military action, including a blockade, but we have yet to see whether this will materialize. The administration abandoned its early threat to recognize Taiwan and declare China a currency manipulator in return for a promise of cooperation on restraining North Korea.[31]

American hard-balancing efforts have been focused on strengthening its traditional formal alliances with Japan, South Korea, and Taiwan. However, it is not clear whether either Japan or South Korea wants to use the U.S. relationship for an active hard-balancing coalition against China yet. Even during the 2012 crisis involving the Diaoyu/Senkaku Islands, Washington's reaction toward China was muted. The Obama administration initially took a neutral position, and then declared America's determination to defend Japan in the event of an armed conflict with China.[32] The U.S. support of Taiwan has been tepid since the

1970s, although there seems a tacit agreement between the two that, except for some serious military provocation from Beijing, each will not act to change the status quo. The U.S. has been attempting to form limited alignments and strategic partnerships with Asian states such as Vietnam and India. These count as, at most, soft to limited hard balancing as none envisions a coordinated military response to China's potential aggression.

THE PIVOT TO ASIA

In 2012 President Obama brought a measure of hard balancing through a strategic "pivot" to East Asia. In a November 2011 article in *Foreign Policy,* Secretary of State Hillary Clinton called for a new focus as the wars in Afghanistan and Iraq wound down.[33] Even then, however, Clinton did not depict China as a new Soviet Union but argued that "geopolitics today cannot afford to be zero-sum game. A thriving China is good for America, so long as we both thrive in a way that contributes to the regional and global good."[34]

As part of this strategy, the U.S. announced the repositioning of its naval strength from an equal distribution between the Atlantic and the Pacific to a ratio of 40:60. Extra troops were to be deployed in the region, especially in Australia. Other parts of this strategy, which had both hard- and limited hard-balancing dimensions, included building strategic relationships with ASEAN countries such as Vietnam and South Asia's rising power, India. Washington encouraged its allies to turn their attention to the Asia-Pacific as well.[35] In January 2012, the U.S. Department of Defense released its new strategic guidelines, which called for a "rebalancing toward the Asia-Pacific Region."[36] In 2017, the pivot had not made a huge impact by way of balancing China militarily, and the Trump administration's decision to pull out of the Trans-Pacific Partnership (TPP) trade deal in January 2017 marked the policy's official end.[37]

A significant soft-balancing move by the U.S. has been its improving relations with India, with which it had an "estranged relationship" for over five decades.[38] The initial U.S. response to India's nuclear explosion in 1998 was to impose punitive sanctions, but that soon changed to engagement and then limited alignment. President Bill Clinton visited India in 2000, beginning an era of strong relations that improved dramatically with the Bush administration's decision to accept India as a "de facto nuclear weapon state."[39] The Obama administration continued this policy, and the president's visits to New Delhi in November 2010 and January 2015 and Prime Minister Modi's several trips to Washington beginning in September 2014 have indicated warming relations.[40]

With both parties having an interest in limited balance of power in the face of China's rise, economic and strategic ties between the U.S. and India have improved rapidly. They have engaged in joint military exercises, cooperative weapons development, and strategic dialogue around the need to balance against China if Beijing becomes too strong or belligerent. In 2016, India and the U.S. signed an agreement to allow American ships to visit Indian ports and vice versa. The U.S. government and American companies compete for military sales to India with other weapons-exporting countries, and the two governments provide logistical support for each other's military aircraft and naval craft. India also regularly participates in the annual Malabar naval exercises along with the U.S., and Japan (and occasionally involving Australia and Singapore).[41] Although the declared purpose is to develop interoperability among the three navies, guarantee that the sea-lanes remain open in the Indian Ocean, and keep the global commons safe from security threats, the exercises are also a limited hard-balancing message to China, which is increasing its presence in the Indian Ocean.[42] The U.S. now considers India a long-term security provider in the region. In November 2017, a key meeting took place on the sidelines of the East Asia Summit in Vietnam of the leaders of the U.S., India, Japan, and Australia, resurrecting the soft-balancing "Quadrilateral dialogue" on security matters involving the four democracies, an idea that was proposed by Japan in 2007.[43]

Although these interactions have drawn critical statements from Beijing, neither India nor the U.S. seems ready to rush into forming a hard-balancing coalition. For now, soft balancing and limited hard balancing are comfortable for both sides.[44] The arrival of the Trump administration in January 2017 has brought a pause in the improving relations with India, as with all U.S. allies. The administration, however, has reaffirmed India's status, bestowed by the Obama administration in

December 2016, as "a major defence partner."[45] Modi's visit to Washington in June 2017 has helped in resuming the growth of strategic and economic links. Trump's hard line on Pakistan is also helping to improve Washington's relations with India.

Despite some limited efforts at hard balancing and soft balancing, it is clear that the Obama administration made "balancing lite" its essential policy. It aimed to avoid provoking China and constantly emphasized a "mutual-sum" as opposed to a "zero-sum game," judging a hard-balancing competition with Beijing too costly for both sides. The Trump approach seems to take a similar course, despite contrary rhetoric and some increases in defense spending.

India's Balancing Strategy

China's rapid rise has posed major challenges to security planners in New Delhi. China has ratcheted up its territorial conflict with India by renewing its territorial claims in the state of Arunachal Pradesh, issuing stapled visas (that is, not stamping directly on the passports but on a separate stapled page to show nonrecognition of the traveler's nationality) to residents of Jammu and Kashmir and Arunachal Pradesh, and strengthening its military alliance with Pakistan. It has also built militarily significant roads in Tibet and on its borders with Sikkim and Bhutan, areas where India is militarily vulnerable. One such road construction, in an area near the Bhutan-India-China tri-junction that is claimed by both China and Bhutan, produced a crisis in the summer of 2017 when the Indian Army stopped construction in the disputed area. The crisis evoked fears of a war akin to the one in 1962, although both sides were careful to prevent the incident from escalating into armed clashes.[46]

In 2014, China and Pakistan signed an agreement for the China-Pakistan Economic Corridor (CPEC), a $54-billion plan (later increased to $62 billion) to develop roads, ports, and other infrastructure linking Xinjiang with Gwadar, in the Baluchistan province on Pakistan's west coast. This is part of President Xi's BRI project and is expected to be completed by 2030. The major projects in infrastructure, energy, and trade zones include extensive military accommodations.[47] Chinese naval vessels were stationed in Gwadar beginning in fall 2016. The use of Pakistan as a proxy for hard balancing while maintaining a limited rivalry with India has been the hallmark of China's balancing strategy against India for some time. More ominously for India, some experts believe China is pursuing a "string of pearls" strategy of building civilian ports and then bases in India's neighboring countries with the intent of establishing a dominant naval presence in the Indian Ocean. It has acquired a base in Djibouti and built commercial ports in Sri Lanka and Pakistan; both could eventually be converted to military purposes. Chinese naval vessels, including submarines, have increased their visits to the Indian Ocean since 2016.[48] Beijing's acquisition of the Hambantota port in Sri Lanka with a ninety-nine-year lease and the signing of the free-trade agreement with Maldives with provisions that China will develop several small islands for commercial and potentially military purposes all happened in December 2017. In addition, China is reportedly planning to develop a second port near Gwadar in Pakistan for naval purposes. These developments foretell more commercial and naval activism by China and India and a ratcheting up of the cascading security dilemma for the parties.[49]

Yet it is also true that India's economic relations with China have been on the upswing. Total trade between the two countries has increased significantly since the late 1980s, as has China's share of India's imports and exports. Imports from China accounted for over 12 percent of total Indian imports in 2014, although exports to China have remained modest, amounting to a little over 4 percent of total Indian exports. The ratio of mutual trade to GDP has risen remarkably for both countries, and this has affected their behavior. Both are heavily dependent on trade and have emerged as key supporters of free trade and continued globalization.[50] In contrast to its intense competition and crisis-ridden behavior toward Pakistan, with which it trades very little, India maintains a managed and restrained rivalry in its approaches toward China. It was working to reduce friction on the border as early as the 1980s. During a visit to Beijing in 1988, Prime Minister Rajiv Gandhi dropped the condition that a border settlement was a prerequisite for improving relations, a move that paved the way for better trade and political relations.[51]

India has employed a mix of strategies to deal with China's some-times threatening behavior. It has followed limited hard balancing based on an internal arms buildup, and soft balancing relying on limited in-formal ententes with the U.S. and other powers such as Japan, the ASEAN countries, and Australia. It has also worked to improve relations with the United States in ways that combine soft balancing, limited hard balancing, and diplomatic engagement within an overall strategy of hedging toward China. India's economic liberalization since 1991 has brought unprecedented economic growth, with average GDP growth rates of 6.4 percent a year from 1992 through 1999, and 7 percent from 2000 through 2014.[52] This has helped India engage more confidently in international forums.[53] The strategic dialogue with Washington follow-ing the nuclear tests in 1998, America's willingness to accept India as a de facto nuclear state, and its entry into the G-20 and other forums have offered India major opportunities to increase its global status.

The arrival of the Narendra Modi government in May 2014 strengthened American-Indian soft balancing and limited hard balanc-ing toward China. Modi's Bharatiya Janata Party (BJP) ardently pro-motes India's status as an emerging military and economic power and has accelerated the country's arms buildup and military cooperation with the U.S., Japan, and Australia. Although India has not signed for-mal military alliances with any of these states, its strategic partnerships and increased cooperation with these countries display many elements of a soft-balancing/limited hard-balancing coalition. The hard-balanc-ing efforts also involve the purchase and deployment of sophisticated weaponry, including nuclear weapons on the India-China border, the development of long-range missiles, and the improvement of infra-structure in the eastern border areas—all measures specifically aimed at China. Analysts have started to believe that with the deployment of new conventional and nuclear capabilities, the Indian strategy on the border is approaching "deterrence by punishment" as opposed to its long-standing "deterrence by denial."[54] By 2016, India was the world's sixth-largest spender on defense, with an annual budget of U.S.$55.9 billion, and the world's leading weapons importer, even though this defense budget pales in comparison with China's $215 billion. In 2017, India was also negotiating the purchase of a number of weapons systems, such as

Rafale fighter jets, Apache, Chinook and Kamov helicopters, and the M-777 lightweight howitzers.[55] In the naval sphere, hard balancing is evident in India's strengthening of its naval base in the Andaman and Nicobar Islands and its acquisition of submarines and aircraft carriers. Yet all these moves toward modernization and acquisition are not sufficient to support a proper hard-balancing strategy. India must still rely on soft balancing, including limited alignments and ententes with other states threatened by China's rise.

The annual Malabar naval exercises, which the Indian and U.S. navies have mounted since 1992 (joined by Japan in 2015), have assumed a key role in these balancing efforts.[56] India has formed limited ententes with Japan, Australia, Vietnam, and Singapore while attempting to maintain its traditional bonds with island states where China is also making inroads, such as Sri Lanka, Seychelles, and the Maldives. None of these efforts amounts to full-fledged balancing; they are asymmetric responses to China's increased activism. Even though many Indian realists view America's pivot to Asia as an opportunity for balancing China, such postures are constrained by India's desire to "benefit from China's economic growth," the domestic consequences of "military alignment with the United States against China," and the desire of many in India to retain "strategic autonomy."[57] Indians also remain skeptical of U.S. rebalancing policies, partly because of the uncertainty of U.S. domestic politics, Washington's need of Beijing's support for many of its global policy initiatives, and a fear that the U.S. might accommodate rather than challenge China; India is fearful of being seen as too "far out ahead of the United States in dealing with a rising China."[58]

Japan's Strategy toward China

Beyond India, the other major Asia-Pacific power most affected by China's rise has been Japan. It has an active dispute with China over the small islands of Diaoyu/Senkaku, which flared into a crisis in 2012–13. Beijing is a supporter of North Korea, which has threatened Japan for some time with nuclear and missile tests. Moreover, old Chinese grievances over Japanese atrocities in World War II still linger. Although Japan has an operational alliance with the U.S., it has also pursued diplomatic engagement and soft-balancing strategies in dealing with China.[59] In recent years, Beijing's emergence as Japan's leading trading partner has limited Tokyo's ability to pursue intense hard balancing.

The dispute over Diaoyu/Senkaku islands flared up in April 2012 when the Tokyo city government purchased them from private owners. China, which claims the islands as its territory, first sent fishermen and small vessels and then, in November 2013, announced that the islands were covered by an Air Defense Identification Zone. Japan protested loudly and declared Tokyo would ignore China's move. China, which viewed Japan's Shinzō Abe government as a "trouble maker" bent on rearming, saw the conflict as a pretext for revising its ambitious defense policy. Despite the aggressive tones on both sides and some tension-ridden encounters among coast guard vessels, the conflict, surprisingly, de-escalated, and both sides used institutional forums to design a code of conduct for unplanned encounters at sea.[60] Japan's response has been to strengthen its ties with the U.S. and to engage in internal balancing by increasing military spending.

The security threats to Japan have increased in recent years, partially from North Korea's nuclear and missile development. Pyongyang's alliance with China has been taken into account in Japanese defense planning, which includes building and deploying ballistic missile defense systems and exploring counterattack options. In view of the threats from both countries, Japan has increased its defense budget and has sought to buy systems such as F35As, V-22 Osprey Amphibious Assault Vehicles (AAVs), and Global Hawks.[61] Its $50.2 billion in defense spending and revision of the constitution's war renunciation clause have also been part of the Abe government's internal balancing efforts.[62]

Japan has also pursued a soft-balancing coalition with India. Prime Minister Narendra Modi has been an eager partner, given his desire to acquire Japanese technology and military support in addition to civilian nuclear energy capabilities. Prime Minister Abe visited New Delhi in 2014 and was the chief guest at India's Republic Day parade. Since then, Modi has visited Tokyo at least three times, with a civil nuclear agreement and the purchase of Japanese arms as a major plank of the new friendship. Japan has also used institutions in an effort to constrain China's behavior. For example, Japan insisted on inviting three non–East Asian countries, India, Australia, and New Zealand, to join the East Asia

Summit (EAS) in an effort to reduce China's influence in the grouping. This multipronged balancing strategy is a necessary consequence of Japan's deep economic interactions with Beijing, a situation that tempers both sides' desire to escalate their periodic disputes.

China's Response

China's strategy in response includes internal balancing through military modernization and soft balancing using institutions to restrain American power.[63] Since many existing institutions are not cooperating with China's aspirations, it has created new institutions and selectively joined regional institutions, especially those of the ASEAN. It is also using denial of institutional membership to India, especially to the UN Security Council, as a soft-balancing strategy now that India is emerging to challenge its global ambitions.

China has not been passive in the face of other states' hedging policies but instead has actively developed its own strategies. Since 2004, the official Chinese strategy has been "peaceful rise" or, as it was rechristened in 2007 to avoid suggestions of hegemonic intent, "peaceful development." The plan is not to disrupt the international order but to use economic and other soft-power instruments to achieve global power. Deepening trade with all major powers and regional states, especially with Western countries, has been a main component of this strategy. Chinese political elites and scholars claim that China has no intention of challenging the international order but would like to use capitalist instruments of trade and investment to emerge as a major market for the world.[64] Since China remains significantly weaker than the United States, it has sought to avoid direct confrontation wherever possible, and to increase its leverage through diplomatic efforts with other states. It still anticipates a conflict with the U.S. over such issues as Mainland-Taiwan relations and U.S. containment.[65] The upshot is a strategy that combines "acquiescence, competition and low-level resistance."[66] To mitigate regional suspicions, China has resisted U.S. pressure through institutional means. For example, it actively promoted the ASEAN Plus Three after the 1997 financial crisis. Since APT does not include the U.S. as a member, it is a useful diplomatic tool for China to balance U.S. influence in the region.

The strategy of "peaceful development" underwent a major change by 2012 with the arrival of Xi Jinping as leader. Although the Chinese policy still formally adheres to peaceful development, it is no longer "hiding one's capabilities and biding one's time." Peaceful development has been made conditional on reciprocity by others and does not keep China from accelerating its military modernization.[67] After settling many of its border disputes, Beijing began to adopt a more assertive strategy in the South China and East China Seas. Its lingering disputes over the Spratly Islands with Vietnam, Malaysia, and the Philippines, and with Japan over the Diaoyu/Senkaku Islands, rest on questionable claims, but it has nonetheless sent naval vessels to these islands. Part of the reason is the hydrocarbon resources beneath the waters surrounding them.

In South Asia, Beijing seems to be pursuing a hard-balancing strategy, for instance, by deepening its existing strategic relationship with Pakistan. As noted above, China has also been using institutional denial as a strategy: it has blocked India's membership on the UN Security Council and the Nuclear Suppliers Group. While it has outwardly followed diplomatic engagement with India, its alliance with and arms support to Pakistan contain many elements of hard balancing and containment. The CPEC agreement with Pakistan, although is primarily economic, is viewed in New Delhi as exacerbating India's security dilemma with Pakistan. An active Chinese presence in Pakistan will act as a double deterrent to Indian military action in response to Pakistani provocations on the border or in Kashmir. In addition, the Pakistani port in Gwadar, now in Chinese management and touted as a future naval base for China, will bring Chinese naval capabilities closer to India and prevent any possible retaliatory action such as an Indian naval blockade of Pakistan.

In addition to these hard-balancing measures against India, China has been trying (so far with limited success) to create soft-balancing coalitions with smaller states such as Sri Lanka, Bangladesh, Maldives, Nepal, and Myanmar. It is also attempting to gain the smaller states' allegiance through buying them off or silencing them on crucial security matters. China, with its deep pockets and willingness to invest in infrastructure projects in unstable states despite the questionable economic returns from them, has been more successful than India.

China views its embrace of economic globalization as a way to restrain the U.S. In response to President Trump's and other right-wing Western leaders' call for protectionism, Beijing has emerged as the key defender of globalization and free trade, which is not surprising given that almost all of China's trade balances are in its favor. Some see this as a new form of mercantilism.[68] Even the Asian financial crisis did not dampen Chinese enthusiasm for economic globalization or lessen Chinese leaders' determination "to deepen the country's participation in the world economy as the best means available to pursue economic modernization, cope with U.S. hegemony, and fulfill Beijing's great power aspirations."[69]

China's counter–soft balancing involves a wedge strategy aimed at dividing the coalitions engaged in targeting it with soft balancing. A prime example is the willingness of China's friends in Southeast Asia (especially Cambodia) to break up the necessary consensus for ASEAN to act on certain issues. Southeast Asia's consensus-based diplomatic norms make this strategy relatively easy to execute, and in this respect the design of institutions becomes an important element in the efficacy of soft-balancing measures. UN Security Council vetoes are another clear example in which power in institutional structures can inhibit soft balancing.

China and Russia have engaged in a soft-balancing coalition since the end of the Cold War.[70] Sino-Russian diplomatic coordination through the UN and other forums during the Kosovo and Iraq crises were discussed in chapter 5. The two nations' actions in Central Asia, especially in developing institutions such as the Shanghai Cooperation Organization, have important economic and security implications. SCO in particular has given China an opportunity to develop a soft-balancing coalition with Central Asian states, limit U.S. power and influence in the region, and take diplomatic positions that undercut the U.S. military presence. Examples include demanding that the U.S. remove its bases from Central Asia, in particular Uzbekistan, conducting anti-terror military exercises with member states, demanding U.S. nonintervention in internal conflicts, and the creation of norms of cooperation based on the Shanghai spirit.[71] China has actively participated in building institutions such as the Asia-Pacific Telecommunity and East Asia Summit to countervail U.S. pressure and limit the American role in the Asia-Pacific.

China's main hard-balancing strategy has been internal balancing, developing its economic and military strength in relation to other actors in the area. In 2010, the Chinese spent $123 billion for defense, an amount that will increase to $233 billion by 2020.[72] China is building new weapons systems and platforms, modernizing its naval force with nuclear attack submarines, and acquiring submarines, aircraft, and air-defense systems from Russia. Its first aircraft carrier, the *Liaoning*, went into service in 2017. It is small compared to U.S. carriers, holding just seven aircraft, but clearly it is only a start. Although the number of troops in the People's Liberation Army fell by about three hundred thousand in 2017, China has stepped up its efforts in asymmetric warfare, focusing increasingly on developing its considerable strength in cyber-, space-, and information-dominant areas. The major development has occurred in its naval posture: China has abandoned its "near shore" and "near sea" strategies in favor of a "far sea strategy."[73] Although it has accelerated its weapons acquisition and internal hard balancing, none of these presently match American capabilities in the Asia-Pacific.

Balancing Rising China

Considered as a case study, China shows the relevance of soft balancing and limited hard balancing in contemporary world politics. Eurasia has yet to see the formation of an intense, coalition-driven hard-balancing equilibrium as all parties seem reluctant to escalate the conflict to that level. Hard balancing could emerge if the Trump administration imposes protectionist barriers to Chinese products, reestablishes links with Taiwan, initiates a war with North Korea, or steps up its military spending and naval presence in the Pacific, especially if it inserts itself aggressively in the South China Sea disputes. The limited rivalry between China and the U.S. in the Pacific may give the impression that intense balance-of-power competition is returning and that the international system is changing from a near-unipolar order to a multipolar one. While there has been some change from the first two post–Cold War decades, the region's powers are still reluctant to fully commit to coordinated hard balancing, partly because the necessary allies are missing.

The close of the second decade of the twenty-first century is a period of high anxiety in international politics. It feels like a calm before the storm. The powers are steadily showing signs of competitive relations, with increased arms buildups by the U.S., China, and Russia as well as smaller states. The nuclear buildup has also accelerated. But there are no new formal alliances among the great powers or their friends, and the existing alliances are not engaging in intense balance-of-power competition. The prospect of a strengthened balancing coalition is precluded, at least for now, by the low possibility of a military alliance between Russia and China or between Russia and other states in its near abroad. China remains most Asian states' lead trading partner, especially in East and Southeast Asia and indeed in Europe, Canada, and Australia as well. This fact will dampen efforts at forming intense hard-balancing coalitions by these states with the United States. China is also, however, building up its capabilities, especially its navy, and expanding its maritime presence to the Indian Ocean, prompting limited countermeasures from others, especially India, Japan, and Vietnam. Even for them, balance-of-power competition is only one part of a combined strategy for dealing with China's rise.

The preferred U.S. approach toward China mixes soft balancing with limited hard balancing, with hard balancing increasing since 2010. The hesitation to engage in intense hard balancing against China arises from Beijing's involvement in economic globalization through dense economic and social interactions and networks with Western and other economies. Further, it has yet to directly challenge its neighbors' sovereignty and core territorial integrity. Its claims in the South China Sea are different: although it is challenging the territorial order, it is imposing itself on global commons. The Trump administration has declared its intention to increase defense spending by 20 percent and aggressively patrol the South China Sea, and it has unnerved the region with its rhetoric of a nuclear war with North Korea. The possibility exists of an intense balance-of-power competition and arms race reemerging in the Asia-Pacific. The key to preventing that outcome may be to return to soft balancing and diplomatic engagement using existing institutions, or creating new and better institutions that can address the security and economic issues now bedeviling China and its neighbors.

Balancing Resurgent Russia

S econdary states have used soft balancing to constrain the United States, but we should also expect to see balancing against other states, especially rising and resurging powers. In the post–Cold War era, both the U.S. and Europe have made efforts to balance Russia's threatening behavior, and Russia in turn has used both soft-balancing and, increasingly, hard-balancing strategies in response. After a period of strategic retreat in the 1990s, Russia has, with partial success, been resurrecting itself as a global power under Vladimir Putin. Moscow's relations with the West plunged in 2014 following Russia's annexation of Crimea and an aggressive push by President Putin in support of Ukrainian rebels. These policies have elicited both hard- and soft-balancing responses by the U.S. and its European allies.

Balancing by the West

American attitudes toward Russia are well captured by President Barack Obama's statement that "Russia is a regional power that is threatening some of its immediate neighbors, not out of strength but out of weakness," and by Senator John McCain's comment that Russia is "a gas station masquerading as a country."[1] These shows of contempt reflect the deterioration in Western relations with Russia since Moscow began conducting military activities in Syria and Ukraine. Finding themselves in increasing conflict with Russia, Western countries, particularly the U.S., have progressively relied on the hard-balancing tools of arms buildup and alliances. Russia, meanwhile, having followed a soft-balancing strategy against the U.S. and the West since the end of the Cold War, has recently changed its tactics as well. The ongoing Ukrainian conflict has reignited both theoretical and policy questions on the continuing relevance of balance of power among great powers. Russia has also engaged in an intense military buildup along its border with the Baltic states, conducted bombing campaigns in Syria against the rebel forces fighting President Hafez al-Assad's regime, and is alleged to have engaged in cyber attacks during the 2016 U.S. election, harming Democratic candidate Hillary Clinton's campaign in favor of Donald Trump.[2] Some observers speculate that these actions are the harbingers of a new international order based on hard-balancing rivalries between the Western alliance and Russia.

The annexation of Crimea in March 2014 followed the Ukrainian parliament's ouster of pro-Moscow president Viktor Yanukovych in February. Fearing that a pro-Western government in Kiev would bring the NATO alliance to Russia's border, Moscow also began providing political and military support for separatist forces in eastern Ukraine. In response, Western powers adopted both soft-balancing measures, including sanctions, institutional responses, and hard balancing. The latter largely consists of a ratcheting up of NATO forces in the Baltic states. Some other former Soviet republics that are pro-Western have also engaged in limited hard balancing. The Russian case shows that countries can use both hard- and soft-balancing tools in the face of complex threats.

The key institutional arenas for soft balancing against Russia have been the G-7 and the UN General Assembly and Security Council. In response to the Crimean takeover, in March 2014 the G-7 countries decided to suspend Russia as a member of what had been the G-8 as its actions went against the organization's shared values by "violating the independence and territorial integrity of a neighboring nation."[3] The original rationale for including Russia, in 1998, was to support democratic consolidation under Yeltsin and mollify Russian opposition to

NATO's expansion. But under Putin, Russia's positions began to diverge more openly from the West's. In 2013, Russia opposed the Western G-8 states' demand that Syrian leader Bashar al-Assad be removed from power in response to his violent crackdown on those opposing his rule. Russia was scheduled to hold the G-8 summit in Sochi in June 2014, but after the invasion of Crimea, the other members cancelled the meeting and met as the G-7, without Russia, in Brussels. According to the G-7 statement of March 24, 2014, "We will suspend our participation in the G8 until Russia changes course and the environment comes back to where the G8 is able to have a meaningful discussion."[4] This may well be a soft-balancing act, as the suspension was a way to delegitimize Russian policies with the hope of a return to normal relations once Russia amended its behavior.

The Western countries engaged in intense soft balancing at the UN. On March 27, the General Assembly passed a resolution calling on all parties "to desist and refrain from actions aimed at the partial or total disruption of the national unity and territorial integrity of Ukraine, including any attempts to modify Ukraine's borders through the threat or use of force or other unlawful means." It held that the previous day's referendum in Crimea "cannot form the basis for any alteration of the status of the Autonomous Republic of Crimea or the city of Sevastopol."[5]

The soft-balancing measures also included two rounds of sanctions imposed by Western powers. These targeted key sectors of the Russian economy, froze the financial accounts of Russian officials, and curtailed their travel rights in the West. The first wave of sanctions, imposed in March and July 2014, were intended as a signal. After they failed to change Moscow's behavior, more robust sanctions were imposed. Asset freezes and visa bans targeted specific individuals and companies seen as responsible for Russia's actions in Ukraine. Other measures had a broader economic and financial impact. These included the suspension of development loans previously extended by the European Bank for Reconstruction and Development; limits on trading activities with major Russian banks, energy companies, and defense firms; and embargoes on trade in arms, other defense-related products, and some energy equipment.[6] These sanctions have been supported by a variety of countries, including Albania, Australia, Canada, Iceland, Japan, Moldova, Norway, and Switzerland.

Although the European Union was slow to act, the second round of sanctions appeared to have increased the legitimacy of its position and the illegitimacy of Russia's, especially in Western eyes. While they may appear limited, they were expected to have some effect on the Russian economy. Combined with falling oil prices and a sharp depreciation of the Russian ruble beginning in late 2014, the sanctions seem to have done significant harm to the Russian economy and likely contributed to rapidly increasing capital outflows.[7]

Moscow answered with sanctions of its own, placing a ban on food imports from the West. It also made separate deals to supply natural gas to China, and the two states discussed forming a balancing coalition against the U.S. This coalition remains at the soft-balancing level as no formal alliance has been formed. Some commentators have raised the fear of a return to Cold War patterns of behavior, although it is far from clear that Russia has the capacity to challenge the West militarily or diplomatically as it could during the Soviet years.[8] A formal Sino-Russian coalition is also unlikely, given that it is improbable that China will jeopardize its economic relations with the West at a time when its economy is slowing down. In January 2017, U.S. president Donald Trump hinted at a rapprochement with Russia in an effort to isolate China and prevent an alliance between the two states.

While relations between Russia and the West seem to be characterized by soft balancing, both sides have also undertaken hard balancing and limited hard-balancing measures. NATO stepped up its military presence in its Eastern European member states in response to the war in Ukraine. As of January 2017, some seven thousand NATO troops were stationed in Estonia, Latvia, Lithuania, Poland, Bulgaria, and Romania, in addition to over two hundred tanks, Bradley fighting vehicles, and Paladin howitzers. These deployments, the largest by NATO since the end of the Cold War, were accompanied by large increases in defense spending by some of the states nearest to Russia.[9] NATO is planning to add several battalions over the next two years in response to some twenty-two battalions Russia has deployed in the region. Both sides have considerable firepower, including fighter aircraft, assault helicopters, tanks, artillery, rocket launchers, and short-range missiles. Russia is also reportedly using hybrid warfare involving nonkinetic or soft-power tools to undermine popular confidence in democracy in the Baltic states and reportedly elsewhere. More ominously, Russia now has a first-use policy for nuclear weapons. Combined with NATO's own first-use poli- cy, this creates the danger of nuclear escalation.[10] Moscow's continued support for Syrian president Bashar al-Assad and its growing military involvement in the Syrian civil war have also caused tension between Russia and NATO. In late 2015, Russia increased its campaign of aerial bombardment of strategic targets in Syria, to the particular concern of NATO member Turkey. Incursions by Russia into Turkish airspace in October 2015 elicited a sharp response from Ankara and a reminder of NATO's collective defense mandate. NATO's buildup in several Eastern European states and Russia's countermeasures should be seen as hard balancing. Still, European states annually spend less than 2 percent of their GDP on defense, and these states' overall defense preparation is less than one would expect for intense internal hard balancing relying on arms buildup. A force deployment equivalent to what we saw in the Cold War era is far off.[11] The difference between Europe's and America's positions on the Russia threat also makes the degree of hard balancing difficult to predict.

Balancing Responses to the Ukrainian Crisis

The Ukrainian crisis emerged out of two decades of Western-Russian conflict over spheres of influence and the geopolitical role of a weak- ened Russia. This conflict was somewhat contained during Dmitry Medvedev's presidency, when there was some limited cooperation between Russia and the West. But Vladimir Putin's return as Russian president in May 2012 and Western policies in Syria and Iran have pushed disagreements into the open. For the West, balance of power implies the expansion of the Western liberal coalition under NATO and the European Union into the former Soviet republics, with the intent of preventing aggressive actions by Russia in what it calls its "near abroad." This strategy amounts to balancing against anticipated threats as opposed to balancing against power, as Russia's capabilities in the short run are too small to elicit full military balancing by the West.[12] Russia, not surprisingly, takes a different view. Under Putin's leadership in particular, it has interpreted the West's expansion into former Soviet republics as a breakdown in the balance-of-power system and as the containment policy resurrected. The inability to agree on what constitutes each side's minimal strategic interests has contributed to the breakdown of balance-of-power equations between them.

The rivalry between Russia and the West goes back to the end of the Cold War, when Russian expectations of better treatment did not materialize. Western efforts to expand into Russia's sphere of influence, especially the enlargement of NATO to include former Soviet republics, facilitated the emergence of a nationalist leadership in Russia determined to gain more status and legitimacy. The West has tried to expand and consolidate liberal democracy to prevent the rise of challengers and deter any threats that might emanate from Russia or China. Underpinning this policy is the conviction that spreading democracy and liberal institutions would create peace throughout Europe. Extending the Western European model of liberal market capitalism to Eastern Europe was conceived as a preventive measure against the emergence of an aggressive power that might threaten the regional order. Russia would thus be balanced using both hard (NATO) and soft (EU) mechanisms.[13]

The question is why the Western responses to Russian versus Chinese expansionism were so dissimilar. An important difference between Russia and China is the nature of the economic relationships they have built with the West. Figures 3 and 4 show the level of Russian trade with the European states and the U.S. It is very skewed, consisting largely of oil and gas exports to the EU. Russia lacks the product specialization that China offers. Although it had a total export of $316 billion and an import of $184 billion in 2017, these respectively constituted the thirteenth and twenty-fourth positions among 221 countries.[14] China, meanwhile, in 2015 exported some $2.7 trillion and imported $1.27 trillion, placing it first and second in world ranking. Unlike Russia, China's key exports are computers, broadcasting equipment, telephones, integrated circuits, and office machines, and its imports are crude petroleum, integrated circuits, gold, iron ore, and cars. The Chinese export-import model is both larger and more sophisticated.[15]

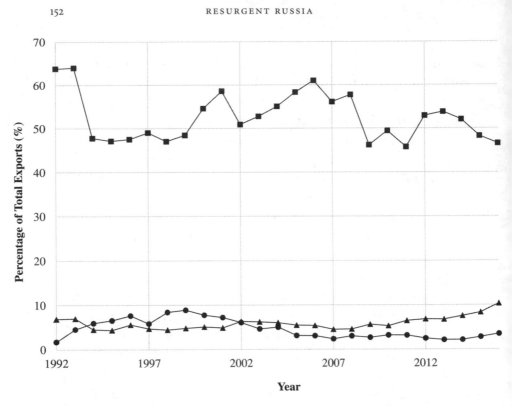

Figure 3. Russia's Export Dependence on Major Partners (Export to a Partner as the Percentage of Total Export): 1992–2016. *(Sources: IMF Direction of Trade Dataset, http://data.imf.org/?sk=9D6028D4-F14A-464C-A2F2-59B2CD424B85&sId=1390030341854; WTO Times Series on International Trade, http://stat.wto.org/StatisticalProgram/WSDBStatProgramHome. aspx?Language=E. Adapted by Erik Underwood and Daniel Smit.)*

The eastward expansion of the liberal pacific union began in March 1999 when Poland, Hungary, and the Czech Republic were added to NATO. In March 2004, seven more states were given membership: Estonia, Latvia, Lithuania, Slovenia, Slovakia, Bulgaria, and Romania. Albania and Croatia joined in 2009, and NATO has also held membership discussions with Georgia, Moldova, and Ukraine—three states that share long borders with Russia. In May 2004, the European Union expanded to include ten Central

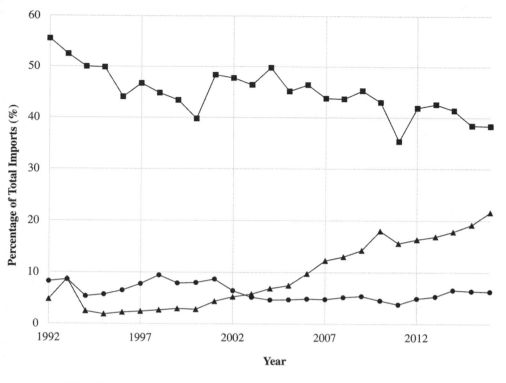

Figure 4. Russia's Import Dependence on Major Partners (Import from a Partner as the Percentage of Total Import): 1992–2016. *(Sources: IMF Direction of Trade Dataset, http://data.imf.org/?sk=9D6028D4-F14A-464C-A2F2-59B2CD424B85&sId=1390030341854; WTO Times Series on International Trade, http://stat.wto.org/StatisticalProgram/WSDBStatProgramHome. aspx?Language=E. Adapted by Erik Underwood and Daniel Smit.)*

and East European states—the Czech Republic, Estonia, Cyprus, Latvia, Lithuania, Hungary, Malta, Poland, Slovakia, and Slovenia—many of which had been members of the Warsaw Pact. In 2007, it further enlarged to include Romania and Bulgaria, and it added Croatia in 2013.[16] The NATO expansion thus created an enlarged hard-balancing coalition among former allies or constituent units of the old Soviet Union, but instead of providing stability, it has provoked the intended target.

NATO tried to mollify Russian concerns by creating a Partnership for Peace in January 1994. This provided "a framework for enhanced political and military cooperation for joint multilateral crisis management activities, such as humanitarian assistance and peacekeeping," allowing a signatory to "consult with NATO when faced with a direct threat to its security, although doing so "doesn't extend NATO security guarantees."[17] But the partnership, which Russia joined, has not been particularly effective. The NATO-led invasion of Serbia in 1999 and the eventual separation of Kosovo increased Russian fears about NATO's actual goals. Georgia's efforts to punish the breakaway regions of Abkhazia and South Ossetia caused a violent Russian reaction and a short war in the summer of 2008. This crisis marked the beginning of the West's current soft-balancing and limited hard-balancing approach.[18] NATO suspended practical cooperation at the civilian and military levels after the Russian invasion of Crimea, although the program was never completely abandoned. This may be another example of the failure of institutional balancing and restraint attempted by the Western countries toward Russia.

In the face of the military and economic disparity between the U.S. and Russia since the end of the Cold War, Moscow has used institutions to balance U.S. power as well as perceived threats. Early efforts included the creation of the Commonwealth of Independent States (CIS) in 1991, the adoption of a collective security treaty in 1992, and a proposal to replace NATO with the Conference on Security and Cooperation in Europe, which later became the Organization for Security and Cooperation Europe (OSCE). Later, in 1996, the Shanghai Cooperation grouping began among the five Central Asian states—China, Russia, Kazakhstan, Kyrgyzstan, and Tajikistan—and in 2001, with the addition of Uzbekistan, it was renamed the Shanghai Cooperation Organization (SCO). In 2002, Russia created the Collective Security Treaty Organization (CSTO) involving many Central Asian states as a quasi-military grouping to counter NATO. This may be considered a semi-hard-balancing coalition as it has proved to be of limited value since the members diverge on collective actions and it has no equivalent to NATO's article 5, which calls upon member states to join collective defense if an ally is attacked.[19] Russia has been attempting to use institutions such as CSTO to contain the West and keep regional states in its orbit. But none of these balancing efforts was able to prevent NATO's expansion to former Soviet republics and Eastern European allies. Since the 2014 Ukrainian crisis, however, NATO has stopped further expansion.[20]

Diplomatic engagement has also been part of the U.S. strategy toward Russia. The Obama administration initiated a "reset policy" toward Russia (2009–12), which produced a new Strategic Arms Reduction Treaty (START) in April 2010. Russia also agreed with the U.S. on imposing tougher sanctions on Iran for its nuclear program, offered supply routes for NATO to Afghanistan, and signed agreements to secure nuclear materials in different parts of the world. But this improved relationship was bedeviled by differences on important issues, including Syria and the deployment of U.S. missile defenses in Europe. Russia accepted commitments demanded at the OSCE meetings, including one at the 2010 meeting in Kazakhstan that all member states respect democracy, rule of law, human rights, fundamental freedoms, and, most important, the right to pursue economic integration with the EU. This agreement led Ukraine, Moldova, and Georgia to begin negotiating with the EU to enter into a free-trade association.[21] It may be that Russia saw trade as a precursor to security alignment.

The Ukrainian crisis also suggests this kind of fear emanating from potential externalities of trade relations. The crisis escalated in 2014 when negotiations for increased trade and economic aid started between Ukraine and the European Union. The EU gave Kiev the option of either joining the European Union or accepting a Russian offer for a financial and economic deal, including concessional purchases of Russian gas. Ukraine's democratically elected, pro-Russian government under Viktor Yanukovych accepted the Russian aid and trade terms, but street protests against the Yanukovych government in favor of joining the EU forced his resignation in February 2014. Yanukovych and his Moscow allies portrayed the rallies as a coup engineered by the West. A successor government headed by Petro Poroshenko was voted into power in May 2014 on a promise of continuing pro-EU policies. Following a popular referendum, the EU and Ukraine signed an association agreement in June 2014. President Putin reacted by instigating ethnic Russian-led revolts in Crimea and eastern Ukraine. When Kiev attempted to suppress them, Russia invaded and annexed Crimea in March 2014, while offering material and political assistance to Russian co-nationalists fighting for autonomy or independence in the eastern Ukrainian provinces of Donetsk and Luhansk. The response of Western countries has been to impose sanctions and to belittle Russia and Putin. President Obama's description of Russia as a "regional power" happened in this context. By imposing limited economic sanctions, the West attempted to soft-balance Russia, but the Russians see this move as overly aggressive.

Russian leaders have never been convinced by the Western position that former Soviet states should be free to join the EU and NATO and that no aggressive intent is directed toward Moscow. They fear that the expansion into Eastern Europe and the former Soviet republics is designed to "encircle" Russia, and that these efforts are comparable to similar attempts by Napoleon and Nazi Germany.[22] These fears, and Russia's belligerence in Eastern Europe, are a departure from the ingratiating policy toward the West that Russia indicated by its initial expression of interest in joining Western coalitions such as the NATO Partnership for Peace. Russia has shown increasing reluctance to accept Western ideas or to expand liberal democracy to its former sphere of influence. Instead, it wants to retain its status as a great power and/or *primus inter pares* among its former republics and Eastern European allies.

Russia's foreign-policy statements—especially the military doctrines Moscow issues periodically—reveal determined opposition to NATO and EU expansion. The Russian military doctrine of December 2014, for instance, states that the "main external military danger" comes from the increasing power of NATO "and giving it global functions carried out in violation of international law," citing the bringing of "military infrastructure of NATO to the borders of Russian Federation," "the expansion of the bloc," the destabilization of "individual countries and regions," and "the deployment of military contingents of foreign states in the territories bordering Russian Federation and its allies." From this perspective, the Ukrainian conflict reflects an "intensification of global competition" and the "rivalry of value orientations and models of development." According to the doctrine, America's strategic ballistic missile defense, its Global Strike concept, and its strategic non-nuclear systems form key threats to Russia.[23] The doctrine shows that Russia's ruling elite are deeply committed to the notion of balance of power.

Russia's motive has been to regain its status as the leading power in Eastern Europe. The status competition this ambition creates is not easy for its neighbors to reconcile.[24] As early as 2001, Putin declared his intent to return "Russia [to] its [rightful] place among the truly strong, economically advanced and influential states of the world" and highlighted economic growth as essential for this purpose.[25] Most former Soviet republics and former allies do not see Russia as having equivalent status to the West. For Russia's current leaders, however, it was the misguided policies of Mikhail Gorbachev and Boris Yeltsin that made the West unwilling to treat Moscow as an equal. Clearly, balance of power is not simply a competition over power or influence, but over status and position in the world system.[26] The 2014 military doctrine showed this clearly when it declared that Russia was willing to engage the U.S., NATO, and the EU in "a dialogue of equals" on issue areas such as "European and Asia-Pacific security, arms control, countering WMD proliferation, and confidence building measures."[27] Putin appears to believe that the West offers Russia scant respect, as evident in its rejection of Moscow's 2008 proposal for the creation of a new European security architecture and the decision to admit new members to NATO over Russian opposition.[28]

The Return of Hard Balancing?

The actions of both sides have combined soft balancing, limited hard balancing, and hard balancing. Russia has been constrained by falling oil and gas prices, and it has not succeeded in creating a hard-balancing coalition with China, which needs to maintain its trade and economic relations with the West. India, a former ally, has also been inching toward the West as New Delhi sees its main challenge as coming from China and Pakistan. At most, such former allies are likely to remain neutral in Moscow's conflict with the West, given the legal implications of Russia's having forcefully annexed the territory of a sovereign state.

The Russia-China relationship has evolved toward soft balancing and increasingly limited hard balancing. In addition to their ad hoc collaboration during the Kosovo and Iraq Wars, they have formed strategic partnerships in 1994, 1996, 2001, 2012, and 2014, but these in no way add up to a hard-balancing alliance. The two countries' strategic goals seem to diverge, and their strategies also look different. Russia's exports to China—weapons and natural gas—do not constitute a diversified export base. China exports diversified products, making the economic relationship uneven. It is also unclear whether China completely approves of Russia's military policies, especially in Ukraine and Syria. Russia and China do hold summit meetings, and whenever a threat comes from the West they tend to take joint positions at the UN.[29] Their activities at SCO also take the form of soft balancing or limited institutional coordination. Under Xi Jinping and Vladimir Putin, who have a good personal rapport, the relationship has evolved into more economic and limited strategic cooperation. The 2014 agreement for a Russian natural gas company to export billions of dollars' worth of gas to China, Russia's key role in the Belt and Road Initiative, the 2014 currency swap agreement, and increasing exports of manufactured goods to China all indicate a strengthening economic relationship. Russia has also sympathized with China's position in the South China Sea, and China has given verbal support to Russia's military actions in Ukraine and Syria.[30] But suspicions still exist, and China's rapid rise constitutes a challenge to Russia's status aspirations, given that China's goal is to replace the U.S. as the world's most powerful country. For all these reasons, if the rivalry between Russia and the West intensifies, it is unlikely that China will automatically form a military coalition with Russia unless the West threatens China as well.

The Russian actions in Ukraine and the Baltics seem to have at least stopped the Western expansion to the former Soviet republics. Among NATO member states, Poland, the Czech Republic, and a few others have expressed opposition to NATO expansion or the deployment of troops to protect Ukraine.[31] Western efforts to bolster the military power of Eastern European states such as Poland, Romania, and the Baltic states are still limited. The possibility that Ukraine may join NATO remains low, given that if Russia were to invade openly, Ukraine's full membership would entail the invocation of article 5 and thus the possibility of NATO fighting a nuclear-armed state. Continuing fiscal strains in the EU and the resurgence of right-wing leaders suggest that the member states are unlikely to form an active balancing coalition against Russia, and it is improbable that NATO members such as Greece and Turkey would support military action by the alliance in Ukraine. The U.S. under Obama had given Ukraine limited military support, but this has not stopped Putin from backing the separatists in eastern Ukraine. Although President Trump is sympathetic to Russia, the administration's policy toward it has yet to crystallize.

Western soft-balancing efforts continue against Russian involvement in Syria. In addition, the Arab League has suspended Russia's observer status at its meetings and recognized the Syrian opposition. The U.S. and Britain have regularly denounced Russian bombing campaigns, especially at the UN, and Turkey has made efforts to build a diplomatic coalition with the Gulf States. In response, Russia has engaged in counter–soft balancing by using its UN Security Council veto against resolutions on Syria.[32] Both Russia and China have repeatedly vetoed Western efforts to delegitimize Bashar al-Assad's regime and to send UN troops to aid Syrian civilians. In September 2015, Russia intervened directly by bombing opposition forces and Islamic State positions, an action that generated intense criticism from the U.S. and its Western allies. More important, Russia has also created new balance-of-power dynamics among states in the region, especially Iran, Iraq, and Saudi Arabia, while constraining U.S. military and diplomatic options in the civil conflict.[33]

Thus, key Western powers and many of their smaller neighbors are pursuing a strategy of hedging toward Russia based on limited hard balancing, engagement, and soft balancing, while Russia reciprocates with similar behavior toward the U.S. and EU. These patterns, however, are not set in stone, and there are several scenarios in which the current approach could turn into an active balance-of-power competition. The first scenario would be if Russia and China were to form a more formal coalition in the face of Western efforts to contain them. Hard balancing might also reemerge if Western powers led by the U.S. became more active in courting former Soviet states, or if Russia managed to gain the support of a number of them along with some disgruntled EU members such as Greece. Moreover, even if Russia fails in its coalition-building efforts with its neighbors, it still has considerable ability to generate tensions by spoiling peace processes in different parts of the world, especially in the Middle East, and fomenting unrest. In the short run, Russia's asymmetrical military power in its region gives it an edge over NATO. Balance-of-power politics is always dependent on strategic context, and the Russian sphere of influence shows that abundantly.

While these scenarios of hard balancing are hypothetical, some elements are already occurring. NATO's expansion, for example, has unintentionally emboldened states on Russia's periphery, such as Georgia and Ukraine, to undertake rash actions toward their Russian ethnic minorities in the belief that NATO would come to their rescue if Moscow reacted militarily. The problem is that NATO can provide only limited aid. On the other side of the equation, Russian minorities are also emboldened to seek the autonomy of the provinces they dominate, fueling ethnic hatred and violence. Russia has been using asymmetric warfare techniques in Ukraine by generating a fait accompli for future negotiations.[34] Its use of cyber warfare and of military and political support for ethnic Russian enclaves in neighboring countries is part of this strategy. The inability of Russia and its neighbors to agree on a modus vivendi reflecting minimal shared interests is a genuine threat to peace as each side seeks a new balance-of-power equation in the hope the other side will blink first.

Russia and the West need to synchronize their conceptions of balance of power if they want to prevent a major hard-balancing competition from reemerging in Europe and Eurasia. Unless it is economically and ideologically integrated in the globalized world, Russia is unlikely to be convinced of the benefits of expanding the liberal union to its spheres of influence. The Russian leadership is driven by a desire to regain Moscow's old status as a superpower, and it seems to believe that its security depends on its retaining semialigned buffer states that will accord it dominant regional status. Its playbook is realism, while the Western conception is based on a combination of liberal internationalism and realpolitik. For their part, liberals rarely acknowledge the power motivations behind their behavior, as their ideology offers good cover for such intentions. They can believe their own claim to stand for universal values of liberty, freedom, and self-determination. The West's message to Russia is that it has to accept a secondary role as a co-opted power in a European order built around liberal principles and headed by the EU and NATO. But Western idealism has little resonance in Moscow, which does not see liberal hegemony as either benign or without power considerations.

The challenge for Russia is that its former republics are moving away from its sphere, partly due to the attraction of the West, but partly also because of Russian policies toward them and the unpredictability of its future intentions and behavior. Where Moscow wants them to accept its hegemony, the West has a better record of treating smaller allies with respect and dignity. They tend to have a strong voice in the European Union and NATO, which make many crucial decisions based on consensus. Many of the ex-Soviet states still depend on Russia for core products such as subsidized oil and gas, but others are trying "exit," as loyalty to Russia has been based on limited economic opportunities and sometimes on ethnic affinities.[35] Yet the smaller states of Eastern Europe and former Soviet space should be wary of isolating Russia. Henry Kissinger has suggested that countries such as Ukraine should endeavor to be bridging states and may have to reduce their appetite for fully abandoning their economic and security relationship with Russia in favor of the Western alliance. They should not promote policies that make their Russian minority populations and regions unhappy.[36] Instead, they can help revitalize regional institutions and cooperation with the West by creating joint groupings rather than exclusive ones. Eventually Russia may come around to joining the pacific union if the strategies its neighbors adopt do not generate violent reactions and arouse intense nationalism on both sides.

Russia has been able to place considerable strain on Western unity, create divisions among Eastern European states, and stop NATO's and the EU's expansion plans. By meddling in American and European elections, Russia has also become a key player in these countries' domestic politics. In Syria, Russian activism continues, although the U.S. under Trump has also increased its bombing activity. Russia's hard-, soft-, and asymmetrical balancing efforts remain potent.

Balancing Russia

Eurasia has yet to see the formation of an intense hard-balancing equilibrium, as the parties appear reluctant to escalate the conflict to an intense level. The Russia-NATO relationship is the closest thing to a hard-balancing rivalry in the world today. Yet even the tense relationship between Russia and the West contains a mixture of hard and soft balancing. Substantial American military aid to Ukraine or a military alliance of Kiev with NATO could change the situation. However, an intense hard-balancing effort by either the West or Russia will be hampered by a lack of allies, disunity between the U.S. and European states, the fear of economic losses, and the realization that the escalation of conflict is undesirable. Instead we are seeing continued hedging based on soft balancing, diplomatic engagement, and limited hard balancing. This situation may continue for years, until threats crystallize and Russia's power capabilities increase to the point of upsetting the present order. In the meantime, Russia is challenging the West using asymmetrical military and cyber means as well as soft balancing.

Until 2013, the West also preferred a mix of soft balancing and hard balancing. Now, however, Western policies toward Russia increasingly tilt toward hard balancing, relying on the NATO alliance, and more aggressive soft balancing that depends on economic sanctions. One reason may be that except for its gas exports to Eastern Europe, Russia is not economically globalized. China, on the other hand, is heavily globalized and has a dense web of economic and social interactions with Western economies, especially the U.S., and also with the rest of East Asia. A second reason is that Russia is directly challenging the sovereignty and territorial integrity of Ukraine and the Baltic states, while China's challenges are less overt and not focused on direct military interference or the threat of a land offensive of its neighbors. The existence of the NATO coalition makes it easy to ratchet up hard-balancing activity against Russia through arms buildup and frontline military deployments.

The arrival of the Donald Trump administration in 2017, with its aggressive policy postures, once again challenges many axioms of balance-of-power theory and policy. The president appears to be positioning himself to demand more sharing of the burden from U.S. allies, backed up with a threat of a return to isolationist policies. His effort to befriend Russia and to create a wedge in Sino-Russian relations suggests the reintroduction of a divide-and-rule balancing strategy. But the shortcoming of this approach quickly became apparent when Trump had to seek China's cooperation in containing North Korea's nuclear program. And despite its demand that its NATO allies contribute more toward their common defense, the administration has increased defense spending. Vladimir Putin, who appears to have hoped that President Trump would eliminate the West's economic sanctions against his state, may now try to reunite the lost Soviet empire in some fashion—an effort that would most likely draw strong responses from European states and the United States.

The Future of Balance of Power

The Greek historian Polybius's admonition still resonates in world politics: "We should never contribute to the attainment of one state of a power so preponderant, that none dare dispute it even for their acknowledged rights."[1] Many Greek city-states, especially Athens, believed in a balance of power to prevent their dominance by others, especially Sparta. The same idea appears in Roman, Chinese, and Indian statecraft, and modern versions were practiced by medieval Europeans, especially Italian city-states. In post-Westphalia Europe, balance of power became a mythical science and an art but was often practiced imperfectly. Central to the concept is the contention that power must be met by power in order to prevent aggression and dominance. If no equilibrium exists, the most powerful state will be tempted to use its advantage to subjugate or even eliminate the less powerful.

Balance of power took its modern form in the predatory world of European empires and great powers of the seventeenth to twentieth centuries, where it was central to the conduct of international relations. The philosophers of the Enlightenment, as they did with so much else, tried to turn it into a scientific principle, but they could never eliminate the need for human agency or resolve the contentions among theorists and practitioners: What does balance of power mean? How is it obtained? Do states balance against power or threats? Should we see balance of power as an automatic process or as a strategy that statesmen adopt in the hope of achieving stability? Is it the dominant approach to security among great powers, or one among several tools? If the latter, should we privilege it as the principal instrument for stability, as many realist scholars and practitioners do?

The end of the Cold War and the rise of America's near-unipolar position in the 1990s have not produced the balance-of-power dynamics predicted by some scholars, nor have most key states merely bandwagoned with America. This lack of traditional balancing behavior in the face of centralized power in a single state presents a puzzle for mainstream balance-of-power scholarship. In this book, I have explained this puzzle by demonstrating that balancing was considerably more widespread than it initially appears, but it took the form of a less intense mechanism, soft balancing. In recent decades, states have adopted hard-balancing behavior, relying on arms buildup and formal alliances, only in a few instances. Instead, in an illustrative case involving the U.S., states have used international institutions to steer American behavior toward legitimacy and thereby curtail Washington's appetite to use its power too aggressively, especially in the Middle East.

This approach has produced mixed results. Soft balancing did not prevent the U.S. from launching offensive action in Iraq. The U.S. under George W. Bush disregarded even the soft-balancing efforts of American allies. As a consequence, however, Washington found little support from its traditional allies for its invasion of Iraq in 2003, and its failure to achieve its objectives there compelled American policy makers to rethink their strategic options. President Barack Obama came to power determined to restore America's credibility and legitimacy in the world. In December 2011, he pulled the last U.S. forces from Iraq, claiming that the U.S. invasion and military presence had done much damage to America's reputation, credibility, and power position.[2] One might conclude that despite their failure to prevent an invasion, the soft-balancing efforts of other states contributed to the U.S. decision to withdraw. America's subsequent reluctance to enter other theaters of conflict, such as Libya and Syria, without multinational participation and UN authorization suggests that soft balancing played a role in U.S. national security behavior under the Obama administration. The idea of soft balancing is also premised on Raymond Aron's contention that "either a great power will not tolerate equals, and then must proceed to the last degree of empire, or else it consents to stand first among sovereign units, and must win acceptance for such pre-eminence."[3] Having tried on Aron's first category under George W. Bush and found it a poor fit, America under Obama attempted the second strategy.

In this book, I have shown that soft balancing is not an invention of the post–Cold War era, used only to restrain American behavior. It is found in unipolar, bipolar, and multipolar world orders. While observers have typically emphasized hard balancing as the currency of power politics during the past three centuries, soft balancing at least for two centuries has acted as either a complement or an alternative to hard balancing. The form balance-of-power politics and diplomacy takes has always been dependent on context. States pursued hard and soft balancing predicated on their expectations of the costs and benefits of each course of action, based on the anticipated reactions from their targets and their own states' ability to withstand retaliation.

The larger finding is that balance of power is not, as the traditionalists believe, an immutable or permanent fixture of international politics with unbreakable laws. Its functioning is very much dependent on the international politics of the day, capability configurations, and how leading statesmen operate strategically.[4] In Europe between the seventeenth and nineteenth centuries, the transformation of feudal and dynastic politics into empires changed the balance-of-power dynamics. In the nineteenth century, a small group of European great powers balanced each other using both traditional "hard" instruments such as alliances, arms buildups, and wars, and "soft" instruments such as institutions. Leaders had to adjust their balancing strategies to the threat environment they perceived and by assessing the costs and benefits of balancing with military means against using other instruments of statecraft.

During the eighteenth century, predatory great powers were keen to diminish the territorial size and power status of their peers. But in the aftermath of the Napoleonic Wars their objectives changed, and in exchange for stability they became willing to maintain the status and power positions of their fellow powers. By the early twentieth century this had changed, as offensive doctrines and predatory policies once again became the cornerstone of the European powers' strategies, lending renewed importance to the balance of military power. With the rise of nationalism among great powers, intense hard balancing grew resurgent. The peak of traditional balance-of-power politics was in the twentieth century. Two world wars and a Cold War raised questions about balance-of-power's automatic presence. During the Cold War, when nuclear weapons were added to the equation, there emerged a symbiotic relationship between balance of power and mutual assured destruction.

Since the end of the Cold War, economic globalization has affected the key instruments of balancing. Although international institutions have been part of the great powers' attempts to balance and restrain one another since at least the nineteenth century, the post–Cold War era brought them higher salience. But then, under what conditions has soft balancing succeeded or failed? What insights do these cases hold for diplomacy and for the peaceful conduct of great-power politics in an increasingly globalized and interdependent world? Another important question is whether balancing works only as a strategy for survival, or for both autonomy and survival. Kenneth Waltz equates a balance-of-power strategy with a requirement for survival and maintaining "a state's autonomous way of life."[5] The primary question in the world today is whether survival is the major concern it once was, and if not, to what extent states rely on hard-balancing instruments versus softer instruments to deal with lower-level challenges. The severity of the threat environment and the intensity of rivalry are key factors in determining whether states adopt intense hard balancing or lower-level forms, which may range from limited hard balancing to soft balancing.

Critics of soft balancing have argued that it is akin to simple diplomatic friction. The case studies show that it is different from simple diplomacy—it is diplomacy aimed at restraining threatening behavior or policies. This diplomatic pressure has to be applied consistently over some length of time, with the use of institutions and limited ententes aimed at restraint and delegitimation.

This book represents a key attempt to develop a theory of soft balancing. In the first two chapters, I argued that states are more likely to pursue soft-balancing strategies against great powers challenging regional or international orders when one or more of the following conditions are present:

- In the aftermath of major wars or enduring great-powers rivalries, when the perceived costs of unilateral rearmament or the formation of "tight" alliances with similarly positioned states are too high;
- When the great power's actions do not directly threaten the territorial integrity or the core security interests of status quo great powers;
- When the power differentials between threatening great powers and others attempting to restrain their behavior appear to make the costs of hard balancing prohibitive.

The case studies in this book show that formal alliances and arms buildups have not characterized the entire period of the modern international system of the past three centuries. Great powers also shaped the international order by using the institutions they devised as well as other instruments of statecraft, such as sanctions, to balance the power and threatening behavior of other states. Smaller countries have used soft balancing individually and collectively for the same purpose. Since the nineteenth century especially, the most common condition of international relations has been a mixture of hard and soft balancing by key states.

The first two decades following great-power wars were the golden years of soft balancing through international institutions. The fatigue of war and efforts to create new norms of international conduct led to great-power restraint through institutional means. In addition, great-power relationships take time to evolve into intense rivalries. The role of soft balancing was most prominent in the immediate aftermath of major wars such as the Napoleonic Wars and the two world wars. It took center stage in the two decades following the end of the Cold War, which was history's greatest systemic rivalry and thus like a world war, though without actual violence in the central theaters where the U.S. and USSR directly confronted each other.

Soft balancing has been employed irrespective of the distribution of power in the international system—whether multipolar, bipolar, or unipolar. It was used during the multipolar system of Europe after the Napoleonic Wars, during the post-1919 world, and in the near-unipolar post–Cold War era. While it has once again emerged as a strategy of choice alongside hard balancing in the new multipolar order, soft balancing reached its peak during the period of unquestioned U.S. supremacy, when second-tier great powers increasingly adopted institutional and diplomatic means to counter the unilateralist tendencies of the United States while trying not to disturb their economic ties with the hegemonic power.

This choice may have been facilitated by the hard-power differential among key powers, and as that power differential decreased during the second decade of the twenty-first century, rising powers began to rely on limited hard balancing, especially internal military buildups. Both established and rising powers still used soft-balancing techniques, however, even as they intensified their hard balancing. Hence the transformation to a limited hard-balancing system has been occurring since approximately 2010. But if the rising power emerges as a powerful and threatening center, a bipolar or multipolar order can generate more demand for hard-balancing coalitions. Similarly, if a declining power such as the U.S. engages in reckless military behavior, this may also propel hard-balancing coalitions. Thus either a rising or a declining power's threatening policies could elicit countervailing coalitions. On the other hand, if neither the U.S. nor the rising powers engage in military adventures challenging states' sovereign existence or frontally violating their territorial integrity, soft balancing may coexist with limited hard balancing for some time, but it may evolve into hard balancing depending on the severity of the threat posed by the challenger.

Neither hard nor soft balancing will necessarily prevent wars, a point recognized by Henry Kissinger in his claim that balance of power is intended to limit the extent of aggression, not to prevent it.[6] Even that argument is problematic. As Gulick contends, "The history of balance of power is littered with the carcasses of violated pledges, broken treaties and abortive friendships among nations," and "the pursuit of balance of power policies has often shown itself most immoderate; coalition wars cannot be called moderate; and the extinction of weak powers under the plea of balance of power surely cannot be termed moderate."[7] The outbreak of two world wars despite intense hard-balancing efforts by the major powers would suggest that this mechanism did not limit aggression either.[8] States, especially those with revisionist goals, may perceive balancing efforts as highly threatening. Status quo states could likewise view challengers' balancing efforts as illegitimate and worth quashing through coercive means.

Much like hard balancing, soft-balancing efforts can also produce unnecessary conflict. During the interwar period, the soft-balancing mechanisms against the revisionist states—Japan, Italy, and Germany— backfired: they only made those states more nationalistic. Economic sanctions as a tool of soft balancing have often produced adverse reactions in the targeted countries. Current efforts to soft-balance Russia have not produced the desired outcome—at least not yet. Moscow has managed to occupy Crimea and use pro-Russian proxy forces to destabilize eastern Ukraine. It has also engaged in cyber attacks and strengthened Russia's military presence in surrounding Baltic states, prompting NATO to augment its capabilities. It has engaged in intense bombing in Syria, defying Western pressure. In 2016, Moscow was alleged to have intervened in U.S. elections and promoted the candidacy of Donald Trump while exposing Hillary Clinton's and Democratic Party officials' emails through hacking.[9]

This discussion generates important questions about institutions, sanctions, and legitimacy. Rising powers could view institutions and their use by established powers as illegitimate acts to restrain their power, ambition, and interests. In contrast, established powers can view institutions as legitimate tools and believe that their policies are also legitimate given that they have institutional backing. Declining powers can use institutions to arrest their decline. In fact, this is an argument for the U.S. supporting the norms inherent in institutions and hoping that rising powers may internalize some of them and refrain from disregarding them to engage in system-changing wars. But rising powers may be turned against such institutions if they are overused or selectively used against their interests. Similarly, the soft-balancing instrument of sanctions could be viewed as a mechanism to punish or coerce secondary powers rather than a peaceful means of behavior modification. The creative use of international institutions and the preservation of their legitimacy are necessary to prevent them becoming irrelevant to rising power behavior.

In chapter 3, I acknowledged that soft-balancing strategies directed at Russia during the Concert of Europe era (1815–53) and toward Germany and Japan during the interwar period (1919–39) succeeded in holding off war for a time, but they were not sufficient. In both the Concert era and the interwar period, status quo great powers embarked on hard-balancing strategies relatively late. More important, hard balancing did not ultimately prevent the outbreaks of the Crimean War and World War II in the European and Pacific theaters. In all three cases, soft balancing was a clear signal to aggressive great powers that further provocation might bring a hard-balancing response. But in all three cases, the revisionist great power did not accept that negative feedback. Elites in St. Petersburg in the 1840s and elites in Berlin, Rome, and Tokyo in the 1930s were unreceptive to soft balancing because they saw the international order as greatly tilted against them. There was also an expectation among the Axis powers that their position would deteriorate if they did not adopt an offensive posture. The emerging balance-of-power dynamics in favor of the Allied powers were thus viewed as highly threatening to their existence as great powers. These historical instances show that both hard and soft balancing can provoke rather than temper revisionist states, especially if they possess grand ambitions of transforming the international order by force. The expectation of an unfavorable balance of power in the future can put pressure on them to break the logjam.

Table 3 summarizes the key balancing strategies of states during different historical eras, the facilitating conditions or lack thereof, and the outcomes the strategies produced.

What is noticeable from the table is that both hard balancing and soft balancing are important and that the crucial time element in their prevalence is often neglected by realists and institutionalists alike. As I have argued in this book, in the immediate aftermath of wars or similar events (such as the end of the Cold War), states rely more on institutional mechanisms for balancing. This happened after the Napoleonic

Table 3 Historical evolution of balancing

Historical era	Key balancing strategy	Facilitating conditions	Outcomes
1815–53	Soft balancing	Low threat environment Legitimacy valued Strong participation in institutions Absence of expansionist ideologies Defensive weapons/strategies Economic interdependence (unclear) Domestic support (unclear)	Favoring success
1853–90	Hard/soft balancing	High/moderate threat environment Declining value of legitimacy Weak institutions Nationalism becoming stronger Defensive and increasingly offensive weapons/doctrines Increasing economic interdependence Domestic support (unclear)	Not favoring success
1890–1914	Hard balancing	Increasingly high threat environment Weak institutions Offensive weapons/doctrines Economic interdependence Lack of territorial integrity norm	Not favoring success

Period	Balancing	Characteristics	Outcome
1919–39	Hard/soft balancing	High threat environment Legitimacy not valued Weak institutions Expansionist ideologies Offensive weapons/doctrines/strategies	Not favoring success
1945–91	Hard balancing	Weak institutions Weak economic interdependence Territorial integrity norm Defensive/deterrent weapons/doctrines Perception of offensive intent Expansionist ideologies	Not favoring success
1991–2010	Soft balancing	Widespread institutions Legitimacy partially valued Globalization/economic interdependence Territorial integrity norm Defensive/deterrent weapons/doctrines	Favoring success
2010–	Soft/limited/hard balancing	Widespread yet weakening institutions Globalization/economic interdependence under challenge—but still present Territorial integrity norm moderately present Defensive/deterrent/asymmetric weapons/doctrines/strategies	Favoring partial success

Wars, World War I, and the Cold War. But this preference does not necessarily last long: institutional soft balancing may lead to hard balancing as political conditions change. Today, the world is going through another phase in this evolutionary process. After three decades of intense globalization, forces favoring de-globalization are emerging, although they have yet to acquire full power. Most of Europe and rising powers such as China and India still favor globalization over de-globalization, which in turn might have dissuaded them from pursuing intense hard balancing.

Globalization and Balance of Power Today

What is the relevance of balance-of-power theory today? Neorealist theory, originally developed by Kenneth Waltz, predicts balancing behavior repeating with law-like regularity, but this theory struggles to explain the dearth of hard balancing in contemporary world affairs. Two main realist arguments have been put forward to explain this anomaly.[10] The first is associated with William Wohlforth, who argues that the cost of creating a powerful counter-coalition against the U.S. has become prohibitive because the U.S. has crossed a "threshold concentration of power."[11] No other great power or coalition of powers has achieved the protection magnet status to attract a counter-coalition.[12] Similarly, Stephen Brooks and Wohlforth argue that "the larger, more comprehensive, and more entrenched the hegemon's lead, the more formidable the collective action and coordination barriers to balancing, and the higher the likely domestic autonomy and opportunity costs of pursuing this strategy. Given the current distribution of capabilities, we would thus not expect the counterbalancing constraint to be operative." Hence China, the most likely candidate for a magnet power, is unlikely to pursue intense counterbalancing.[13] In the decade since Brooks and Wohlforth made these arguments, events have proven them partially incorrect as they did not take into account asymmetric challenges presented by weaker great powers. Russia's increased arms buildup, aggressive behavior in Ukraine and Syria, and cyber attacks, and more nuanced aggressiveness from China in the South China Sea, suggest that despite the cost, these states are already engaging in limited expansion and counterbalancing efforts. These efforts today are indirect and asymmetrical. China is also rapidly expanding its commercial and naval reach into the Indian Ocean through the Belt and Road Initiative, which indirectly challenges American hegemony. Much of international relations (IR) theory ignores the power of asymmetric strategies, but these strategies can sometimes slowly whittle down the strongest power on earth.

The American policy of supporting economic globalization and the integration of rising powers through international institutions played a significant role in preventing active hard balancing by second-ranking states. Had the U.S. emulated previous revisionist powers and tried to take away the sovereignty and economic well-being of other great powers, it would have seen more hard balancing directed against it. Twenty-five years after it became a near-unipolar power, we are in a slow transition phase for balancing behavior, even though the costs of frontally confronting the U.S. remain high. Great powers such as China and Russia are using multiple strategies, including soft and hard balancing, to restrain the U.S. as and when appropriate. Moreover, the potential challengers are more concerned with regional balancing, but these regions, especially the Asia-Pacific and Europe, are crucial to the hegemon's dominant global position. But if the cost of active balancing is an influence on states contemplating different mechanisms of restraint, how long does it remain the dominant consideration if the hegemonic power presents a greater threat? What specific costs do states have to consider, especially in the era of deepened globalization?

The second realist explanation for a lack of contemporary balancing is that the U.S. does not threaten other states because it is not geographically close to them. The oceans that protect the U.S.—as much as the English Channel protected Britain from Europe in the era of European classical hard balancing—reduce the threat the U.S. presents to others and thus the need for balancing against American power.[14] This is a problematic assertion given that American military power extends to all continents and the U.S. is part of the security complex of every region. It is indeed the most threatening power to Russia and China, the two great powers that are potentially capable of balancing it.

In addition to these realist perspectives, liberals have argued that American hegemony is benign and constitution-like because it offers order and economic stability to other powerful actors.[15] The problem

with this argument is that nonliberal states have not often been beneficiaries of American-led order, and they have strong apprehensions over
the use of armed intervention to propagate liberal values. Even a country like China, which has benefited from economic liberalism, is deeply
concerned about American security overreach in East Asia and its pro-
pensity to intervene in the internal affairs of the nonliberal states.

    In contrast to these perspectives, the one I have outlined focuses on
the contemporary role of globalization, especially in determining states'
cost-benefit calculations about their security. Globalization has generated
two competing forces in world politics (although there is no guarantee
these will last forever). One is the increased economic strength of rising
powers such as China, which are pushing their claim for a larger role in
international governance. The other is that in order to sustain economic
growth and development, rising powers must maintain open ties with
other major economies and especially with the U.S. This forces them to
tread carefully on security matters. One major change from the past is that
with the onset of rapid communications and transportation, geographic
barriers do not matter as much as before. The new powers operate in a
highly networked world, and to fulfill their economic and strategic goals
they have to make links wherever possible.[16] As Jonathan Kirshner states,
globalization has "raised the opportunity costs of going to war, reduced
the expected gains from territorial conquest, and diluted pristine formula-
tions of the 'national interest' that can be effectively advanced by interstate
war."[17] This does not mean that globalization-generated constraints will
continue forever. In 2016–17, less than three decades after the onset of intense economic globalization, de-globalization efforts have gained momentum, with populist forces pressuring for more resources and power in
response to the employment, wealth, and income inequalities generated
by globalization. As the Chinese leader Xi Jinping told the 2017 Davos
World Economic Forum: "Economic globalization was once viewed as the
treasure cave found by Ali Baba in The Arabian Nights, but it has now
become the Pandora's box."[18] If globalization fails and states enter an intense phase of neo-mercantilist competition, the geopolitical consequences could include arms races, alliance buildups, and perhaps wars.

    Countries gaining from globalization could, after a period of
restraint, engage in stepped-up arms acquisitions, generating pressures

on their neighbors and others to respond with their own arms buildups. The security dilemma can be accentuated, as higher wealth and purchasing power allow a rising power to spend more on arms. Whether these are offensive or defensive weapons, and whether the rising power deploys them offensively, will help determine the balancing options other countries may pursue against it. If the rising power sees a nonthreatening posture as essential for commercial interaction with others, it may refrain from deploying its capabilities offensively. Even though it may engage in internal balancing through weapons acquisition, by its restrained behavior, it may reduce others' coalition building for balance-of-power purposes.

Scholars often compare today's world to the period prior to 1914, when interdependence was high, but the two eras are very different. One difference is the quantity of foreign direct investment in the contemporary era. According to one study: "A 10% increase in FDI leads to on average to a 3 per cent decrease in conflict."[19] FDI increases have facilitated greater interactions and raised the cost of conflict for states. Others contend that globalization and interdependence do not make countries reluctant to impose tariffs. The huge increases in the flow of capital, labor, and goods did not prevent Europe and America from imposing tariffs and protectionism, despite the lessons of the Great Depression.[20] The risk that globalization may recede is not discounted in this analysis. What is noticeable is that globalization can go smoothly for a period, but then countries can feel its negative effects on employment and wages, prompting them to pursue revanchist or mercantilist policies.[21] Karl Polanyi powerfully argues that the balance-of-power system and the "pragmatic peace" of the nineteenth century were built around the international gold standard, the self-regulating market system, and the liberal state. The self-regulating market was a "utopia," and when states took measures to protect domestic industries, all the other edifices collapsed.[22] Polanyi argues there was a "double movement." The first aspect of it was based on the "principle of economic liberalism, aiming at the establishment of self-regulating market, relying on the support of the trading classes, and using largely laissez-faire and free trade as its methods." The second was "the principle of social protection aiming at the conservation of man and nature as well as productive organization, relying on the varying support of those most immediately affected by the deleterious action of the market—primarily, but not exclusively the working and landed classes—and using protective legislation, restrictive associations, and other instruments of intervention as its methods."[23] Polanyi views the outcome as twofold: "the clash of the organizing principles of economic liberalism and social protection ... led to a deep-seated institutional strain," and "the conflict of classes ..., interacting with the first, turned the crisis into a catastrophe."[24] What is relevant here is that as globalization-led costs and benefits change, so do balancing strategies. They can be fluid as globalization-led growth waxes and wanes.

Great powers, especially the beneficiaries of economic globalization, can at least temporarily restrain their policies and rely on institutional mechanisms to soft-balance each other. Compared to their early twentieth-century counterparts, today's major powers have pursued a considerably more nuanced approach to balancing, relying mainly on soft balancing and limited hard balancing. This trend can be upset if globalization fails and domestic politics propels the rising powers' military expansion, against which regional states—in alignment with the U.S.— would be impelled to respond more powerfully. Or the U.S., as the declining power, could engage in military operations to forestall a peer competitor's rise. Nothing is permanent in international politics. Intense hard balancing could return if the United States engages in nationalist policies, foreclosing the trade and economic opportunities for others while stepping up military expansion. China and Russia could increase their belligerent behavior toward other states in their respective regions, or they could aggressively threaten U.S. primacy in the Pacific. Alternatively, hard and soft balancing could emerge as parallel mechanisms for dealing with China's rise. At least some Asian states would welcome institutions to constrain Chinese behavior. They might also form limited balance-of-power coalitions and engage in internal balancing through arms buildups.

If trade and investment are strong among great powers, the need for intense competition and balance of power could be reduced. During the eighteenth and nineteenth centuries, European powers had many territories available for conquest, and their competition was conducted at the expense of non-European third parties. Once the opportunities for expansion began to close at the end of the nineteenth century, alliances became rigid.[25] By the same token, the opportunities offered by economic globalization need not be infinite either, and when the available resources become scarce, rivalry and intense balancing among great powers could resurface.

The election of populist leader Donald Trump in the U.S. in 2016, the rising prominence of right-wing candidates and parties in Europe, and the British electorate's choice to leave the EU (Brexit) all point to discontent with globalization, especially among the middle- and lower-income segments of the population. As the possibility of protectionist policies by the U.S. increases, so has the prospect of greater international tensions among major powers, especially between the rising power China and the U.S. If the promise of globalization decreases dramatically for Beijing, the chances of a nationalist upsurge in China are high. Military competition and hard balancing could return to the international arena, especially in the Indo-Pacific region. Moreover, if President Trump withdraws from U.S. treaty commitments to Asian and European allies, they may consider building their own military capabilities to replace American protection. Balance-of-power competition could get more intense and diffused among many actors.

The idea inherent in this book that states' balancing behavior may be more nuanced than merely hard balancing is an advance over other perspectives in international relations, and especially over neorealist and offensive realist theories' contentions on balancing. These theories predict that (hard-) balancing behavior will come back, but they cannot state the timing of this return. They do not, in general, connect security and economics in predicting balancing behavior. They also assume that what states do before hard balancing begins has nothing to do with balancing. If balance of power is one of several strategies and its arrival is indeterminate, then we need to pay attention to state policies when intense hard balancing is not taking place. We need to explain the nonemergence of balancing coalitions in key instances—like that of the contemporary international order—when the most powerful state enjoys an overwhelming preponderance of power.

Moreover, while realists have offered explanations for the lack of hard balancing against the U.S., they have focused less on a dearth of hard balancing against rising powers such as China. Why has China not faced intense balancing despite being neither a hegemon (with a "threshold concentration of power") nor a democracy? Although the U.S. has a preponderance of power in the Pacific, it has not prevented China from building naval facilities, including runways, and installing antiaircraft guns in the disputed South China Sea islets. Since 2015, the U.S. has stepped up its patrolling, but the Chinese response has been to further militarize the waters, which now include the Indian Ocean. Granted, China has yet to threaten the existence of other states or global maritime transportation, and while it has started to make claims on territories in the South and East China Seas that are also claimed by other states, these are not the same as existential challenges. China is a land power, and an ocean separates it from the U.S. In fact, the ocean is the source of the limited hard balancing we are witnessing against China today.

One sees this in the limited balancing efforts against China by its neighbors even though Beijing has yet to pose a formidable threat to other states' sovereign existence. Indeed, China provides collective goods to the region as a leading trading partner. It offers infrastructure support through lending agencies such as the Asian Infrastructure Investment Bank (AIIB) to regional countries. In fact, some of the states of the region have increased their response from soft balancing to limited hard balancing, and others have accommodated China's position while stopping well short of bandwagoning. They have not, for instance, openly supported China's territorial claims in the South China Sea. It should be noted that observers have questioned whether balance-of-power theory even applies in East Asia. Some suggest that the Chinese order is evolving toward an inclusive hierarchical model that makes European models of balance of power less relevant.[26] Yet others have explained the lack of balancing in East Asia by describing mechanisms that are actually tools of soft balancing. Institutional binding may well be the major reason that Asia has not witnessed intense balance-of-power competition, at least during the 1990s.[27] In either case, if China adopts a more threatening grand strategy, we are likely to see more intense hard balancing in the wider region.

The type of state behavior that exists today calls for a more eclectic view of balancing and of IR theory itself. State behavior cannot be placed in a straitjacket, and the soft-balancing approach offers a mechanism for explaining international politics during key periods. From a policy perspective, it has much merit as well. It calls for the creative use of international institutions by states and the evocation of legitimacy to restrain powerful actors who threaten regional or international order. This creative balancing should include soft- and hard-balancing techniques along with other forms of engagement to avoid massive conflicts or escalation to violence. Institutional mechanisms could be used to engage and reduce friction points where active hard balancing may produce unwanted outcomes.

Bridging Theory and Policy

In previous chapters I have tried to make some major advancements in bridging the theory/policy divisions among different IR paradigms. The diplomatic history I have discussed offers insights for policy makers contemplating balance-of-power strategies. The case studies show the strengths and limitations of diverse strategies and that the argument in favor of hard balancing, popular among realpolitik-oriented policy makers, needs revision, as hard balancing does not necessarily produce benign outcomes or even security. Soft balancing has much potential as a tool of statecraft during periods of globalization and peace among great powers. Institutions are useful tools for delegitimizing aggressive behavior when powers are not in intense rivalries. But statesmen should also be familiar with the limitations of soft balancing. They should have a sense of when, why, and how institutions produce positive outcomes—or not. A strategy can be applied more effectively when we understand its facilitating conditions. Realists in general do not pay much attention to different phases in the evolution of the balancing process, and they thus make balancing a somewhat static approach. Institutionalists fail to distinguish when institutions can be useful for restraining great powers and when they are not. By highlighting the evolutionary nature of balancing, we can add an element of nuance often missing from IR theory and policy.

The eclectic approach offered in this book explains the mechanisms by which states choose hard balancing, soft balancing, or a combination of both. It shows that a liberal mechanism of institutions can be used for realist ends. Similarly, the normative foundations of state-craft, such as the territorial integrity norm, can be important for states pursuing softer instruments of balancing. I have also tried to link an English School concern, legitimacy, especially for great powers of the international system, with realist notions of power and liberal ideas of institutions as vehicles for engagement among states. Bridging theoretical and epistemological divides among various IR traditions should be one goal of the soft-balancing research program.

An eclectic approach has virtues in a complex international system. Atomized theory development has created challenges for understanding key phenomena like balance of power, as the behavior of states tends to vary. Sometimes they underbalance, and sometimes they resort to non-military instruments even during periods of hard balancing. History shows that past patterns were not either/or, whereas mainstream, single-paradigm perspectives tend to ignore or pigeonhole behavior that is difficult to explain. As David Lake and others have argued, scholars should be "developing contingent, mid-level theories of specific phenomena," rather than reifying one tradition or other as always correct.[28] I have tried to modify balance of power as both a strategy and a theory, and suggest that realists need to pay more attention to the role that institutions and norms play in achieving balance and restraint. The evidence also shows that soft balancing occurred in different systems—multipolar, bipolar, and near-unipolar worlds. Also, the case studies show that the approach is being used in the current transition and emerging order against a rising China and a more assertive Russia. Weaker states attempted limited forms of soft balancing during the bipolar era also by way of nonalignment.

A final point is that both power structures and agency matter in balance of power. Structure is important because the distribution of power in the international system certainly influences the strategies adopted by states and their decisions about whether to balance a rising or hegemonic power. It is a myth that national elites have little role in determining the strategic options they adopt. National leaders with poorly developed strategies or clever asymmetric strategies can upset the balance of power and undermine deterrence strategies, leading to war even when it is not intended. Similarly, ambitious leaders with revisionist intentions can adopt different strategies—including asymmetric ones—to frustrate other powers' efforts to maintain the status quo. When leaders think they can break their power status, they may design clever strategies to do so. In order for balance of power to work, leaders have to make choices and take actions that augment their preferred position. The international power structure constrains and shapes those choices, but how deterministic that structure is is a matter of contention.

Institutions play a multifaceted role in the international arena, especially in the areas of peace and security. New research shows that they strongly influence systemic, structural processes and thus state behavior. Steven Lobell has argued that institutions can have two major impacts: they change the interaction capacity among states in the international system, and they change the structure of the system itself.[29] Yet it is important to note that not all institutions and not all sanctions produce peace. History advises against the notion that one strategy will work in all great-power conflicts. Sometimes institutional sanctions have caused conflict, and soft balancing through institutions has worked only when the targeted power saw it as a legitimate course of action.

A long line of liberal thinkers has shown how institutions encourage cooperation and prevent costly arms races and sudden military reaction by opposing sides, suggesting that a rising power can hope to obtain changes in the status quo without violence. Yet it also seems that power politics via institutions can generate conflict and violence among great powers. Russia's cyber warfare following European and American sanctions in response to its actions in Ukraine supports this position. A more prominent case is how economic sanctions against Japan and Italy in the 1930s produced nationalism and militarism in those countries. IR scholars have yet to explore this dimension of sanctions adequately, and we clearly need to better understand the implications of using institutions and sanctions to obtain peace among major powers.

In a fluid international environment like today's, states may use hybrid strategies of soft and hard balancing. Hybrid balancing is more feasible, both politically and economically, than following only one dominant approach. States that rely too much on hard balancing may hurt themselves economically by creating enmity with a powerful state that also offers them many public goods. Similarly, there is a growing literature on sanctions arguing that they can work if they are carefully calibrated against the powerful economic sectors of a country rather than the whole country, as the latter approach can generate humanitarian catastrophes, high levels of nationalism in the target states, and sanctions fatigue among the sanctioning states.[30] "Smart power," combining hard and soft power, drew much interest among U.S. policy makers under the Obama administration.[31] Likewise, "smart balancing" could involve a deft application of hard, limited hard, and soft balancing depending on the situation—a flexible hedging strategy for states concerned about preserving both their security and their economic growth.

Soft balancing also serves to build bridges across theory and policy. Alexander George, who has argued that the theory/practice divide remains very high in international relations, urges scholars to pay more attention to addressing the conditions under which their propositions work or do not work.[32] Knowing when and how soft balancing is likely to succeed, as well as its limitations, is very important for policy makers as a guard against blindly following one approach or another. Realpolitik-oriented leaders tend to carelessly employ hard balancing out of an attraction to "security through strength," a widespread conception among political and bureaucratic elites. Whether or not it has any chance of working, looking tough attracts some. Liberal-oriented policy makers, on the other hand, often give too much prominence to institutions and economic sanctions, not realizing that these policies can also produce bad outcomes. Knowing when both types of mechanisms work and don't work is vital to applying them effectively.

Balance of Power in the Emerging International Order

The emerging international order offers states many opportunities for conflict as well as for cooperation and restraint. Soft balancing can be an invaluable tool for states attempting to adapt and respond to the growing power or threatening postures of both rising and established states. The emergence in both the West and the East of nationalist leaders with no particular commitment to globalization and free trade may cause turbulence in coming years. To avert conflict, leaders of great-power states will need to learn from past mistakes and avoid seeking purely unilateral gains. Strengthening institutions and agreeing on the legitimate uses of power is of prime importance, as is respecting the status and interests of peers. Rising powers need to be integrated peacefully into the international order. Here the United States has a major role to play. The question is whether the U.S. under the Trump administration will continue the policies of preceding administrations or revert to a protectionist path. National choices need not follow a linear path: elites with different ideas can always attempt to scuttle previous policies. As I write this, over a year into the Trump presidency, it is not clear that he has any coherent foreign-policy strategy at all, except that his preference for putting hawkish individuals into key positions suggests he may be intuitively drawn to hard balancing.

Will soft balancing help make an emerging power transition peaceful?[33] The historical record is mixed. As a strategy, soft balancing successfully maintained order among the Concert powers for a short period in the nineteenth century. But in the 1930s, it failed to work against the actively revisionist policies of Germany, Japan, and Italy. The timing and the application of these strategies matter just as they do with any other strategy in world politics. The behavior of established and rising powers in the post–Cold War era gives mixed hope for soft balancing as a mechanism for peaceful power transition. In the coming era, soft balancing and limited hard balancing may be more effective than frontal collision, as full-fledged arms buildup or alignment can generate excessive competitions, misperception, and militarized crises. As Graham Allison recently argued, the "Thucydides trap," in which a waning power tries to forestall its decline by engaging in war with a rising power, is not inevitable.[34]

BALANCING RISING CHINA

For the first three decades of the post–Cold War era, hard balancing toward China has been limited. Even though Chinese power has increased greatly in both economic and military terms, until China adopted a more belligerent approach to its territorial claims in the South China Sea, the other powers preferred to deal with it through limited hard balancing, soft balancing, and diplomatic engagement. Since 2010, China's neighbors have been understandably concerned about its change in strategy and have begun to form limited coalitions and strengthened military alliances with the United States. Even so, balancing efforts remain limited.

In the future, whether countries pursue hard or soft balancing or a combination of the two will largely depend on China's behavior. If it adopts an imperialist strategy toward other states in the region, they will likely form hard balancing coalitions among themselves as well as with the U.S. If China remains engaged in international institutions, other states are likely to pursue soft balancing. The context of intensified globalization in which China's rise is occurring makes the imperialist policy more difficult to adopt—both for China and for competing states.

Yet China appears to be periodically asserting its military muscle and coercive instruments to achieve compliance from regional states, as indicated by the naval clashes between China and Japan in 2013, the subsequent economic sanctions on Japan, and the 2017 border skirmishes with India. Beijing may be taking its cue from U.S. foreign policy, applying coercive diplomacy as and when it pleases. It may also expect regional states to comply or eventually to bandwagon with it from fear of adverse consequences.[35] China's BRI project, although aimed at increased trade and maritime connectivity, has the potential to go either way, generating either more conflict or widespread peace and prosperity. Is China above the temptation of the European East India companies that preceded the colonial era, in which trade motives produced the desire for territorial conquest and militarization? The British East India Company was originally interested in trading rights and trading posts, and not until it obtained these did its ambitions change. Thinking it needed additional lands, the company eventually conquered much of South Asia. Military might was the servant of economic and trade interests.

China's intentions following its rise to global power status are less clear. Its neighbors and other interested states cannot yet tell whether China aims for hegemony, partial hegemony, or complete dominance, or indeed whether it will behave like any rising power bent on enlarging its influence and settling long-running territorial disputes with neighbors through military threats. Chinese decision makers and strategic planners are likely asking themselves profound questions now. What kind of international and regional order does China want to help create? What is the ultimate purpose of the "peaceful rise/development strategy"? Can China acquire security and power by offering a different conception of international order than that of the U.S., and will other states accept it as legitimate? China has placed very high importance on sovereignty—maintaining its own freedom of action while slowly integrating internationally.[36] But we don't know whether its leaders truly believe in the sovereignty norm for other Asian states and whether it will respect their territorial boundaries. Some have argued that China's increasing participation in international institutions has encouraged Beijing to accept more cooperative and "self-constraining commitments" in areas such as arms control.[37] Recently, a Chinese spokesman asserted that China wants to reform and not upset the international order.[38] Even if this is true, it is less clear how long this socialization will last. Can other states in the region accept Chinese pronouncements at face value in the context of its increasing power and changing aspirations?

The policy instruments adopted by states to deal with China have been mixed, involving diplomatic engagement, soft balancing, limited forms of bandwagoning, and limited hard balancing, with the latter increasingly favored. This calibrated strategy of limited alignments is meant to avoid the pitfalls of "entrapment" or "abandonment," the two dangers associated with a full-fledged balance-of-power strategy.[39] China's continuing conflicts with India, Japan, and the ASEAN states, however, would suggest that balance-of-power politics relying on hard instruments may return, although deep alignment through new formal alliances is unlikely in the near term, even when the Asian states seek an American presence as a pacifying force.

In the post–Cold War era, deepened globalization and America's near-unipolar status made power competition more nuanced than in previous eras. States today make security choices in a more calibrated manner, avoiding black-and-white choices and leaving themselves room to register their opposition to China's expansionist policies while keeping open the possibility of engagement with Beijing. Since China is the lead trading partner of almost all Asian states, they cannot follow traditional balance-of-power strategies. Their adaptive response follows the dictum: "Necessity is the mother of invention."

Whether soft balancing will work in the long run depends ultimately on China as well. If Beijing wants its rise to be peaceful, it has to follow a less belligerent policy. The coercive diplomacy China has pursued since 2009 with respect to Japan, India, Bhutan, and the ASEAN states has only alienated those who believe in a benign China. The resulting concern shows in the flurry of diplomatic visits by leaders of the U.S., Japan, India, and ASEAN states to each other's capitals in 2010. Worryingly, China's inability or unwillingness to temper North Korea's pursuit of nuclear weapons as well as its increasing support for Pakistan's revisionist policies in South Asia suggests that China may use client states to advance revisionist goals. The danger is that some of these states may take Chinese support for granted and make reckless military choices.

Soft balancing can also be a useful strategy for China toward other great powers. It has used this strategy at the UN Security Council to deny legitimacy to the Kosovo and Iraq invasions, and later the Syrian and Libyan interventions. Soft balancing may also be necessary for Beijing to mobilize the international community in opposition to U.S. hegemony, particularly any reckless policies the Trump administration or its successors may follow on Iran, Syria, or North Korea. It may help avoid a massive arms race with the U.S. Regional states as well could be soft balanced more than hard balanced, and it is in China's interests to use institutions like BRICS, ASEAN, and SCO to restrain its regional neighbors. In addition to binding them in institutional frameworks, these organizations may become useful tools for balancing and restraint.

BALANCING RUSSIA

Europe and the United States have responded to Russia's territorial revanchism with a combination of hard and soft balancing. They have imposed limited sanctions on Russia, and NATO has deployed additional forces on its eastern flank and in the Baltic states. Even in this instance, however, the deployments have been limited. As Russia's relative power position has declined, President Putin has engaged in coercive policies toward neighbors. He has also made Moscow an important player in the Middle East by intervening militarily in the Syrian civil war. President Trump appeared ready to befriend Russia, perhaps in an effort to divide the Russo-Chinese soft-balancing and limited hard-balancing coalition, but this move seems to have stalled.

The European states have been less than successful in using regional institutions or the UN to soft-balance Russia, partially because

Moscow doesn't allow such institutions to get in the way of protecting its security and status. The absence of strong institutions that include Russia may be a reason for the ineffectiveness of soft balancing. Europe should consider developing better regional institutions similar to the Conference on Security and Cooperation in Europe, a mechanism that existed during the Cold War. The expansion of NATO to Russia's erstwhile member states, a hard-balancing act, has caused more damage to regional security than anticipated.

At the same time, Russia has used institutional mechanisms to restrain Americans' interventions. In Kosovo, it used such mechanisms to limit the extent of the Kosovo intervention, and in 2003 it worked along with some of America's Western allies to delegitimize the U.S. invasion of Iraq. Without the UN, Moscow would have fewer tools. Russia's membership in BRICS and the SCO can be useful for future soft-balancing efforts toward China if the need arises. Its desire to be recognized as a lead actor will be more plausible if its positions in international institutions are strong and legitimate.

These insights also apply to other rising powers such as India and Brazil. BRICS could become an arena of soft balancing, but that has not happened yet as its main focus has been economic. The G-20 states could also lead in preventing their regions from sliding into hard-balancing rivalries. In regions such as the Asia-Pacific, institutional mechanisms need to be strengthened to prevent arms races.

SOFT BALANCING THE UNITED STATES IN THE TRUMP ERA AND BEYOND

President Trump, who wishes to halt American decline and regain the country's hegemonic position, has been paying less attention to soft power and international institutions than his predecessors did. Those predecessors' policies elicited limited defensive arms buildup and asymmetric strategies by second-ranking great powers, but not direct alliance formation. Soft balancing will appeal to U.S. public opinion more effectively than hard balancing, and it may affect popular choices in the next elections. Hard balancing by other states would surely harden American public opinion—or a significant part of it—around militaristic responses. The Trump administration's turn toward a more abrasive foreign policy and its use of military force against regional states such as Iran and North Korea could propel more calls for hard-balancing coalitions. In addition, if the Trump administration does not properly attend to its allies, alliances might break or weaken. The U.S. could lose its benign hegemonic status and become a revisionist power with little to gain. It could be one of the few established powers in history to initiate a global conflict, even though its decline was not that sharp relative to its peers. Dramatic policy changes would bring dramatic responses from affected countries. An abandonment of economic and security institutions that have served many purposes, including soft balancing, would hurt international order and global security as well as American and allied security. If the U.S. becomes more aggressive toward Iran or China, allies and adversaries alike may resort to soft balancing by seeking institutional means to show the illegitimacy of American policies. But the changes in the U.S. that result from the delegitimation of these policies may or may not immediately work in the balancers' favor.

The Trump administration's strategy of arms buildup—the chief mechanism for internal balancing—aimed at restoring American predominance may produce an unwanted arms race in Europe and the Asia-Pacific. Encouraging allies to spend more on arms also generates arms competition and may even prompt Germany and Japan to acquire nuclear weapons. Further, America's abandonment of institutions is deeply problematic for the goal of maintaining American hegemony. Institutions are difficult to create, and once destroyed they are even harder to rebuild. Reforming institutions with the aim of achieving engagement and soft balancing should be the core of U.S. strategy.

The soft-balancing research agenda has much to offer in understanding state behavior over the past two hundred years, when institutions began to flourish in international politics. In this book, I have made a modest effort to explain the conditions under which soft balancing is employed as a strategy as well as when it works. More work is needed on conditions that lead states to adopt soft balancing versus other strategies such as bandwagoning, hard balancing, and buck-passing. Hard balancing presupposes intense rivalry, whereas soft balancing can occur among either rivals or nonrivals. The interesting questions arise, as they often do, at the margins: how and when allies and rivals attempt to soft-balance, and when do they instead resort to other strategies? Answering these questions may be essential to understanding the characteristics of the emerging international order, in particular the conflictual and cooperative behavior of rising and established powers, as well as to seeing whether or not states accommodate one another peacefully.

Notes

ONE Balance of Power Today

1. These wars are the Thirty Years' War (1618–48), the Dutch War of Louis the XIV (1672–78), the War of the League of Augsburg (1688–97), the War of the Spanish Succession (1701–14), the Seven Years' War (1756–63), the French Revolutionary and Napoleonic Wars (1792–1815), World War I (1914–18), and World War II (1939–45). See Jack S. Levy, *War in the Modern Great Power System, 1495–1975* (Lexington: University Press of Kentucky, 1983), 75.

2. See *Encyclopedia Britannica* for World War I statistics: https://www.britannica.com/+6event/World-War-I/Killed-wounded-and-missing; and Second World War History for World War II statistics: http://www.secondworldwarhistory.com/world-war-2-statistics.asp.

3. These estimates are rough. See James A. Lucas, "Deaths in Other Nations since WW II Due to U.S. Interventions," Countercurrents.org, April 24, 2007, http://www.countercurrents.org/lucas240407.htm.

4. Data is from "Iraq Body Count," May 22, 2017, https://www.iraqbodycount.org.

5. Barbara Tuchman, *The March of Folly: From Troy to Vietnam* (New York: Random House, 1965).

6. In modern times, chiefly three categories of people have granted themselves the ability and right to ask their people to lay down their lives for collective goals. First are national leaders, second are leaders of cataclysmic terrorist groups such as al-Qaeda, and third are violent nationalist/liberation/insurgent movements. The difference is that the first group has the legitimate sanction of the state, while the latter two are viewed as illegitimate. National leaders may get away with committing senseless acts of violence, including genocide, while the latter, if caught, can be killed or punished by states even without the due process of law.

7. Jack Snyder, *Myths of Empire: Domestic Politics and International Ambition* (Ithaca: Cornell University Press, 1993), 1–2. Similarly, Jeffrey Taliaferro argues that great powers often get entrapped in "prolonged," costly, and "self-defeating" wars due to a desire among elites not to lose the conflicts for reasons such as relative power and international status, even when withdrawal from such enterprises makes much rational sense. Jeffrey W. Taliaferro, *Balancing Risks: Great Power Intervention in the Periphery* (Ithaca: Cornell University Press, 2004).

8. Paul Kennedy, *The Rise and Fall of Great Powers* (New York: Random House, 1987). On the state causing aggression and warfare, see T. V. Paul, "Recasting Statecraft: International Relations and Strategies of Peaceful Change," *International Studies Quarterly* 61, no. 1 (March 2017): 1–13.

9. For the positive aspects of great powers and order building, see Robert A. Pastor, ed., *A Century's Journey: How the Great Powers Shape the World* (New York: Basic Books, 1999); Benjamin Miller, *When Opponents Cooperate: Great Power Conflict and Collaboration in World Politics* (Ann Arbor: University of Michigan Press, 2002).

10. On this, see T. V. Paul, ed., *Accommodating Rising Powers: Past, Present and Future* (Cambridge, Cambridge University Press, 2016).

11. For instance, see A. F. K. Organski, *World Politics* (New York, Knopf, 1958); Jacek Kugler and Douglas Lemke, eds., *Parity and War* (Ann Arbor: University of Michigan Press, 1996); Robert Gilpin, *War and Change in World Politics* (Princeton: Princeton University Press, 1981); John J. Mearsheimer, *The Tragedy of Great Power Politics,* rev. ed. (New York: Norton, 2014); Immanuel Wallerstein, *The Capitalist World-Economy* (Cambridge: Cambridge University Press, 1984); George Modelski, *Long Cycles in World Politics* (London: Macmillan, 1987).

12. John Mueller, *Retreat from Doomsday: The Obsolescence of Major War* (New York: Basic Books, 1989).

13. For a discussion of balance of power in the Greco-Roman world, see Michael Sheehan, *The Balance of Power: History and Theory* (London: Routledge, 1996), 24–29. For balance of power in ancient China, especially during the Qin period, see Victoria Tin-bor Hui, *War and State Formation in Ancient China and Early Modern Europe* (Cambridge: Cambridge University Press, 1995), 54–78. For a brief discussion of balance of power in ancient India, see Subrata K. Mitra and Michael Liebig, *Kautilya's Arthashastra* (Baden-Baden: Nomos, 2016), 118–26. There is skepticism regarding the extent to which balance of power was practiced in various parts of the world other than post-Westphalia Europe. According to this view, most regions were under the control of empires, and hence hegemony or preponderance seems to be the key structure of international order in much of the world. For these historical practices, see various chapters in Stuart Kaufman, Richard Little, and William Wohlforth, eds., *Balance of Power in History* (New York: Palgrave Macmillan, 2007). Empires, as Kissinger warned, have "no interest in operating within an international system; they aspire to *be* the international system. Empires have no need for a balance of power." Henry Kissinger, *Diplomacy* (New York: Simon & Schuster, 1994), 21.

14. Raymond Aron, *Peace and War: A Theory of International Relations* (New York: Prager, 1970), 126. The absence of a balancing coalition against the U.S. in the nineteenth

century, especially between Mexico and British Canada, is also an interesting topic, although this may have been due to the preponderance of British naval power, which prevented the emergence of strong nation-states supported by other European great powers, in particular France. See Daniel H. Deudney, *Bounding Power: Republican Security Theory for the Polis to the Global Village* (Princeton: Princeton University Press, 2007), 172. The British ceding of the dominant position in North America to the U.S. in the late nineteenth and early twentieth centuries also constitutes a limited challenge to balance-of-power theory. The British preoccupation with Europe, which was emerging as its main theater of security challenge, may be a key reason in this case. Ali Zeren and John A. Hall, "Seizing the Day or Passing the Baton? Power, Illusion, and the British Empire," in *Accommodating Rising Powers: Past, Present and Future*, ed. T.V. Paul (Cambridge: Cambridge University Press, 2016), 111–49.

15. James Der Derian, *On Diplomacy: A Genealogy of Western Estrangement* (Oxford: Blackwell, 1987), 132.

16. Henry Kissinger, *World Order* (New York: Penguin, 2014), 30. See also Hendrik Spruyt, *The Sovereign State and Its Competitors* (Princeton: Princeton University Press, 1996); Stephen D. Krasner, *Sovereignty: Organized Hypocrisy* (Princeton: Princeton University Press, 1999).

17. J. Dumont, *Corps universel diplomatique du droit des gens* (Amsterdam, 1731), cited in Edward Vose Gulick, *Europe's Classical Balance of Power* (Ithaca: Cornell University Press, 1955), 35.

18. Der Derian, *On Diplomacy*, 133.

19. Cited in Gordon A. Craig and Alexander L. George, *Force and Statecraft: Diplomatic Problems of Our Time*, 2nd ed. (New York: Oxford University Press, 1990), 8.

20. Ibid., 9.

21. J. Rousseau, "Extrait du projet de paix perpetuelle de M. l'Abbé de Saint Pierre," cited in Ernst Haas, "Balance of Power: Prescription, Concept, or Propaganda?" *World Politics* 5, no. 4 (July 1953): 453.

22. Real, "Science du gouvernement," cited in Gulick, *Europe's Classical Balance of Power*, 58.

23. Hans J. Morgenthau, *Politics among Nations*, 5th ed. (New York: Knopf, 1973), 220.

24. Ibid.

25. Richard Little, *The Balance of Power in International Relations: Metaphors, Myths and Models* (Cambridge: Cambridge University Press, 2007), 102. On nationalism, see Ernest Gellner, *Nationalism* (New York: NYU Press, 1997); Benedict Anderson, *Imagined Communities: Reflections on the Origin and Spread of Nationalism*, rev. ed. (London: Verso, 2016); Perry Anderson, *Lineages of the Absolutist State* (London: Verso, 2013); John A. Hall and Sinisa Malesevic, eds., *Nationalism and War* (Cambridge: Cambridge University Press, 2013).

26. Craig and George, *Force and Statecraft*, 38.

27. Sheehan, *The Balance of Power*, 135–36.

28. Craig and George, *Force and Statecraft*, 28.

29. Little, *The Balance of Power*, 118–19.

30. On the nuclear revolution, see Robert Jervis, *The Meaning of the Nuclear Revolution* (Ithaca: Cornell University Press, 1990).

31. Ibid., 231–32.

32. On the significance of balance of power, see Morgenthau, *Politics among Nations*, ch. 11; David Hume, "Of the Balance of Power," in *Balance of Power*, ed. Paul Seabury (San Francisco: Chandler, 1965), 32–36; Henry A. Kissinger, *A World Restored: Metternich, Castlereagh and the Problems of Peace* (Boston: Houghton Mifflin, 1973); Inis L. Claude Jr., *Power and International Relations* (New York: Random House, 1962).

33. Kenneth Waltz, *Theory of International Politics* (New York: Random House, 1979), 127; Mearsheimer, *The Tragedy of Great Power Politics*, 13.

34. As Andrew Hurrell states: "Radically unbalanced power will permit the powerful to 'lay down the law' to the less powerful, to skew the terms of cooperation in its own favor, to impose its own values and ways of doing things, and to undermine the procedural rules on which stable and legitimate cooperation must inevitably depend." Hurrell, "Hegemony, Liberalism and Global Order: What Space for Would-be Great Powers?" *International Affairs* 82, no. 1 (January 2006): 844.

35. Waltz, *Theory of International Politics*, 127.

36. 32 House of Commons, March 31, 1854, Parliamentary Debates, 3rd ser; vol. cxxxii, col. 279, cited in Great Britain Parliament and Thomas Curson Hansard, *Hansard's Parliamentary Debates* (London: Office for Hansard's Parliamentary Debates, 1854), 279.

37. Gulick, *Europe's Classical Balance of Power*, ch. 2. See also Paul Seabury, "The Status Quo and Balance," in Seabury, *Balance of Power*, 207; Emerich de Vattel, *Balance of Power: 1486–1914* (Totowa, NJ: Rowman & Littlefield, 1975), 72. Sometimes states also pursue balancing for status reasons, as they perceive that their opponent will gain higher status and believe that such gains undermine their own position. They could end up in a status dilemma similar to a security dilemma, whereby one's efforts to achieve status increase lead others to compete, making the status positions of both insecure. On this, see William C. Wohlforth, "Status Dilemmas and Interstate Conflict," in *Status in World Politics*, ed. T. V. Paul, Deborah Welch Larson, and William C. Wohlforth (Cambridge: Cambridge University Press, 2014), 115–40.

38. Jack Levy, "What Do Great Powers Balance against and When?" in *Balance of Power: Theory and Practice in the 21st Century*, ed. T. V. Paul, James Wirtz, and Michel Fortmann (Stanford: Stanford University Press), 32.

39. In fact, it has been argued that the concept is defined differently by diverse writers and practitioners. Ernst Haas has examined some eight meanings ascribed to balance of power by different authors. It has been used to mean: (1) distribution of power, (2) equilibrium, (3) hegemony, (4) stability and peace, (5) instability and war, (6) power politics in general, (7) a universal law of history, and (8) a system and guide to policy making. Haas, "Balance of Power: Prescription, Concept, or Propaganda?" 442–77. For the differences between manual and automatic balancing, see Colin Elman, "Introduction: Appraising Balance of Power Theory," in *Realism and the Balancing of Power: A*

New Debate, ed. John A. Vasquez and Colin Elman (Upper Saddle River, NJ: Prentice Hall, 2003), 9–10.

40. In modern times, this belief in automatic balancing is held by leading realists Morgenthau, Waltz, and Mearsheimer. See Hans J. Morgenthau, *Politics among Nations*, 4th ed. (New York: Knopf, 1966), 163; Waltz, *Theory of International Politics*, 119–20; Mearsheimer, *The Tragedy of Great Power Politics*, 21.

41. Nicholas John Spykman, *America's Strategy in World Politics: The United States and the Balance of Power* (New York: Harcourt, Brace, 1942), 25.

42. Ibid., 21–23.

43. F. R. Bridge and Roger Bullen, *The Great Powers and the European States System, 1814–1914*, 2nd ed. (Harlow, UK: Pearson-Longman, 2005), 15–16.

44. Stephen M. Walt, "Alliance Formation and the Balance of World Power," *International Security* 9, no. 4 (Spring 1985): 3–43.

45. William C. Wohlforth, *The Elusive Balance: Power and Perceptions during the Cold War* (Ithaca: Cornell University Press, 1993).

46. Levy, "What Do Great Powers Balance against and When?"; Christopher Layne, "From Preponderance to Offshore Balancing: America's Future Grand Strategy," *International Security* 22, no. 1 (Summer 1997): 86–124. For a good overview of balance-of-power theory and its various interpretations, see Randall L. Schweller, "The Balance of Power in World Politics," *Oxford Research Encyclopedia of Politics*, 2016, http://politics.oxfordre.com/view/10.1093/acrefore/9780190228637.001.0001/acrefore-9780190228637-e-119.

47. George Liska, *International Equilibrium: A Theoretical Essay on the Politics and Organization of Security* (Cambridge, MA: Harvard University Press, 1957), 34–41; Stanley Hoffmann, "Balance of Power," in *International Encyclopedia of the Social Sciences*, ed. David L. Sills (New York: Macmillan, 1968), 1:507; Claude, *Power and International Relations*, 56.

48. Waltz, *Theory of International Politics*, 126–28.

49. Some scholars have argued that it may be the unipolar order created by American power that produced this outcome. For instance, see Brock F. Tessman, "System Structure and State Strategy: Adding Hedging to the Menu," *Security Studies* 21, no. 2 (May 2012): 192–231. It is unclear why a unipolar power is not viewed as a threat to form a balance of power against. More unconvincing is why China has not balanced according to this logic.

50. On this, see Charles Kindleberger, *The World in Depression*, rev. ed. (Berkeley: University of California Press, 1976); Douglas A. Irwin, *Against the Tide: An Intellectual History of Free Trade* (Princeton: Princeton University Press, 1996).

51. See Dani Rodrik, *The Globalization Paradox* (New York: Norton, 2011), chs. 1–2; Michael D. Bordo, Barry Eichengreen, and Douglas A. Irwin, "Is Globalization Today Really Different Than Globalization a Hundred Years Ago?" (working paper 7195, National Bureau of Economic Research, Cambridge, MA, June 1999). See also Deepak Lal, *In Praise of Empires: Globalization and Order* (New York: Palgrave Macmillan, 2004), chs. 2, 4.

52. Stephen G. Brooks, *Producing Security* (Princeton: Princeton University Press, 2005), 3–4. Dale Copeland argues that interdependence can lead to peace if there is an expectation of greater economic benefits and prosperity, but war can result if great powers expect to lose in a big way in the future. Dale C. Copeland, *Economic Interdependence and War* (Princeton: Princeton University Press, 2015). Going by this argument, rising powers of today are less likely to be initiators of war, as they seem more optimistic about globalization and economic interdependence than established powers.

53. *World Investment Report 2017: Investment in the Digital Economy* (Geneva: United Nations, 2017), xi.

54. Brooks, *Producing Security,* 8, 17, 20.

55. Richard Rosecrance and Arthur Stein, "Interdependence: Myth or Reality?" *World Politics* 25, no. 1 (October 1973): 15–16.

56. Steve Chan, *Looking for Balance: China, the United States, and Power Balancing in East Asia* (Stanford: Stanford University Press, 2012), 4. See also Kai He, "If Not Soft Balancing, Then What? Reconsidering Soft Balancing and U.S. Policy toward China," *Security Studies* 17, no. 2 (June 2008): 363–95.

57. Robert Jervis, "Cooperation under the Security Dilemma," *World Politics* 30, no. 2 (January 1978): 167–214.

58. Stephen Van Evera, "The Cult of the Offensive and the Origins of the First World War," *International Security* 9, no. 1 (Summer 1984): 58–107.

59. For this phenomenon, see Mark W. Zacher, "The Territorial Integrity Norm," *International Organization* 55, no. 2 (Spring 2001): 15–50; Boaz Atzilli, *Border Fixity and International Conflict* (Chicago: University of Chicago Press, 2012). See also Mikulas Fabry, *Recognizing States: International Society and the Establishment of New States since 1776* (Oxford: Oxford University Press, 2010).

60. For theories flowing from different causal explanations for war, see Greg Cashman, *What Causes War?* (New York: Lexington Books, 1993).

61. I concur with Walt that balancing against threat is more prevalent than against power. Walt, "Alliance Formation and the Balance of World Power."

TWO Restraint by Other Means

1. This definition of soft balancing improves on previous definitions, including mine, and makes the concept more specific. Not all diplomatic actions can be termed soft balancing as some previous works on the subject have done. For instance, Robert Pape includes any nonmilitary actions aimed at frustrating or undermining U.S. aggressive policies as soft balancing, and this has been criticized as "concept stretching." See Robert A. Pape, "Soft Balancing against the United States," *International Security* 30, no. 1 (Summer 2005): 7–45. By focusing on three specific mechanisms of restraint, the concept of soft balancing can be made more specific and rigorous. It should be noted that these strategies are used in other contexts, including containment and retribution. However, a strategy qualifies as soft balancing only if it is specifically aimed at frustrating aggressive behavior.

2. Barry R. Posen, *Restraint: A New Foundation for U.S. Grand Strategy* (Ithaca: Cornell University Press, 2014), 30.

3. Kissinger, *World Order*, 263.

4. Robert E. Osgood, *Alliances and American Foreign Policy* (Baltimore: Johns Hopkins University Press, 1968), 17.

5. I realize that sometimes formal alliances were called *ententes*, such as the Anglo-French-Russian alliance, the Triple Entente before World War I. I use the term to mean a flexible agreement that has limited purpose and may not involve military commitment but rather diplomatic convergence on a security challenge that the parties see as threatening.

6. For a discussion of differences between alliances and ententes, see Robert A. Kann, "Alliances versus Ententes," *World Politics* 28, no. 4 (July 1976): 611–21.

7. In this respect, I agree with Stephen Walt's characterization of balancing against threats as opposed to power as the dominant feature of balancing behavior. Walt, *The Origins of Alliances* (Ithaca: Cornell University Press), 21.

8. On rivalries, see Gary Goertz and Paul F. Diehl, "Enduring Rivalries: Theoretical Constructs and Empirical Patterns," *International Studies Quarterly* 37, no. 2 (June, 1993): 147–71.

9. Judith Kelley, "Strategic Non-cooperation as Soft Balancing: Why Iraq Was Not Just about Iraq," *International Politics* 42, no. 2 (June 2005): 153–73.

10. Ibid., 167–68.

11. Robert O. Keohane, *After Hegemony: Cooperation and Discord in the World Political Economy* (Princeton, NJ: Princeton University Press, 1984); Stephen D. Krasner, "Regimes and the Limits of Realism: Regimes as Autonomous Variables," in *International Regimes,* ed. Stephen D. Krasner (Ithaca: Cornell University Press 1983); Arthur A. Stein, "Coordination and Collaboration: Regimes in an Anarchic World," in Krasner, *International Regimes;* and Lisa Martin, "Interests, Power, and Multilateralism," *International Organization* 46, no. 4 (Autumn 1992): 765–92.

12. G. John Ikenberry, *After Victory* (Princeton: Princeton University Press, 2000). See also Ikenberry, *Liberal Leviathan: The Origins, Crisis, and Transformation of the American World Order* (Princeton: Princeton University Press, 2011).

13. Prashanth Parameswaran, "Explaining US Strategic Partnerships in the Asia-Pacific Region: Origins, Developments and Prospects," *Contemporary Southeast Asia* 36, no. 2 (August 2014): 262–89.

14. Ankit Panda, "Why Does India Have So Many 'Strategic Partners' and No Allies?" *Diplomat,* November 23, 2013, http://thediplomat.com/2013/11/why-does-india-have-so-many-strategic-partners-and-no-allies/.

15. Quoted in M. S. Daoudi and M. S. Dajani, *Economic Sanctions: Ideals and Experience* (Boston: Routledge & Kegan Paul, 1983), 26.

16. Daniel W. Drezner, *The Sanctions Paradox: Economic Statecraft and International Relations* (Cambridge: Cambridge University Press, 1999), 8.

17. Ibid., 11–15. See also Lisa Martin, *Coercive Cooperation: Explaining Multilateral Economic Sanctions* (Princeton: Princeton University Press, 1992), 44–45, 243.

18. For these diverse dimensions, see Meghan L. O'Sullivan, *Shrewd Sanctions: Statecraft and State Sponsors of Terrorism* (Washington, DC: Brookings Institution, 2003), 303.

19. Michael Mastanduno, "Strategies of Economic Containment: US Trade Relations with the Soviet Union," *World Politics* 37, no. 4 (July 1985): 503–31.

20. Robert W. Jackman, *Power without Force: The Political Capacity of Nation-States* (Ann Arbor: University of Michigan Press, 1993), 95.

21. Martha Finnemore, "Legitimacy, Hypocrisy, and the Social Structure of Unipolarity," *World Politics* 61, no. 1 (January 2009): 62.

22. Ian Hurd, "Legitimacy and Authority in International Politics," *International Organization* 53, no. 2 (April 1999): 381; Finnemore, "Legitimacy, Hypocrisy," 62.

23. See *The Free Dictionary,* http://www.thefreedictionary.com/legitimacy.

24. Barry Hindess, *Discourses of Power: From Hobbes to Foucault* (Oxford: Blackwell, 1996), 1. See also Mlada Bukovansky, Ian Clark, and Robin Eckersley, *Special Responsibilities: Global Problems and American Power* (Cambridge: Cambridge University Press, 2012).

25. Christian Reus-Smit, *American Power and World Order* (Cambridge: Polity, 2004), 43–44.

26. Adam Watson, *The Evolution of International Society: A Comparative Historical Analysis* (London: Routledge, 1992), 13; Martin Wight, *Systems of States* (Bristol: Leicester University Press, 1977), 153.

27. Posen calls this "balance of power diplomacy" "short of building alliances." *Restraint,* 29, 30.

28. Reus-Smit, *American Power and World Order,* 53.

29. This is not to deny the existence of a scholarship that links security and economics. See Joanne Gowa, *Allies, Adversaries and International Trade* (Princeton: Princeton University Press, 1994); Edward D. Mansfield, *Power, Trade and War* (Princeton: Princeton University Press, 1994); Lars Skalnes, *Politics, Markets and Grand Strategy* (Ann Arbor: University of Michigan Press, 2000); Mark Brawley, *Political Economy and Grand Strategy: A Neoclassical Realist View* (London: Routledge, 2010); Steven E. Lobell, *The Challenge of Hegemony: Grand Strategy, Trade, and Domestic* Politics (Ann Arbor: University of Michigan Press, 2003).

30. Christopher Layne, *The Peace of Illusions: American Grand Strategy from 1940 to the Present* (Ithaca: Cornell University Press, 2006), 145.

31. Jonathan Kirshner, "Political Economy in Security Studies after the Cold War," *Review of International Political Economy* 5, no. 1 (Spring 1998): 61.

32. Ikenberry, *After Victory.*

33. For these, see Kier A. Lieber and G. Alexander, "Waiting for Balancing: Why the World Is Not Pushing Back," *International Security* 30, no. 1 (Summer 2005): 109–39; Stephen G. Brooks and William C. Wohlforth, "Hard Times for Soft Balancing," *International Security* 30, no. 1 (Summer 2005): 72–108. For a response, see Robert J. Art, "Striking the Balance," *International Security* 30, no. 3 (Winter 2005–6): 177–85.

34. Beth Elise Whitaker, "Soft Balancing among Weak States? Evidence from Africa," *International Affairs* 86, no. 5 (September 2010): 1109–27; Nicola Contessi, "Central Asia in Asia: Charting Growing Trans-Regional Linkages," *Journal of Eurasian Studies* 7, no. 1 (January 2016): 3–13; Javier Corrales, "Using Social Power to Balance Soft Power: Venezuela's Foreign Policy," *Washington Quarterly* 32, no. 4 (October 2009): 97–114; Max Paul Freed-

man and Tom Long, "Soft Balancing in the Americas: Latin American Opposition to US Intervention, 1898–1936," *International Security* 40, no. 1 (Summer 2015): 120–56; Mark Eric Williams, "The New Balancing Act: International Relations Theory and Venezuela's Foreign Policy," in *The Revolution in Venezuela: Social and Political Change under Chavez,* ed. Thomas Ponniah and Jonathan Eastwood (Cambridge, MA: Harvard University Press, 2011), 259–80; Weiqing Song, "Feeling Safe, Being Strong: China's Strategy of Soft Balancing through the Shanghai Cooperation Organization," *International Politics* 50, no. 5 (September 2013): 664–85; Ilai Z. Saltzman, *Securitizing Balance of Power Theory* (Lexington: Lexington Books, 2012), ch. 5.

35. Nadav Kedem, "Soft Balancing in Various International Systems" (paper presented at the International Studies Association Conference, New York, February 15–19, 2009); Ilai Z. Saltzman, "Soft Balancing as Foreign Policy: Assessing American Strategy in the Interwar Period," *Foreign Policy Analysis* 8, no. 2 (April 2012): 131–50.

36. Kenneth Abbot and Duncan Snidal, "Hard and Soft Law in International Governance," *International Organization* 54, no. 3 (Summer 2000): 421–56.

37. Joseph S. Nye Jr., *Soft Power: The Means to Success in World Politics* (New York: Public Affairs, 2004), x.

38. John Mearsheimer, "The False Promise of International Institutions," *International Security* 19, no. 3 (Winter 1994–95): 5–49; Susan Strange, *"Cave! hic dragones:* A Critique of Regime Analysis," in Krasner, *International Regimes,* 337–54.

39. Robert O. Keohane, "Multilateralism: An Agenda for Research," *International Journal* 45, no. 4 (Autumn, 1990): 735; E. H. Carr, *The Twenty Years' Crisis, 1919–1939,* 2nd ed. (London: St Martin's, 1946); Hans J. Morgenthau, *Politics among Nations: The Struggle for Power and Peace* (New York: Knopf, 1948); Joseph M. Grieco, *Cooperation among Nations* (Ithaca: Cornell University Press, 1990).

40. Hans J. Morgenthau, *The Purpose of American Politics* (Chicago: University of Chicago Press, 1962), 68.

41. Ikenberry, *After Victory.*

42. Ibid.

43. For these strategies, see Randall L. Schweller, "Managing the Rise of Great Powers: History and Theory," in *Engaging China: The Management of an Emerging Power,* ed. Alastair Iain Johnston and Robert S. Ross (London: Routledge: 2002), 10–18; Mark R. Brawley, "The Political Economy of Balance of Power Theory," in Paul, Wirtz, and Fortmann, *Balance of Power,* 82–85; On bandwagoning versus balancing, see Walt, *The Origins of Alliances,* 18–33.

44. Paul W. Schroeder, "Historical Reality versus Neorealist Theory," *International Security* 19, no. 1 (Summer 1994): 116, 117.

45. See Stefanie Von Hlatky, *American Allies in Times of War: The Great Asymmetry* (Oxford: Oxford University Press, 2013), 18–24.

46. For an alternate view on the Concert as not a success, see Korina Kagan, "The Myth of the European Concert," *Security Studies* 7, no. 2 (Winter 1997–98): 1–57.

47. Posen, *Restraint,* 29; Stephen M. Walt, *Taming American Power: The Global Response to U.S. Primacy* (New York: Norton, 2005), 161–71.

THREE Soft Balancing from Concert to the Cold War

1. Richard B. Elrod, "The Concert of Europe: A Fresh Look at an International System," *World Politics* 28, no. 2 (January 1976): 159.

2. Compiled from Kalevi J. Holsti, *Peace and War: Armed Conflicts and International Order, 1648–1989* (Cambridge: Cambridge University Press, 1991), 167. See also F. H. Hinsley, "The Concert of Europe," in *Diplomacy in Modern European History*, ed. Laurence W. Martin (New York: Macmillan, 1966), 43–57; Elrod, "The Concert of Europe."

3. Elrod, "The Concert of Europe," 166.

4. K. J. Holsti, "Governance without Government: Polyarchy in Nineteenth-Century European International Politics," in *Governance without Government: Order and Change in World Politics*, ed. James N. Rosenau and Ernst-Otto Czempiel (Cambridge: Cambridge University Press, 1992), 43.

5. Carsten Holbraad, "The Concert of Europe," *Australian Outlook*, 25, no. 1 (March 1971): 31.

6. Ikenberry, *After Victory*, ch. 4. For a constructivist account, see Mlada Bukovansky, *Legitimacy and Power Politics* (Princeton: Princeton University Press, 2002), 228.

7. Holsti, *Peace and War*, 139.

8. Ibid.

9. Paul W. Schroeder, "The 19th-Century International System: Changes in the Structure," *World Politics* 39, no. 1 (October 1986): 2.

10. Ikenberry, *After Victory*, 81–82.

11. Kissinger, *A World Restored*, 5.

12. Holsti, *Peace and War*, 168.

13. Sheldon Anderson, "Metternich, Bismarck, and the Myth of the 'Long Peace,' 1915–1914," *Peace & Change* 32, no. 3 (July 2007): 303.

14. Kissinger, *A World Restored*, 145.

15. Liska, *International Equilibrium*, 47.

16. Kissinger, *A World Restored*, 5. See also Hudson Meadwell, "The Long Nineteenth Century in Europe," *Review of International Studies* 27, no. 5 (December 2001): 165–89.

17. Holsti, *Peace and War*, 142.

18. Holsti, "Governance without Government," 43.

19. Ibid.

20. Gordon A. Craig, *Europe, 1815–1914*, 2nd ed. (New York: Holt, Rinehart & Winston, 1966), 12.

21. Craig and George, *Force and Statecraft*, 30.

22. Schroeder, "The 19th-Century International System," 12–13; Seabury, "The Status Quo and Balance," 211.

23. Gulick, *Europe's Classical Balance of Power*, 75–76.

24. Ibid., 16.

25. Ibid., 18–19.

26. Craig and George, *Force and Statecraft*, 31–32.

27. Matthew Rendall, "A Qualified Success for Collective Security: The Concert of Europe and the Belgian Crisis, 1831," *Diplomacy & Statecraft* 18, no. 2 (June 2007): 272.

28. Craig and George, *Force and Statecraft*, 46.

29. Rendall, "A Qualified Success for Collective Security," 272.

30. Ibid.

31. Robert Jervis, "Security Regimes," in Krasner, *International Regimes*, 178–87.

32. Rendall, "A Qualified Success for Collective Security," 272.

33. Matthew Rendall, "Russia, the Concert of Europe, and Greece, 1821–29: A Test of Hypotheses about the Vienna System," *Security Studies* 9, no. 4 (Summer 2000): 53; Paul W. Schroeder, "Containment Nineteenth-Century Style: How Russia Was Restrained," *South Atlantic Quarterly* 82, no. 1 (Winter 1983): 4.

34. Paul W. Schroeder, *Systems, Stability and Statecraft* (New York: Palgrave Macmillan, 2004), 127.

35. Bridge and Bullen, *The Great Powers*, 114–15.

36. Ibid., 115–25.

37. A. J. P. Taylor, *The Struggle for Mastery in Europe: 1848–1918* (Oxford: Clarendon, 1954), 60–61.

38. Rendall, "Russia, the Concert of Europe, and Greece," 54.

39. Richard Hart Sinnreich, "In Search of Military Repose: The Congress of Vienna and the Making of Peace," in *The Making of Peace: Rulers, States and the Aftermath of War,* ed. Williamson Murray and Jim Lacey (Cambridge: Cambridge University Press, 2009), 156.

40. Schroeder, "The 19th-Century International System," 11.

41. Cited in Elrod, "The Concert of Europe," 161–62.

42. Ibid.

43. Kennedy, *The Rise and Fall of Great Powers,* 250.

44. Ibid., xviii.

45. Ibid., 253.

46. Bernadotte E. Schmitt, "Triple Alliance and Triple Entente, 1902–1914," *American Historical Review* 29, no. 3 (April 1924): 450.

47. Anderson, "Metternich," 305–6, 309.

48. Van Evera, "The Cult of the Offensive."

49. On the causes of the war, see Jack S. Levy and John A. Vasquez, eds., *The Outbreak of the First World War* (Cambridge: Cambridge University Press, 2014); A. J. P. Taylor, *The First World War: An Illustrated History* (New York, Penguin, 1966); Barbara Tuchman, *The Guns of August* (New York: Random House, 1962); John Keegan, *The First World War,* 5th ed. (New York, Knopf, 1999).

50. Kissinger, *World Order,* 267.

51. John Milton Cooper Jr., *Breaking the Heart of the World: Woodrow Wilson and the Fight for the League of Nations* (Cambridge: Cambridge University Press, 2001).

52. For the text of the Covenant, see Ruth B. Henig, ed., *The League of Nations* (Edinburgh: Oliver & Boyd, 1973), 179–89.

53. Thomas J. Knock, *To End All Wars: Woodrow Wilson and the Quest for a New World Order* (New York: Oxford University Press, 1992), 198–99; Ikenberry, *After Victory*, 144.

54. See the Covenant text in Henig, *The League of Nations*, 182.

55. Ikenberry, *After Victory*, 147.

56. See Wilson's Guild Hall address in London, December 28, 1918, in Ray Stannard Baker and William E. Dodd, eds., *The Public Papers of Woodrow Wilson: War and Peace* (New York: Harper & Brothers, 1927), 1:342.

57. John Gerard Ruggie, *Winning the Peace: American and World Order in the New Era* (New York: Columbia University Press, 1996), 79.

58. Wilson's speech at Indianapolis, September 4, 1919, cited in Cooper, *Breaking the Heart of the World*, 159.

59. Cooper, *Breaking the Heart of the World*, 199–200.

60. Randall L. Schweller, *Unanswered Threats: Political Constraints on the Balance of Power* (Princeton: Princeton University Press, 2006).

61. Joseph Nye, *Understanding International Conflicts* (New York: Harper Collins, 1993), 77.

62. Richard Rosecrance and Zara Steiner, "British Grand Strategy and the Origins of World War II," in *The Domestic Bases of Grand Strategy*, ed. Richard Rosecrance and Arthur A. Stein (Ithaca: Cornell University Press, 1993), 126.

63. E. H. Carr, "The Future of the League—Idealism or Reality?" *Fortnightly* 140 (July–December 1936): 386, cited in Charles Jones, *E. H. Carr and International Relations* (Cambridge: Cambridge University Press, 1998), 31.

64. Nye, *Understanding International Conflicts*, 77; Ian Kershaw, ed., *Weimar: Why Did German Democracy Fail?* (London: Weidenfeld & Nicolson, 1990); Hans Mommsen, *The Rise and Fall of Weimar Democracy* (Chapel Hill: University of North Carolina Press, 1996).

65. Scott A. Silverstone, "The Legacy of Coercive Peacebuilding," in *The Challenge of Grand Strategy: The Great Powers and the Broken Balance between the World Wars*, ed. Jeffrey W. Taliaferro, Norrin M. Ripsman, and Steven E. Lobell (Cambridge: Cambridge University Press, 2012), 68, 71.

66. Peter Jackson, "Deterrence, Coercion, and Enmeshment: French Grand Strategy and the German Problem after World War I," in Taliaferro, Ripsman, and Lobell, *Challenge of Grand Strategy*, 37.

67. Ibid., 45.

68. Andrew Webster, "The League of Nations and Grand Strategy: A Contradiction in Terms," in Taliaferro, Ripsman, and Lobell, *Challenge of Grand Strategy*, 93.

69. Henig, *The League of Nations*, 58.

70. Kennedy, *The Rise and Fall of Great Powers*, 290.

71. Nye, *Understanding International Conflicts*, 79.

72. For the list of goods, see Henig, *The League of Nations*, 128–32.

73. Martyn Housden, *The League of Nations and the Organization of Peace* (London: Longman, 2012), 104.

74. John Whittam, *Fascist Italy* (Manchester: Manchester University Press, 1995), 111.

75. William A. Podmore, "The Making of the Anglo-Italian Agreement, 1937–1938," *Italian Studies* 49, no. 1 (January 1994): 112.

76. Housden, *The League of Nations,* 104.

77. Viscount Templewood, *Nine Troubled Years* (London: Collins, 1954), 152.

78. Housden, *The League of Nations,* 105.

79. Podmore, "The Making of the Anglo-Italian Agreement," 112.

80. Ibid., 113.

81. George W. Baer, *Test Case: Italy, Ethiopia and the League of Nations* (Stanford: Stanford University Press, 1976), 2.

82. Henig, *The League of Nations,* 119.

83. Reynolds M. Salerno, "The French Navy and the Appeasement of Italy, 1937–9," *English Historical Review* 112, no. 445 (February 1997): 70, 97.

84. Nye, *Understanding International Conflicts,* 81.

85. George W. Baer, "Sanctions and Security: The League of Nations and the Italian-Ethiopian War, 1935–1936," *International Organization* 27, no.2 (Spring 1973): 179.

86. Elisabeth Wiskemann, *Prologue to War* (New York: Oxford University Press, 1940); 172–76; MacGregor Knox, *Common Destiny: Dictatorship, Foreign Policy and War in Fascist Italy and Nazi Germany* (Cambridge: Cambridge University Press, 2000), 141.

87. James W. Davidson, "The Roots of Revisionism: Fascist Italy, 1922–39," *Security Studies* 11, no. 4 (Summer, 2002): 125–59.

88. Baer, *Test Case,* xiv.

89. Nye, *Understanding International Conflicts,* 81.

90. Housden, *The League of Nations,* 106.

91. F. S. Northedge, *The League of Nations: Its Life and Times, 1920–1946* (New York: Holmes & Meir, 1986), 145.

92. Ibid., 146.

93. Ibid., 148.

94. For the report, see Henig, *The League of Nations,* 148.

95. Northedge, *The League of Nations,* 160.

96. Ibid., 157.

97. Housden, *The League of Nations,* 101.

98. Henig, *The League of Nations,* 96.

99. Thomas W. Burkman, "Japan and the League of Nations," *World Affairs* 158, no. 1 (Summer 1995): 45.

100. Yale Candee Maxon, *Control of Japanese Foreign Policy: A Study of Civil-Military Rivalry, 1930–1945* (Berkeley: University of California Press, 1957), 72–90.

101. Robert J. C. Butow, *Tojo and the Coming of the War* (Princeton, Princeton University Press, 1961), 80–81; Maxon, *Control of Japanese Foreign Policy,* 108–12.

102. Ben-Ami Shillony, *Revolt in Japan: The Young Officers and the February 26, 1936 Incident* (Princeton: Princeton University Press, 1973), 209–10; Toshikazu Kase, *Journey to the Missouri* (New Haven: Yale University Press, 1950), 33–34.

103. Burkman, "Japan and the League of Nations," 55.

104. Northedge, *The League of Nations,* 161.

105. For an excellent analysis of the U.S. strategy of soft balancing toward Japan, see Saltzman, "Soft Balancing as Foreign Policy." The long-term strategies of the U.S. and Britain called for a blockade of Japan, employing naval fleets operating from bases in the Philippines, Singapore, and the Pacific. It was envisioned that this would lead to the eventual defeat of Japan in an attrition warfare. It was hoped by the Allies that this strategy would deter Japan. However, the early approach revolved around soft balancing more than hard balancing.

106. Ibid.

107. Ibid., 145–46.

108. For the Washington Naval Conference, see "The Washington Naval Conference, 1921–1922," https://history.state.gov/milestones/1921–1936/naval-conference.

109. "The London Naval Conference, 1930," https://history.state.gov/milestones /1921–1936/london-naval-conf.

110. James H. Belote and William M. Belote, *Titans of the Seas: The Development and Operations of Japanese and American Carrier Task Forces during World War II* (New York: Harper & Row, 1975), 19–20.

111. Ibid., 20; Ian Nish, *Japanese Foreign Policy, 1869–1942: Kasumigaseki to Miyakezaka* (London: Routledge & Kegan Paul, 1977), 167.

112. Ibid., 32; Masanori Ito, *The End of the Imperial Japanese Navy* (New York: Praeger, 1984), 11.

113. For a discussion of the incompatibility between Japan's dependence and its search for autarky, see Michael A. Barnhart, *Japan Prepares for Total War: The Search for Economic Security, 1919–1941* (Ithaca: Cornell University Press, 1987), 19.

114. George Morgenstern, "The Actual Road to Pearl Harbor," in *Perpetual War for Perpetual Peace: A Critical Examination of the Foreign Policy of Franklin Delano Roosevelt and Its Aftermath,* ed. Harry E. Barnes (Caldwell, ID: Caxton, 1953), 322–23, 327–28.

115. Memoirs of Prince Konoye, cited by Butow, *Tojo and the Coming of the War,* 267.

116. Kissinger, *A World Restored,* 6.

FOUR Balancing during the Cold War

1. For the UN Charter, see http://www.un.org/en/charter-united-nations/index. html.

2. On this, see Patrick M. Morgan, "Collective-Actor Deterrence," in *Complex Deterrence: Strategy in the Global Age,* ed. T. V. Paul, Patrick M. Morgan, and James J. Wirtz (Chicago: University of Chicago Press, 2009), 158–82.

3. On aspects of cooperation, see Alexander L. George, Philip J. Farley, and Alexander Dallin, eds., *U.S.-Soviet Security Cooperation: Achievements, Failures, Lessons* (New York: Oxford University Press, 1988).

4. Mastanduno, "Strategies of Economic Containment."

5. On this, see Layne, *The Peace of Illusions*, 57–58. See also Melvin P. Leffler, *A Preponderance of Power: National Security, the Truman Administration, and the Cold War* (Stanford: Stanford University Press, 1992).

6. See "The Sinews of Peace" ("Iron Curtain Speech"), March 5, 1946, Westminster College, Fulton, Missouri, http://www.winstonchurchill.org/resources/speeches/1946–1963-elder-statesman/120-the-sinews-of-peace.

7. George F. Kennan ("X"), "The Sources of Soviet Conduct," *Foreign Affairs* 25, no. 4 (July 1947): 570. On the impact of Kennan on containment strategy, see John Lewis Gaddis, *Strategies of Containment* (Oxford: Oxford University Press, 1982), ch. 2.

8. Denise M. Bostdorff, *Proclaiming the Truman Doctrine: The Cold War Call to Arms* (College Station: Texas A&M University Press, 2008); Howard Jones, *A New Kind of War: America's Global Strategy and the Truman Doctrine in Greece* (New York: Oxford University Press, 1989).

9. Deborah Larson argues that the Cold War was not bound to happen the way it did, and that cognitive-psychological theories can shed considerable light on how it emerged. See Deborah Larson, *Origins of Containment* (Princeton: Princeton University Press, 1985).

10. "A Report to the National Security Council—NSC 68," April 12, 1950, 4, President's Secretary's File, Truman Papers, https://www.trumanlibrary.org/whistlestop/study_collections/coldwar/documents/pdf/10-1.pdf. See also Gaddis, *Strategies of Containment*, 91.

11. Alexander L. George and Richard Smoke, *Deterrence in American Foreign Policy: Theory and Practice* (New York: Columbia University Press, 1974), 26–34.

12. On these, see Osgood, *Alliances and American Foreign Policy*, ch. 5.

13. Richard W. Baker, ed., *The ANZUS States and Their Region* (New York: Praeger, 1994).

14. George R. Packard, "The United States–Japan Security Treaty at 50," *Foreign Affairs* 89, no. 2 (March–April 2010): 92–103; on the U.S.-Korea treaty, see Jae-Jung Suh, *Power, Interests and Identity in Military Alliances* (New York: Palgrave Macmillan, 2007).

15. On the COMECON, see Jenny Brine, *COMECON: The Rise and Fall of an International Socialist Organization* (New Brunswick, NJ: Transaction, 1992).

16. On this, see Jervis, *The Meaning of the Nuclear Revolution*, 231–32.

17. In 1990, the U.S. arsenal had 21,390 nuclear warheads and Russia possessed 37,000. Robert S. Norris and Hans M. Kristensen, "Global Nuclear Weapons Inventories, 1945–2010," *Bulletin of the Atomic Scientists* 66, no.4 (July–August 2010): 82.

18. Gunnar Adler-Karlsson, *Western Economic Warfare, 1947–1967* (Stockholm: Almqvist & Wiksell, 1968).

19. David P. Calleo, *Beyond American Hegemony: The Future of Western Alliance* (New York: Basic Books, 1987), 31–33.

20. Dietmar Rothermund, "The Era of Non-alignment," in *The Non-Aligned Movement and the Cold War*, ed. Natasa Miscovic, Harald Fischer-Tine, and Nada Boskovska (London: Routledge, 2014), 20.

21. *New York Times*, June 15, 1946, 1.

22. *New York Times,* June 20, 1946, 1.

23. Keith Kyle, *Suez: Britain's End of Empire in the Middle East* (London: I. B. Tauris, 2003); John Lewis Gaddis, *We Now Know: Rethinking Cold War History* (New York: Oxford University Press, 1997), 173.

24. Diane B. Kunz, *The Economic Diplomacy of the Suez Crisis* (Chapel Hill: University of North Carolina Press, 1991), 192–93.

25. Greg Thielmann, "The Missile Gap Myth and Its Progeny," *Arms Control Today* 41, no. 4 (May 2011).

26. John J. Mearsheimer, "Back to the Future: Instability in Europe after the Cold War," *International Security* 15, no. 1 (Summer 1990): 10–11.

27. For perceptive analyses, see Robert J. McMahon, *Cold War in the Periphery: The United States, India and Pakistan* (New York: Columbia University Press, 1994); Yezid Sayigh and Avi Shlaim, eds., *The Cold War and the Middle East* (Oxford: Clarendon, 1997); Albert Laued, *Southeast Asia and the Cold War* (London: Routledge, 2012); Tanya Harmer, "The Cold War in Latin America," in *The Routledge Handbook of the Cold War,* ed. Artemy M. Kalinovsky and Craig Daigle (London: Routledge, 2014), 133–48; and Jeffrey James Byme, "The Cold War in Africa," in Kalinovsky and Daigle, *Routledge Handbook of the Cold War,* 149–62.

28. Fred Halliday, "The Middle East, the Great Powers, and the Cold War," in Sayigh and Shlaim, *The Cold War and the Middle East,* 9.

29. The term *Third World* was first used by French anthropologist Alfred Sauvy in 1952 to distinguish the states from the Western and Eastern Bloc countries. On this, see Amandeep Sandhu, "Third World," in *Encyclopedia of the Developing World,* ed. Thomas M. Leonard (New York; Routledge, 2003), 3:1542–45. Later it became a somewhat pejorative term and the preferred term today is *developing world.*

30. See Wohlforth, *The Elusive Balance,* 188–89.

31. See Steve Coll, *Ghost Wars* (New York: Penguin, 2004).

32. See Lorenz M. Luthi, "The US Accommodation of Communist China," in Paul, *Accommodating Rising Powers,* 131–49. See, for example: Margaret MacMillan, *Nixon in China: The Week That Changed the World* (New York: Penguin, 2006); William C. Kirby, Robert S. Ross, and Gong Li, eds., *Normalization of U.S.-China Relations: An International History* (Cambridge, MA: Harvard University Press, 2005); Enrico Fardella, "The Sino-American Normalization: A Reassessment," *Diplomatic History* 33, no. 4 (September 2009): 545–78.

33. Raymond L. Garthoff, *Détente and Confrontation* (Washington, DC: Brookings Institution, 1985), 33.

34. See Fareed Zakaria, "The Reagan Strategy of Containment," *Political Science Quarterly* 105, no. 3 (Autumn, 1990): 373–95.

35. Jawaharlal Nehru, "Free India's Foreign Policy," March 15, 1946, in *Selected Works,* 2nd ser., 55 vols. (New Delhi: Nehru Memorial Museum and Library, 1984–2014), 15:525; Nehru, "2. Basic Principles," September 12, 1948, in *Selected Works,* 7:612.

36. Nehru, "2. Basic Principles," 7:612.

37. See Rahul Mukherji, "Appraising the Legacy of Bandung: A View from India," in *Bandung Revisited: The Legacy of the 1955 Asian African Conference for International Order,* ed. See Seng Tan and Amitav Acharya (Singapore: National University of Singapore Press, 2008), 168.

38. Amitav Acharya and See Seng Tan, "The Normative Relevance of the Bandung Conference for Contemporary Asia and International Order," in Tan and Acharya, *Bandung Revisited,* 8–10.

39. George McTurnan Kahin, *The Asia-African Conference* (Ithaca: Cornell University Press, 1956), 80–81; Clive Christie, *Ideology and Revolution in Southeast Asia, 1900–1980* (Richmond, UK: Curzon, 2001), 132.

40. Final communiqué of the Asian-African Conference held at Bandung, April 18–24, 1955, reprinted in *Interventions* 11, no. 1 (March 2009): 94–102.

41. Tan and Acharya, *Bandung Revisited,* 169. On the importance of the Bandung conference for the emergence of a pluralistic conception of international society, see Richard Devetak, Tim Dunne, and Ririn Tri Nurhayati, "Bandung 60 Years On: Revolt and Resilience in International Society," *Australian Journal of International Affairs,* 70, no. 4 (June 2016): 358–73.

42. M. S. Rajan, *Nonalignment & Nonaligned Movement* (New Delhi: Vikas, 1990), 9–10.

43. Cairo Summit Declaration, 24, cited in ibid., 5.

44. Cited in Rajan, *Nonalignment & Nonaligned Movement,* 7.

45. Radovan Vukadinovic, "The Various Conceptions of European Neutrality," in *Between the Blocs: Problems and Prospects for Europe's Neutral and Nonaligned States,* ed. Joseph Kruzel and Michael H. Haltzel (Cambridge: Cambridge University Press, 1989), 30.

46. Rajan, *Nonalignment & Nonaligned Movement,* 10.

47. Cyril E. Black and Richard A. Falk, *Neutralization and World Politics* (Princeton: Princeton University Press, 2015), 18.

48. Vukadinovic, "The Various Conceptions," 40

49. Rajan, *Nonalignment & Nonaligned Movement,* 25.

50. For these efforts, see A. W. Singham and Shirley Hune, "Principles of Nonalignment," in U. S. Bajpai, ed., *Non-alignment: Perspectives and Prospects* (New Delhi: Lancers, 1983), 4, 15.

51. P. R. Chari, "Nonalignment and Disarmament," in Bajpai, *Non-alignment,* 118.

52. On the role of the nonaligned states in nuclear disarmament campaigns, see Alva Myrdal, *The Game of Disarmament* (New York: Pantheon Books, 1982), 84–89; M. A. Husain, "Third World and Disarmament: Shadow and Substance," *Third World Quarterly* 2, no. 1 (January 1980): 76–99; T. T. Poulose, *United Nations and Nuclear Proliferation* (New Delhi: B. R. Publishing, 1988).

53. On these, see Myrdal, *The Game of Disarmament,* 84–89.

54. International Court of Justice, "Legality of the Threat of Use of Nuclear Weapons, Advisory Opinion," *ICJ Reports 1996,* July 8, 1996, 15–16.

55. T. V. Paul, *The Tradition of Non-use of Nuclear Weapons* (Stanford: Stanford University Press, 2009), 159–60; Nina Tannenwald, *The Nuclear Taboo* (Cambridge: Cambridge University Press, 2007).

56. Roy Allison, *The Soviet Union and the Strategy of Non-alignment in the Third World* (Cambridge: Cambridge University Press, 1988), 105.

57. Ibid., 85–86.

58. Lorenz M. Luthi argues that it was the Arab-Asian group at the United Nations that took the initiative in bringing this to the UN, although the Afro-Asian Movement played a role as well. Luthi, "Non-alignment, 1946–1965: Its Establishment and Struggle against Afro-Asianism," *Humanity* 7, no. 2 (Summer 2016): 206.

59. Michael Brecher, *The New States of Asia: A Political Analysis* (New York: Oxford University Press, 1966), 167.

60. Rinna Kullaa, *Non-alignment and Its Origins in Cold War Europe* (London: I. B. Tauris, 2012), 49.

61. Ibid., 50.

62. Natasa Miscovic, "Between Idealism and Pragmatism: Tito, Nehru and the Hungarian Crisis, 1956," in Miscovic, Fischer-Tine, and Boskovska, *Non-Aligned Movement and the Cold War*, 121–22. See also George Mikes, *The Hungarian Revolution* (London: André Deutsch, 1957).

63. Kullaa, *Non-alignment*, 109–10.

64. Swapna Kona Nayudu, "Responses to Russian Interventionism: India and the Questions of Hungary, 1956 and Crimea, 2014," January 12, 2015, Center for the Advanced Study of India, Philadelphia, https://casi.sas.upenn.edu/iit/swapnakonanayudu.

65. On this war, see Srinath Raghavan, *1971: A Global History of the Creation of Bangladesh* (Cambridge, MA: Harvard University Press, 2013).

66. Allison, *The Soviet Union and the Strategy of Non-alignment*, 3.

67. Garthoff, *Détente and Confrontation*, 679.

68. Allison, *The Soviet Union and the Strategy of Non-alignment*, 4; Peter Lyon, "The Non-aligned Movement: Performance and Prospects," in Bajpai, *Non-alignment*, 29.

69. Allison, *The Soviet Union and the Strategy of Non-alignment*, 5.

70. For these French efforts, see Layne, *The Peace of Illusions*, 100–102.

71. Vukadinovic, "The Various Conceptions."

72. Immanuel Adler, "Seeds of Peaceful Change: The OSCE's Security Community-Building Model," in *Security Communities*, ed. Immanuel Adler and Michael Barnett (Cambridge: Cambridge University Press, 1998), 127.

FIVE The Post–Cold War Era

1. Ann Devroy and R. Jeffrey Smith, "Clinton Reexamines a Foreign Policy under Siege," *Washington Post*, October 17, 1993, A1.

2. Eligible states are those great powers that are most concerned by the growth of American power and those that possess the actual or potential capabilities to engage in balance-of-power coalition building vis-à-vis the U.S. On U.S. dominance, see also

Nuno P. Monteiro, *Theory of Unipolar Politics* (Cambridge: Cambridge University Press, 2014).

3. On comparative military spending, see Stockholm International Peace Research Institute, *SIPRI Yearbook* (Oxford: Oxford University Press, 2004). On R&D spending, see www.bicc.de/publications/survey/2004/press_release_survey2004.html.

4. William Wohlforth, "Revisiting Balance of Power Theory in Central Eurasia," in Paul, Wirtz, and Fortmann, *Balance of Power*, 214–38.

5. Stephen G. Brooks and William C. Wohlforth, *World out of Balance: International Relations and the Challenge of American Primacy* (Princeton: Princeton University Press, 2008), 45.

6. John M. Owen IV, "Transnational Liberalism and U.S. Primacy," *International Security* 26, no. 3 (Winter 2001–2): 117–52. For alternative views, see William C. Wohlforth, "The Stability of a Unipolar World," *International Security* 24, no. 1 (Summer 1999): 5–41; Charles A. Kupchan, "After Pax Americana: Benign Power, Regional Integration, and the Sources of Stable Multipolarity," *International Security* 23, no. 2 (Fall 1998): 40–79; Michael Mastanduno, "A Realist View: Three Images of the Coming International Order," in *International Order and the Future of World Politics*, ed. T. V. Paul and John A. Hall (Cambridge: Cambridge University Press, 1999), 19–40.

7. G. John Ikenberry, "Liberal Hegemony and the Future of American Postwar Order," in Paul and Hall, *International Order*, 123–45; Ikenberry, *After Victory*.

8. On this, see the chapters in Edward D. Mansfield and Brian M. Pollins, eds., *Economic Interdependence and International Conflict* (Ann Arbor: University of Michigan Press, 2003); Thomas L. Friedman, *Lexus and the Olive Tree: Understanding Globalization* (New York: Farrar, Straus & Giroux, 2000).

9. On liberal imperialism as argued in Machiavelli's *Discourses on Levy* and Schumpeter's *Sociology of Imperialisms*, see Michael Doyle, "Liberalism and World Politics," *American Political Science Review* 80, no. 4 (December 1986): 1154–55.

10. An example is the U.S.-China-Pakistan alliance versus the Russia-India quasi-alliance in the 1970s in which both sides had one liberal-democratic state as a member.

11. Kenneth N. Waltz, "Structural Realism after the Cold War," *International Security* 25, no. 1 (Summer 2000): 5–41; Colin Gray, "Clausewitz Rules, OK? The Future Is the Past—with GPS," *Review of International Studies* 25, no. 5 (December 1999): 169.

12. Christopher Layne, "The War on Terrorism and Balance of Power: The Paradoxes of American Hegemony," in Paul, Wirtz, and Fortmann, *Balance of Power*, 103–26.

13. For arguments for and against this, see Sean M. Lynn-Jones, ed., *The Cold War and After: Prospects for Peace* (Cambridge, MA: MIT Press, 1992); Waltz, "Structural Realism After the Cold War"; Mearsheimer, *The Tragedy of Great Power Politics*, ch. 10; Gilpin, *War and Change in World Politics*; Christopher Layne, "The Unipolar Illusion: Why New Great Powers Will Rise," *International Security* 17, no. 4 (Spring 1993): 5–51.

14. Schroeder, "Historical Reality versus Neorealist Theory"; Brawley, "The Political Economy of Balance of Power Theory," 76–99.

15. Kennedy, *The Rise and Fall of Great Powers*. Theorists of power transition, power cycles, and hegemonic cycles of various hues believe in the rise and fall of great

powers. See A. F. K. Organski and Jacek Kugler, *The War Ledger* (Chicago: University of Chicago Press, 1980); Kugler and Lemke, *Parity and War;* and Ronald Tammen et al., *Power Transitions: Strategies for the 21st Century* (New York: Chatham House, 2000).

16. Levy, "What Do Great Powers Balance Against and When?" 45.

17. Posen, *Restraint,* 29.

18. Walt, *Taming American Power,* 161–71.

19. On these, see T. V. Paul, "Introduction: The Enduring Axioms of Balance of Power Theory and Their Contemporary Relevance," in Paul, Wirtz, and Fortmann, *Balance of Power,* 1–25.

20. Walt, *Taming American Power,* 126–32, 25.

21. For this concept, see Inis L. Claude Jr., *The Changing United Nations* (New York: Random House, 1967), ch. 4. See also Martha Finnemore, *The Purposes of Intervention* (Ithaca: Cornell University Press, 2003).

22. On the events that led to the war, see Human Rights Watch, *World Report 1999* (Federal Republic of Yugoslavia) (New York: Human Rights Watch, 1999); Alan K. Henrikson, "The Constraint of Legitimacy: The Legal and Institutional Framework of Euro-Atlantic Security," in *Alliance Politics: Kosovo and NATO's War: Allied Force or Forced Allies?* ed. Pierre Martin and Mark R. Brawley (New York: Palgrave, 2000), 48; *International Herald Tribune,* October 2, 1998.

23. The Russian posture was driven by the assumption that Kosovo was Yugoslavia's internal affair and centrifugal forces within Russia dictated caution. Oleg Levitin, "Inside Moscow's Kosovo Muddle," *Survival* 42, no. 1 (Spring 2000): 131; Simon Saradzhyan, "Russia Won't Back Down on Kosovo," *Moscow Times,* October 8, 1998, quoted in Levitin, "Inside Moscow's Kosovo Muddle," 136.

24. Ekaterina A. Stepanova, "Explaining Russia's Dissention on Kosovo," *PONARS Policy Memo* 57 (Moscow: Carnegie Center, March 1999).

25. For these considerations, see Oksana Antonenko, "Russia, NATO and European Security After Kosovo," *Survival,* 41, no. 4 (Winter 1999–2000): 124–44.

26. Ibid., 136.

27. Rebecca J. Johnson, "Russian Responses to Crisis Management in the Balkans," *Demokratizatziya* 9, no. 2 (Spring 2001): 298–99.

28. Ibid., 300.

29. Steven L. Burg, "Coercive Diplomacy in the Balkans: The Use of Force in Bosnia and Kosovo," in *The United States and Coercive Diplomacy,* ed. Robert J. Art and Patrick M. Cronin (Washington, DC: U.S. Institute of Peace Press, 2003), 100.

30. On this, see Marc Weller, *Contested Statehood: Kosovo's Struggle for Independence* (Oxford: Oxford University Press, 2009), 229–37; Tim Judah, *Kosovo: What Everyone Needs to Know* (Oxford: Oxford University Press, 2008).

31. For documents outlining these changes, see Alexei G. Arbatov, *The Transformation of Russian Military Doctrine: Lessons Learned from Kosovo and Chechnya,* Marshall Center Papers #2, www.eng.yabloko.ru/Brooks?Arbatov/rus-military.html.

32. Russell Ong, *China's Security Interests in the Post–Cold War Era* (London: Curzon, 2002), 142. According to one Chinese analyst, the U.S. intervention in Kosovo was

part of a "python strategy" of using "its thickest body to coil tightly around the world and prevent any country from possessing the ability to stand up to it." Cheng Guang-zhong, "Kosovo War and the US 'Python Strategy,'" Hong Kong, Ta Kung Pao, June 2, 1999, www.mtholyoke.edu/acad/intrel/cheng.htm. Rosemary Foot, "China and the Idea of a Responsible State," in *Power and Responsibility in Chinese Foreign Policy*, ed. Yongjin Zhang and Greg Austin (Canberra: Asia-Pacific, 2001), 41.

33. Evan A. Feigenbaum, "China's Challenge to Pax Americana," *Washington Quarterly* 24, no. 3 (January 2001): 31–43.

34. "Security Council Rejects Demand for Cessation of Use of Force against Fed-eral Republic of Yugoslavia," UNSC press release, March 26, 1999, https://www.un.org/press/en/1999/19990326.sc6659.html.

35. Yu Bin, "NATO's Unintended Consequence: A Deeper Strategic Partnership . . . or More," *Comparative Connections* 1, no. 1 (July 1999): 67–72.

36. Tyler Marshall, "Anti-NATO Axis Poses Threat, Experts Say," *Los Angeles Times*, September 27, 1999, A1.

37. John Cheriyan, "A Strategic Partnership," *Frontline*, October 14–27, 2000; Julie M. Rahm, "Russia, China, India: A New Strategic Triangle for a New Cold War?" *Param-eters* (Winter 2001–2): 87–97. The Russian efforts continued in 2002 when Putin visited China and India. "Putin Keen on Triangle," *Hindu*, December 9, 2002.

38. Raju G. C. Thomas, "South Asian Security Balance in a Western Dominant World," in Paul, Wirtz, and Fortmann, *Balance of Power*, 322, 324.

39. Ariel Cohen, "The Russia-China Friendship and Cooperation Treaty: A Stra-tegic Shift in Eurasia," *Backgrounder*, July 18, 2001 (Washington, DC: Heritage Founda-tion); see also Igor S. Ivanov, *The New Russian Diplomacy* (Washington, DC: Brookings Institution Press, 2002); J. L. Black, *Vladimir Putin and the New World Order* (Lanham, MD: Rowman & Littlefield, 2004), ch. 11.

40. Chaka Ferguson, "The Strategic Use of Soft Balancing: The Normative Di-mensions of the Chinese-Russian 'Strategic Partnership,'" *Journal of Strategic Studies* 35, no. 2 (January 2012): 197–222.

41. Song, "Feeling Safe, Being Strong."

42. *Washington Post*, October 23, 2002, A23.

43. Sergey Lavrov, Russian ambassador to the UN, stated to the Security Council: "The Resolution deflects the direct threat of war" and, according to France's UN ambassador, Jean-David Levitte, "as a result of intensive negotiations, the resolution that has just been adopted does not contain any provision about automatic use of force." Colum Lynch, "Security Council Resolution Tells Iraq It Must Disarm; Baghdad Ordered to Admit Inspectors or Face Consequences, *Washington Post*, November 10, 2002, A26.

44. *Washington Post*, January 21, 2003, A01.

45. Peter Finn, "U.S.-Europe Rifts Widen over Iraq," *Washington Post*, February 11, 2003, A01.

46. Peter Finn, "Chirac, Schroeder Make Counterproposal," *Washington Post*, February 25, 2003, A17.

47. The United Nations (New York), Security Council, Joint Statement by Mr. de Villepin, Mr. Ivanov, and Mr. Fischer, Paris, March 5, 2003, S/2003/253, https://unispal. un.org/DPA/DPR/unispal.nsf/0/C00BA18B56C76BAF85256CE20056898F.

48. *Washington Post,* March 6, 2003, A19. For a chronology of events, see Michael J. Glennon, "Why the Security Council Failed," *Foreign Affairs* 82, no. 3 (May–June 2003), 16–35.

49. Bradley Graham, "U.S. Official Appeals to NATO for Military Support," *Washington Post,* January 17, 2003, A15.

50. *Washington Post,* January 23, 2003, A01; *Washington Post,* February 12, 2003, A18.

51. Keith B. Richburg, "E.U. Unity on Iraq Proves Short-lived; France Again Threatens to Veto U.N. Resolution Mandating Force," *Washington Post,* February 19, 2003, A24.

52. Glen Frankel, "Chirac Fortifies Antiwar Caucus; 52 African Leaders Endorse French Stance toward Iraq," *Washington Post,* February 22, 2003, A19.

53. *Washington Post,* March 22, 2003, A30.

54. Michael Wines, "3 War Critics Want U.N. Effort to Rebuild but Say Allies Must Act Now," *New York Times,* April 12, 2003, 10.

55. Keith B. Richburg, "French Sees Iraq Crisis Imperiling Rule of Law; Concern Focuses on Future International Order," *Washington Post,* March 6, 2003, A19. See also *Le Figaro,* March 21, 2003, 14, www.figaro.fr.

56. Peter Finn, "U.S.-Style Campaign with Anti-U.S. Theme: German Gain by Opposing Iraq Attack," *Washington Post,* September 19, 2002, A1.

57. Klaus Larres, "Mutual Incomprehension: U.S.-German Value Gaps beyond Iraq," *Washington Quarterly* 26, no. 2 (2003): 23–42; Anja Dalgaard-Nielsen, "Gulf War: The German Resistance," *Survival* 45, no. 1 (Spring 2003): 99–116.

58. David B. Rivkin Jr. and Lee A. Casey, "Leashing the Dogs of War," *National Interest,* no. 73 (Fall 2003): 57–69; Joachim Krause, "Multilateralism: Behind European Views," *Washington Quarterly* 27, no. 2 (2004): 43–59.

59. William Pfaff, "The Iraq Issue: The Real Issue Is American Power," *International Herald Tribune,* March 14, 2003.

60. Reus-Smit, *American Power and World Order,* 53–61.

61. Richard A. Falk, *The Cost of War: International Law, the UN, and World Order after Iraq* (New York: Routledge, 2008), 145.

62. In Obama's words: "Now, when I ran for President eight years ago as a candidate who had opposed the decision to go to war in Iraq, I said that America didn't just have to end that war—we had to end the mindset that got us there in the first place. It was a mindset characterized by a preference for military action over diplomacy; a mindset that put a premium on unilateral U.S. action over the painstaking work of building international consensus; a mindset that exaggerated threats beyond what the intelligence supported. . . . More than a decade later, we still live with the consequences of the decision to invade Iraq. Our troops achieved every mission they were given. But thousands of lives were lost, tens of thousands wounded. That doesn't count the lives

lost among Iraqis. Nearly a trillion dollars was spent. Today, Iraq remains gripped by sectarian conflict, and the emergence of al Qaeda in Iraq has now evolved into ISIL." Remarks by the President on the Iran Nuclear Deal, American University, Washington, DC, August 5, 2015, https://obamawhitehouse.archives.gov/the-press-office/2015/08/05/remarks-president-iran-nuclear-deal.

63. On the diplomatic and military interactions between the U.S. and Iraq prior to the war, see Frank P. Harvey and Patrick James, "Deterrence and Compellence in Iraq, 1991–2003: Lessons for a Complex Paradigm," in Paul, Morgan, and Wirtz, *Complex Deterrence*, 222–56.

64. See the UNSC press release: https://www.un.org/press/en/2004/sc8117.doc. htm. France, Russia, and China had called for stronger language to ensure full sovereignty after June 30: www.IHT.com, June 7, 2004.

65. Barack Obama, "Renewing American Leadership," *Foreign Affairs* 86, no. 4 (July–August 2007): 11.

66. For a timeline of the war in Iraq, see http://content.time.com/time/specials /packages/completelist/0,29569,1967340,00.html.

67. Pew Research Center, "America's Image in the World: Findings from the Pew Global Attitudes Project," March 14, 2007, http://www.pewglobal.org/2007/03/14 /americas-image-in-the-world-findings-from-the-pew-global-attitudes-project/.

68. Michael Cox, "Too Big to Fail? The Transatlantic Relationship from Bush to Obama," *Global Policy* 3, no. 1 (2012): 71–78.

69. Remarks by Hillary Clinton during Senate Foreign Relations Committee Hearing on January 13, http://www.npr.org/templates/story/story.php?storyId=99290981.

70. On the last U.S. troops leaving in December 2011, see Greg Jaffe, "Last American Troops Cross Iraqi Border into Kuwait," *Washington Post,* December 18, 2011, A10.

71. David A. Lake, *Hierarchy in International Relations* (Ithaca: Cornell University Press, 2009), x. There is also a deep reflection on the war and the role of legitimacy in President Obama's decision to adopt a pragmatic approach toward regional conflicts; in order for America "to leverage its power, it needed to cooperate with allies and facilitate intermediaries rather than always accepting the costs of leadership." Jacob Shively, *Hope, Change, Pragmatism: Analyzing Obama's Grand Strategy* (New York: Palgrave Macmillan, 2016), 2.

72. On this, see Thomas Henriksen, *American Foreign Policy in the 21st Century* (New York: Palgrave Macmillan, 2017), 266–67. On the Security Council resolution authorizing a no-fly zone over Libya to protect civilians, see United Nations Security Council, 6,498th Meeting, SC/10200, March 17, 2011, https://www.un.org/press/en/2011/sc10200.doc.htm.

six Rising China and Soft Balancing

1. For the Xi speech, see World Economic Forum, January 17, 2017, https://www. weforum.org/agenda/2017/01/full-text-of-xi-jinping-keynote-at-the-world-economic-forum.

2. Charles Clover, "Russia Resumes Advanced Weapons Sales to China," *Financial Times,* November 3, 2016, https://www.ft.com/content/90b1ada2-a18e-11e6-86d5-4e36b35c3550.

3. I owe Kai He for this line of argument.

4. For the rationale behind hedging, see Kuik Cheng-Chwee, "The Essence of Hedging: Malaysia and Singapore's Response to a Rising China," *Contemporary Southeast Asia* 30, no. 2 (August 2008): 159–85; David Shambaugh, "Containment or Engagement of China: Calculating Beijing's Responses," *International Security* 21, no. 2 (Fall 1996): 180–209.

5. John D. Ciorciari, *The Limits of Alignment: Southeast Asia and the Great Powers since 1975* (Washington, DC: Georgetown University Press, 2010); Cheng-Chwee, "The Essence of Hedging."

6. George W. Bush, *National Security Strategy of the United States* (Washington, DC: White House, 2006), 41–42.

7. Fareed Zakaria, "A 'Hedge' Strategy toward China," *Washington Post,* November 15, 2010.

8. Ibid.

9. In one of the most recent such statements, Foreign Minister Wang Yi "compared world order to a well-designed building, with multilateralism as the most important cornerstone and international organizations such as the united nations the most important pillars." Benny Kung, "China to Reform World Order, Not Create New One," *Asia Times,* March 9, 2017, http://www.atimes.com/article/china-reform-world-order-not-create-new-one/.

10. Thomas J. Christensen, *The China Challenge: Shaping the Choices of a Rising Power* (New York: Norton, 2015), 295.

11. David Shambaugh, "China Engages Asia: Reshaping the Regional Order," *International Security* 29, no. 3 (Winter 2004–5): 64–99. See also Evan S. Medeiros, *China's International Behavior* (Santa Monica, CA: RAND Corporation, 2009).

12. David C. Kang, "Hierarchy, Balancing, and Empirical Puzzles in Asian International Relations," *International Security* 28, no. 3 (Winter 2003–4): 165–80; David C. Kang, "Getting Asia Wrong: The Need for New Analytical Frameworks," *International Security* 27, no. 4 (Spring 2003): 57–85; Amitav Acharya, "Will Asia's Past Be Its Future?" *International Security* 28, no. 3 (Winter 2003–4): 149–64; Steve Chan, "Unbalanced Threat or Rising Integration? Explaining Relations across the Taiwan Strait," in *New Thinking about the Taiwan Issue,* ed. Jean-Marc F. Blanchard and Dennis V. Hickey (New York: Routledge, 2012), 92–115.

13. On the ASEAN Regional Forum, see Rosemary Foot, "China in the ASEAN Regional Forum," *Asian Survey* 38, no. 5 (May 1998): 425–40; Kai He, *Institutional Balancing in the Asia Pacific* (London: Routledge, 2008).

14. Denny Roy, "Southeast Asia and China: Balancing or Bandwagoning?" *Contemporary Southeast Asia* 27, no. 2 (August 2005): 305–22; Evelyn Goh, "Great Powers and Southeast Asian Regional Security Strategies: Omni-enmeshment, Balancing and Hierarchical Order" (working paper 84, Institute of Defence and Strategic Studies, Singapore, 2005).

15. Paul, "Introduction: The Enduring Axioms of Balance of Power Theory."

16. Chan, *Looking for Balance*, 5.

17. David C. Kang, "Between Balancing and Bandwagoning: South Korea's Response to China," *Journal of East Asian Studies* 9, no. 1 (April 2009): 1–28.

18. Chan, *Looking for Balance*.

19. For these data, see UNCTAD, *World Investment Report, 2017*, 12–14, http://unctad.org/en/PublicationsLibrary/wir2017_en.pdf?lien_externe_oui=Continue.

20. Roy, "Southeast Asia and China."

21. I thank John Ciorciari for pointing out these initiatives. On various ASEAN initiatives, see Kishore Mahbabuni and Jeffery Sng, *The ASEAN Miracle: A Catalyst for Peace* (Singapore: National University of Singapore Press, 2017).

22. Fu Ying and Wu Shicun, "South China Sea: How We Got to This Stage," *National Interest*, May 9, 2016, http://nationalinterest.org/feature/south-china-sea-how-we-got-stage-16118; Linda Jakobson, *China's Unpredictable Maritime Security Actors* (Sydney: Lowy Institute for International Policy, December 2014); M. Taylor Fravel, "U.S. Policy towards the Disputes in the South China Sea since 1995," *Policy Report* (Singapore: S. Rajaratnam School of International Studies, 2014); Hugh White, "Explaining China's Behaviour in the East and South China Seas," *Interpreter*, May 22, 2014, http://www.lowyinterpreter.org/post/2014/05/22/Explaining-Chinas-behaviour-in-the-East-and-South-China-Seas.aspx.

23. Michael Leifer, *The ASEAN Regional Forum: Extending ASEAN's Model of Regional Security* (Oxford: Oxford University Press, 1996); Sheldon W. Simon, "Security Prospects in Southeast Asia: Collaborative Efforts and the ASEAN Regional Forum," *Pacific Review* 11, no. 2 (1998): 195–212; Foot, "China in the ASEAN Regional Forum."

24. Alastair Iain Johnston, *Social States: China in International Institutions, 1980–2000* (Princeton: Princeton University Press, 2008); Evelyn Goh, "Great Powers and Hierarchical Order in Southeast Asia: Analyzing Regional Security Strategies." *International Security* 32, no. 3 (Winter 2007): 113–57.

25. Amitav Acharya, "Foundations of Collective Action in Asia: Theory and Practice of Regional Cooperation" (working paper 344, ADBI, February 2012), https://www.econstor.eu/bitstream/10419/101269/1/685361837.pdf.

26. "2002 Declaration on the Conduct of Parties in the South China Sea," adopted by the foreign ministers of ASEAN and the People's Republic of China at the 8th ASEAN Summit in Phnom Penh, November 4, 2002, https://cil.nus.edu.sg/rp/pdf/2002%20Declaration%20on%20the%20Conduct%20of%20Parties%20in%20the%20South%20China%20Sea-pdf.pdf.

27. Simon Denyer and Emily Rauhala, "Territorial Claims by China Dealt Sharp Blow," *Washington Post*, July 13, 2016, A12.

28. US Economic and Security Review Commission, "China's Economic Ties with ASEAN: A Country-by-Country Analysis," March 17, 2015, https://www.uscc.gov/sites/default/files/Research/China%27s%20Economic%20Ties%20with%20ASEAN.pdf.

29. Barry Desker, "The Eagle and the Panda: An Owl's View from Southeast Asia," *Asia Policy* 15, no. 1 (January 2013): 30.

30. For the slow U.S. response to Chinese activities in the South China Sea, see "Flaws in the Diamond," *Economist*, September 21, 2013, 81–82. For the constraints on the U.S. in this regard, see Ashley J. Tellis, *Balancing without Containment: An American Strategy for Managing China* (Washington, DC: Carnegie Endowment for international Peace, 2014).

31. Jethro Mullen, "Why Is Trump Backing Off His China Threats?" CNN Wire Service, February 10, 2017.

32. Justin McCurry and Tania Branigan, "Obama Says US will Defend Japan in Island Dispute with China," *Guardian*, April 24, 2014, https://www.theguardian.com/world/2014/apr/24/obama-in-japan-backs-status-quo-in-island-dispute-with-china.

33. Hillary Clinton, "America's Pacific Century," *Foreign Policy* 189 (November 2011).

34. Hillary Clinton, Forestall Lecture at the Naval Academy, Annapolis, April 10, 2012, http://iipdigital.usembassy.gov/st/english/texttrans/2012/04/201204113625.html.

35. For Obama's rebalance/pivot strategy, see the CRS report: http://oai.dtic.mil/oai/oai?verb=getRecord&metadataPrefix=html&identifier=ADA584466.

36. Department of Defense, *Sustaining U.S. Global Leadership: Priorities for 21st Century Defense*, January 2012, http://archive.defense.gov/news/Defense_Strategic_Guidance.pdf, called for a "rebalancing toward the Asia-Pacific Region."

37. *Christian Science Monitor*, May 3, 2017, https://www.csmonitor.com/USA/Foreign-Policy/2017/0503/In-rejecting-Obama-s-Asia-pivot-did-Trump-leap-before-he-looked.

38. It was Dennis Kux, a former U.S. diplomat, who coined the term *Estranged Democracies* to characterize U.S.-India relations. See his *India and the United States: Estranged Democracies* (Washington, DC: National Defense University Press, 1992).

39. On this, see T. V. Paul and Mahesh Shankar, "Why the US-India Nuclear Accord Is a Good Deal," *Survival* 49, no. 4 (Winter 2007): 111–22.

40. For the China angle in Obama's visit, see David Brunnstrom, "Obama Will Visit India Again as Ties Expand," Reuters, November 21, 2014, http://www.reuters.com/article/2014/11/21/us-usa-obama-india-idUSKCN0J51Q320141121.

41. Sushant Singh, "LEMOA Agreement Signed: India, US Sign Key Defence Pact to Use Each Other's Bases for Repair, Supplies," *Indian Express*, August 31, 2016, http://indianexpress.com/article/india/india-news-india/manohar-parrikar-signs-key-logistics-defence-pact-with-us-3004581/.

42. C. Uday Bhaskar, "Malabar 2017 Isn't Aimed at China," *Hindustan Times*, July 11, 2017, 10.

43. *Hindu*, November 12, 2017, http://www.thehindu.com/news/national/india-highlights-indo-pacific-cooperation-at-the-first-quad-talks/article20317526.ece?homepage=true.

44. Ajay Kumar Das, "Can India Balance between China and America?" *National Interest*, May 10, 2016, http://nationalinterest.org/feature/can-india-balance-between-china-america-16137.

45. "India, US Reaffirm Strategic Partnership," *Times of India*, April 19, 2017, http://timesofindia.indiatimes.com/india/us-reaffirms-major-defence-partner-status-for-india/articleshow/58242327.cms.

46. "Why India and China Are Facing Off over a Remote Corner of the Himalayas," *Economist,* August 9, 2017, https://www.economist.com/blogs/economist-explains/2017/08/economist-explains-6.

47. Hanan Zaffar, "CPEC: Boon or Bane for Pakistan?" *Diplomat,* November 16, 2016, http://thediplomat.com/2016/11/cpec-boon-or-bane-for-pakistan/.

48. Rahul Singh, "From Submarines to Warships: How Chinese Navy Is Expanding Its Footprint in Indian Ocean," *Hindustan Times,* July 5, 2017, http://www.hindustantimes.com/india-news/from-submarines-to-warships-how-chinese-navy-is-expanding-its-footprint-in-indian-ocean/story-QeJp31UtBphNjya2z8L7gM.html.

49. On this, see Rajesh Basrur, Anit Mukherjee, and T. V. Paul, eds., *The Security Dilemma at Sea: India-China Maritime Competition* (London: Routledge).

50. The World Bank, World Development Indicators, 2013 and 2015, cited in Aseema Sinha, *Globalizing India: How Global Rules and Markets Are Shaping India's Rise to Power* (Cambridge: Cambridge University Press, 2016), 3.

51. Shalendra D. Sharma, *China and India in the Age of Globalization* (Cambridge: Cambridge University Press, 2009), 171. On the limited and managed nature of this rivalry, see *The China-India Rivalry in the Globalization Era,* ed. T. V. Paul (Washington, DC: Georgetown University Press, 2018).

52. For this, see World Bank, Indian GDP data (2000–2015) http://data.worldbank.org/country/india?view=chart.

53. David Malone and Rohan Mukherjee, "Polity, Security, and Foreign Policy in Contemporary India," in *South Asia's Weak States,* ed. T. V. Paul (Stanford: Stanford University Press, 2010), 147–69.

54. Anit Mukherjee and Yogesh Joshi, "Competing on Land and Sea: India's China Strategy" (paper presented at the RSIS South Asia Program Workshop, Singapore, January 20, 2017).

55. On India's defense spending, see *SIPRI Fact Sheet,* April 2017, https://www.sipri.org/sites/default/files/Trends-world-military-expenditure-2016.pdf.

56. "Malabar Naval Exercise to Feature Largest Warships of India, US, Japan," *Economic Times,* July 6, 2017, http://www.public.navy.mil/surfor/cg53/Pages/Three-nations-set-sail-for-exercise-Malabar-2016.aspx#.WV_Y7cYZNR4.

57. C. Rajamohan, "India: Between 'Strategic Autonomy' and 'Geopolitical Opportunity,'" *Asia Policy* 15, no. 1 (January 2013): 21–25.

58. Ibid., 25.

59. Michael Jonathan Green, "Managing Chinese Power: A View from Japan," in *Engaging China,* ed. Alastair Iain Johnston and Robert S. Ross (London: Routledge, 2002), 161–70.

60. On these, see International Crisis Group, "Old Scores and New Grudges: Solving Sino-Indian Tensions," *Asia Report,* no. 258 (July 2014): 1–52.

61. Yuki Tatsumi, "Japan Eyes 'Counter-Attack' Capability against North Korea Missile Threat," *Diplomat,* March 31, 2017, http://thediplomat.com/2017/03/japan-eyes-counter-attack-capability-against-north-korea-missile-threat/.

62. Motoko Rich, "Budget Plan for Japanese Armed Forces Urges a Boost: Missile Defense Is Focus amid Challenges from North Korea and China," *International New York Times,* September 1, 2016, 1.

63. Yuan-kang Wang, "China's Response to the Unipolar World: The Strategic Logic of Peaceful Development," *Journal of Asian and African Studies* 45, no. 5 (October 2010) 554–67.

64. Zheng Bijian, "China's 'Peaceful Rise' to Great Power Status," *Foreign Affairs* 84, no. 5 (September–October 2005): 18–24.

65. Rosemary Foot, "Chinese Strategies in a US Hegemonic Global Order: Accommodating and Hedging," *International Affairs* 82, no. 1 (January 2006): 93.

66. Denny Roy, "China's Reaction to American Predominance," *Survival* 45, no. 3 (Autumn 2003): 57–78.

67. Jian Zhang, "China's New Foreign Policy under Xi Jinping: 'Towards Peaceful Rise 2.0'?" *Peace, Security & Global Change* 27, no. 1 (January 2015): 5–19.

68. Neo-mercantilism is defined as deliberately depreciating the exchange rate of a national currency to support export-oriented industrialization. Going by this definition, China is characterized as a classical example of a neo-mercantilism state today. M. P. Dooley, D. Folkerts-Landau, and P. Garber, "The Revived Bretton Woods System," *International Journal of Finance and Economics* 9, no. 4 (October 2004): 307–13.

69. Yong Deng, "China Views Globalization: Toward a New Great Power Politics," *Washington Quarterly* 27, no. 3 (Summer 2004): 118.

70. On China's strategic partnership with Russia, see Vidya Nadkarni, *Strategic Partnerships in Asia: Balancing without Alliances* (New York: Routledge, 2010), ch.3.

71. Song, "Feeling Safe, Being Strong."

72. Alanna Petroff, "China's Defense Spending to Double to 233 Billion," http://money.cnn.com/2016/12/12/news/china-military-defense-defence-spending/.

73. For China's weapons development and acquisitions, see *Military Balance* 117, no. 1 (February 2017): 251, 254, 278.

SEVEN Balancing Resurgent Russia

1. Julian Borger, "Obama: Russia Just a Regional Power Showing Its Weakness: US President Restates G7 Threat of More Sanctions; Nuclear Terrorism 'More Worrying Than Putin,'" *Guardian,* March 26, 2014, 21; David Sherfinski, "McCain: 'Russia Is a Gas Station Masquerading as a Country,'" *Washington Times,* March 16, 2014, http://www.washingtontimes.com/news/2014/mar/16/mccain-russia-gas-station-masquerading-country.

2. Kathy Gilsinan and Krishnadev Calamur, "Did Putin Direct Russian Hacking? And Other Big Questions," *Atlantic,* January 6, 2017, https://www.theatlantic.com/international/archive/2017/01/russian-hacking-trump/510689/.

3. Tamara Cohen, "G8 Becomes the G7 as Leaders Kick Russia Out: It's Not a Big Problem, Says Russia's Foreign Minister," *Daily Mail,* March 24, 2014, http://www.dailymail.co.uk/news/article-2588490/G8-G7-leaders-kick-Russia-Its-not-big-problem-says-Putins-foreign-minister.html.

4. See the Group of 7 CFR Backgrounders, http://www.cfr.org/international-organizations-and-alliances/group-seven-g7/p32957; on the G-7 statements, see "The Hague Declaration," March 24, 2014, http://www.cfr.org/international-organizations-and-alliances/hague-declaration/p32647.

5. United Nations General Assembly (New York) Resolution, 68th Session, A/Res/68/262, April 1, 2014, http://www.un.org/press/en/2014/ga11493.doc.htm.

6. Iana Dreyer and Nicu Popescu, "Do Sanctions against Russia Work?" *European Union Institute for Security Studies Brief* 35 (December 2014): 1–4, https://www.iss.europa.eu/content/do-sanctions-against-russia-work.

7. Tim Daiss, "Prolonged Sanctions Rip into Russian Economy, Causing Angst for Putin," *Forbes*, August 19, 2016, https://www.forbes.com/sites/timdaiss/2016/08/19/prolonged-sanctions-rip-into-russia-causing-angst-for-putin/#5fe1fec439e5.

8. For instance, see Walter Russell Mead, "The Return of Geopolitics: The Revenge of the Revisionist Powers," *Foreign Affairs* 93 (June 2014): 69–79.

9. Tom Batchelor, "The Map That Shows How Many NATO Troops Are Deployed along Russia's Border," *Independent*, March 5, 2017, http://www.independent.co.uk/news/world/europe/russia-nato-border-forces-map-where-are-they-positioned a7562391.html.

10. On these, see Richard Sokolsky, "New NATO-Russia Military Balance: Implications for European Security," Carnegie Endowment for International Peace, Washington, DC, March 2017, http://carnegieendowment.org/2017/03/13/new-nato-russia-military-balance-implications-for-european-security-pub-68222.

11. "Europe Dodges Trump's Defense Spending Ultimatum," Reuters, February 21, 2017, http://www.reuters.com/article/us-usa-trump-nato-analysis-idUSKBN1601IF.

12. Walt, "Alliance Formation and the Balance of World Power."

13. For the core liberal mechanism of peace, see Bruce Russett and John R. Oneal, *Triangulating Peace: Democracy, Interdependence and International Organizations* (New York: Norton 2001). See also John R. Oneal, "Transforming Regional Security through Liberal Reforms," in *International Relations Theory and Regional Transformation*, ed. T. V. Paul (Cambridge: Cambridge University Press, 2012), 158–82.

14. OEC: Russia, Exports, Imports, and Trade Partners, http://atlas.media.mit.edu/en/profile/country/rus/.

15. OEC, China, Exports, Imports, and Trade Partners, http://atlas.media.mit.edu/en/profile/country/chn/.

16. "European Neighbourhood Policy and Enlargement Negotiations," http://ec.europa.eu/enlargement/policy/from-6-to-28-members/index_en.htm.

17. U.S. Department of State, "Fact Sheet: NATO Partnership for Peace," May 19, 1995, https://www.fas.org/man/nato/offdocs/us_95/dos950519.htm. On the reasons why NATO-Russia relations did not improve much, see Vincent Pouliot, *International Security in Practice: The Politics of NATO-Russia Diplomacy* (Cambridge: Cambridge University Press, 2010).

18. Roy Allison, "Russia Resurgent? Moscow's Campaign to 'Coerce Georgia to Peace,'" *International Affairs* 84, no. 6 (November 2008): 1145–71; Jim Nichol,

"Russia-Georgia Conflict in South Ossetia: Context and Implications for U.S. Interests," *CRS Report for Congress*, October 24, 2008.

19. Albert Hayrapetyan, "Why the Collective Security Treaty Organization Is a Pale Replica of NATO," *Russia Direct*, September 8, 2016, http://www.russia-direct.org/opinion/why-collective-security-treaty-organization-just-pale-replica-nato.

20. For these efforts, see James Siebens, "Russia and China's Emerging Strategy of Institutional Balancing," *THINK: International and Human Security*, November 2011, http://www.thinkihs.org/wp-content/uploads/2011/11/James-Siebens-Russia-China-2011.pdf.

21. Lars-Erik Lundin, "Returning to a Basic Level of Trust in Relations between Russia and the West," *SIPRI in the Media*, July–August 2014, http://www.sipri.org/media/newsletter/essay/lundin_aug14.

22. For a realist view on this, see John J. Mearsheimer, "Why the Ukraine Crisis Is the West's Fault," *Foreign Affairs* 93, no. 5 (September–October 2014): 77–89.

23. Military Doctrine of the Russian Federation, December 2014, http://www.scribd.com/doc/251695098/Russia-s-2014-Military-Doctrine#scribd; see also Dmitri Trenin, "2014: Russia's Military Doctrine Tells It All," December 29, 2014, http://carnegie.ru/eurasiaoutlook/?fa=57607.

24. Paul, Larson, and Wohlforth, *Status in World Politics*, chs. 1 and 2.

25. Cited in William C. Wohlforth, "Russia's Soft Balancing Act," in *Strategic Asia, 2003–4: Fragility and Crisis*, ed. Richard Ellings, Aaron Friedberg, and Michael Wills (Seattle: National Bureau of Asia Research, 2003), 167.

26. See Deborah Welch Larson and Alexei Shevchenko, "Managing the Rise of Great Powers: The Role of Status Concerns," in Paul, Larson, and Wohlforth, *Status in World Politics*, ch. 2.; Thomas J. Volgy, ed., *Major Powers and the Quest for Status in International Politics* (New York: Palgrave Macmillan, 2011); Deborah Welch Larson and Alexei Shevchenko, "Status Seekers: Chinese and Russian Responses to U.S. Primacy," *International Security* 34, no. 4 (Winter 2010): 63–95.

27. Trenin, "2014: Russia's Military Doctrine Tells It All."

28. Ibid.

29. For the Russia-China relationship, see Bobo Lo, *Axis of Convenience: Moscow, Beijing, and the New Geopolitics* (London: Chatham House, 2008); Huiyun Feng, "The New Geostrategic Game: Will China and Russia Form an Alliance against the United States?" *Policy Report*, no. 7 (Danish Institute for International Studies, Copenhagen, 2015).

30. On these, see Bob Savic, "Behind China and Russia's Special Relationship," *Diplomat*, December 7, 2016, http://thediplomat.com/2016/12/behind-china-and-russias-special-relationship/.

31. Jackson Diehl, "Eastern Europeans Are Bowing to Putin's Power," http://www.washingtonpost.com/opinions/jackson-diehl-eastern-europeans-are-bowing-to-putins-power/2014/10/12/2adbf4c2-4fd0-11e4-babe-e91da079cb8a_story.html.

32. On this, see Mordechai Chaziza, "Soft Balancing Strategy in the Middle East: Chinese and Russian Vetoes in the United Nations Security Council in the Syria Crisis," *China Report* 50, no.3 (August 2014): 243–58.

33. David E. Sanger, "Russia's Syria Campaign Cuts U.S. Influence over Outcome," *New York Times,* February 11, 2016, A1.

34. On this, see T. V. Paul, *Asymmetric Conflicts: War Initiation by Weaker Powers* (Cambridge: Cambridge University Press, 1994).

35. Albert O. Hirschman, *Exit, Voice, and Loyalty: Responses to Decline in Firms, Organizations, and States* (Cambridge, MA: Harvard University Press, 1970).

36. Henry Kissinger, "To Settle the Ukraine Crisis, Start at the End," *Washington Post,* March 5, 2014, http://www.washingtonpost.com/opinions/henry-kissinger-to-settle-the-ukraine-crisis-start-at-the-end/2014/03/05/46dad868-a496-11e3-8466-d34c451760b9_story.html.

EIGHT The Future of Balance of Power

1. Polybius, *The Histories,* trans. W. R. Paton (Cambridge, MA: Harvard University Press, 1960), 1:115.

2. For Obama's position on Iraq, articulated prior to the U.S. elections in 2008, see Barack Obama, "Renewing American Leadership," *Foreign Affairs* 86, no. 4 (July–August 2007): 11. The gist of Obama's foreign-policy vision, including his position on interventions and his desire to lead from behind, is nicely captured in Jeffrey Goldberg, "The Obama Doctrine," *Atlantic,* April 2016, https://www.theatlantic.com/magazine/archive/2016/04/the-obama-doctrine/471525/.

3. Aron, *Peace and War,* 70.

4. As Gulick powerfully contends: "One of the few things that we can be sure of in all history is that everything changes. In the long-run, flux will upset the best-laid plans of an earlier epoch. What once balanced nicely will for another generation hang as awkwardly as a wet toga." *Europe's Classical Balance of Power,* 40.

5. Waltz, "Structural Realism after the Cold War," 38. The challenge, as Brooks and Wohlforth argue, is that if balancing is for survival, then the power capabilities of opponents have to be superior to conquer, whereas autonomy can be challenged by concentrations below that threshold. Brooks and Wohlforth, *World out of Balance,* 49.

6. Kissinger, *A World Restored,* 6.

7. Gulick, *Europe's Classical Balance of Power,* 72, 75.

8. Randall Schweller has argued that "under-balancing" was the reason for the outbreak of World War II. See *Unanswered Threats.* However, there is little doubt that there were strong alliances and arms buildups during this era, although one can quibble about whether they were sufficient to balance properly. We may never know, as challengers would probably have devised asymmetric strategies to undercut balancing equilibrium, and they did so by inventing strategies such as blitzkrieg, which were designed to offset opponents' overall superiority.

9. *New York Times,* January 20, 2017, A1. "Assessing Russian Activities and Intentions in Recent US Elections," Washington, DC: Office of the Director of National Intelligence, Intelligence Community Assessment, ICA 2017-01D, January 6, 2017, https://www.dni.gov/files/documents/ICA_2017_01.pdf.

10. For an overview of these arguments and their criticism, see Christopher Layne, "The Unipolar Illusion Revisited: The Coming End of the United States' Unipolar Moment," *International Security* 31, no 2 (Fall 2006): 7–41.

11. William C. Wohlforth, "U.S. Strategy in a Unipolar World," in *America Unrivaled: The Future of the Balance of Power,* ed. G. John Ikenberry (Ithaca: Cornell University Press, 2002), 103–4. See also Wohlforth, "The Stability of a Unipolar World."

12. Layne has used the concept "coalition magnet" to describe this phenomenon. Layne, *The Peace of Illusions,* 135.

13. Brooks and Wohlforth, *World out of Balance,* 45.

14. Levy, "What Do Great Powers Balance Against and When?" 42.

15. G. John Ikenberry, introduction to Ikenberry, *America Unrivaled,* 10. See also Ikenberry, *Liberal Leviathan.*

16. On this, see Anne-Marie Slaughter, *The Chess-Board and the Web: Strategies of Connection in a Networked World* (New Haven: Yale University Press, 2017).

17. Jonathan Kirshner, "Globalization, American Power, and International Security," *Political Science Quarterly* 123, no. 3 (September 2008): 386.

18. For the Xi speech, see World Economic Forum, January 17, 2017, https://www.weforum.org/agenda/2017/01/full-text-of-xi-jinping-keynote-at-the-world-economic-forum.

19. Solomon Polachek, Carlos Seiglie, and Jun Xiang, "Globalization and International Conflict: Can FDI Increase Peace?" (paper presented at the Proceedings of the 10th Annual International Conference on Economics and Security, Thessaloniki, Greece, June 22–24, 2006). http://citeseerx.ist.psu.edu/viewdoc/download?doi=10.1.1.606.9277&rep=rep1&type=pdf.

20. Daniel W. Drezner, "Globalization and Policy Convergence," *International Studies Review* 3, no. 1 (Spring 2001): 76.

21. The earlier globalization era of roughly 1850 to 1914, characterized by open trade and mass migration, lost its momentum because of "political backlash developed in response to the actual or perceived distributional effects of globalization. The backlash led to the reimposition of tariffs and the adoption of immigration restrictions, even before the Great War. Far from being destroyed by unforeseen and exogenous political events, globalization, at least in part, destroyed itself." Kevin H. O'Rourke and Jeffrey G. Williamson, *Globalization and History* (Cambridge, MA: MIT Press, 1999), 287.

22. Karl Polanyi, *The Great Transformation* (Beacon Hill, MA: Beacon, 1957), 3–20.

23. Ibid., 132.

24. Ibid., 134.

25. Craig and George, *Force and Statecraft,* 46.

26. For such an argument, see Kang, "Getting Asia Wrong."

27. Acharya, "Will Asia's Past Be Its Future?"

28. David A. Lake, "Why 'Isms' Are Evil: Theory, Epistemology, and Academic Sects as Impediments to Understanding and Progress," *International Studies Quarterly* 55, no. 2 (January 2011): 465. On the virtues of eclectic theorizing, see Rudra Sil and Peter J. Katzenstein, *Beyond Paradigms: Analytic Eclecticism in the Study of World Politics* (New York: Palgrave Macmillan, 2010).

29. Steven E. Lobell, "Bringing Institutions Back into Realism" (paper presented at "Power Politics and International Institutions" workshop, Copenhagen, November 13, 2015).

30. Hamid Beladi and Reza Oladi, "On Smart Sanctions," *Economics Letters*, 130 (May 2015), 24–27; Joy Gordon, "Smart Sanctions Revisited," *Ethics & International Affairs*, 25, no.3 (October 2011): 315–35.

31. On this, see Joseph Nye, "Get Smart: Combining Hard and Soft Power," *Foreign Affairs* 88, no. 4 (July–August 2009): 160–63; Ernest J. Wilson, "Hard Power, Soft Power, Smart Power," *The ANNALS of the American Academy of Political and Social Science* 616, no. 1 (March 2008): 110–24.

32. Alexander L. George, *Bridging the Gap: Theory and Practice in Foreign Policy* (Washington, DC: U.S. Institute of Peace, 1993), 141–42.

33. A recent assessment of the soft-balancing research agenda calls for more attention to this dimension. See Huiyun Feng and Kai He, "Soft Balancing," in *Encyclopedia of Empirical International Relations Theory* (Oxford: Oxford University Press, 2017), http://politics.oxfordre.com/view/10.1093/acrefore/9780190228637.001.0001/acrefore-9780190228637-e-549.

34. Graham Allison, *Destined for War: Can America and China Escape Thucydides's Trap?* (Boston: Houghton Mifflin Harcourt, 2017).

35. Alexander George, *Forceful Persuasion: Coercive Diplomacy as an Alternative to War* (Washington, DC: U.S. Institute of Peace, 1991).

36. Allen Carlson, *Unifying China, Integrating with the World: Securing Chinese Sovereignty in the Reform Era* (Stanford: Stanford University Press, 2005).

37. Johnston, *Social States*, 197.

38. In the words of Chinese foreign minister Wang Yi, the postwar world order has been like an old building, which "may be aging and eroded but it is still shielding us from wind and rain, playing an indispensable role in maintaining world peace and facilitating human development." See Kung, "China to Reform World Order, Not Create New One."

39. On these, see Glenn H. Snyder, "The Security Dilemma in Alliance Politics," *World Politics* 36, no. 4 (July 1984): 466.

Index